Composing Interactive Music

Composing Interactive Music

Techniques and Ideas Using Max

Todd Winkler

The MIT Press
Cambridge, Massachusetts
London, England

First MIT Press paperback edition, 2001

© 1998 Massachusetts Institute of Technology

This book was set in Stone Serif and Stone Sans by Graphic Composition, Inc. and was printed and bound in the United States of America.

Library of Congress Cataloging-in-Publication Data

Winkler, Todd, 1958–
    Composing interactive music : techniques and ideas using Max /
Todd Winkler.
      p.   cm.
    Includes bibliographical references and index.
    ISBN 0-262-23193-X (hc : alk. paper), 0-262-73139-8 (pb)
      1. Computer composition.   2. Max (Computer program language)
I. Title.
MT56.W5   1998
781.3'45268—dc21   97-34535
                                                                         CIP
                                                                         MN
10 9 8 7 6 5 4

Contents

Preface

Composing Interactive Music: Techniques and Ideas Using Max, is a book about the technical and aesthetic possibilities of interactive music: a music composition or improvisation where software interprets a live performance to affect music generated or modified by computers. It describes musical concepts and programming techniques, and presents some insights into the development and research efforts leading up to this increasingly popular area of computer music.

The initial research for this book was conducted for my dissertation at Stanford University, *Three Interactive Etudes for Clarinet and Computer: Technology and Aesthetics in Interactive Composition* (1992). The dissertation, supervised by John Chowning, included a description of a Max program called *FollowPlay,* a large collection of software modules designed as a general-purpose package for interactive composition. Much of *FollowPlay* was conceived of and created while I was a visiting researcher at Institute de Recherche et Coordination Acoustique/Musique (IRCAM) during 1990–1991, with guidance from Miller Puckette, the original author of Max, and Cort Lippe and Zack Settel, who also contributed to the creation of Max.

The numerous compositions I have created with *FollowPlay* have been the laboratory for ongoing research and development for this book. Most of the programming examples presented here were taken directly from these works. However, the *FollowPlay* program is not presented in its entirety since it was never meant to be a program for public distribution. Instead, the principles and techniques I encountered while designing and redesigning the software are described here, with the idea that readers will create their own software to reflect their personal approach to composition.

How to Use This Book

Max is a graphical programming language, designed by Miller Puckette, for interactive composition. A version of Max, further developed by David Zicarelli, is commercially available from Opcode Systems, Inc. The techniques and ideas presented in this book are demonstrated through programming examples using Max. The examples are described in the text, accompanied by a picture of how they appear on the computer screen. The same examples are included as software on the accompanying CD-ROM, playable on a Macintosh computer, which may be copied and edited for further study. Whenever possible, examples and discussions will show the musical relevance of programming techniques, giving the reader firsthand experience in making and understanding interactive music. In the few software examples that are not my own, I have given credit to the contributor, whose name appears above their work. Because of space limitations, some of the examples on CD-ROM are not printed in their entirety in the book. An index of all examples, cross-referenced with the Opcode's Max manual, appears in appendix A.

Although this book is targeted at composers who will be writing music and software using Max, it has been written so that a casual reader might learn the basic concepts of interactive composition by just reading the text, without running any software at all. For readers who have access to a MIDI setup who do not own Opcode's Max programming environment, the accompanying software will run by itself, in a noneditable form, on most Macintosh computers. However, the complete Max application is highly recommended to accompany the text since it is necessary for editing the examples and for creating new software. Programming interactive works using Max is like learning to play an instrument: a thorough understanding will come only with firsthand experience. There is no substitute for practice.

The examples for this book require a basic MIDI studio, consisting of a Macintosh computer with at least 4 MB of RAM, a MIDI keyboard, and a MIDI interface. Keyboards should send and receive on MIDI channel 1. Although the examples are designed for keyboards, other

MIDI controllers may be used in conjunction with a MIDI sound module.

While no knowledge of Max programming is assumed, it would be helpful for readers to familiarize themselves with the Max tutorial and the manual before or while reading the text. (These are provided by Opcode Systems, Inc.) The information on Max and many of the examples presented here are indebted to these excellent resources. Although some overlap between the Max tutorial and the first chapters of this book is unavoidable, presenting two views of similar information will provide a solid foundation for more advanced work. Experienced Max programmers may want to skip chapters 3 and 4, which provide an introduction to Max programming.

The structure of the book follows a logical progression, keeping in mind composers with few programming skills. The ten chapters were conceived of as four large sections: Introduction, History, and Theory; Programming Foundation; Core Components; and Advanced Techniques. An overview of the chapters is as follows:

I   Introduction, History, and Theory

Chapter 1, *Introduction to Interactive Composition,* presents basic concepts regarding interactive music and continues with a brief history of interactive music compositions and systems.

Chapter 2, *Interactive Music Performance and Theory,* discusses models for interactions, issues of freedom and control, and human/computer relationships.

II   Programming Foundation

Chapter 3, *Graphic Programming using Max,* is designed to build a foundation for writing software using Max. It contains essential information for anyone new to Max and new to programming. It begins with an overview of various programming languages and programming concepts as they relate to Max, continues with an introduction to the basic materials and operations used in Max, and concludes with a section on MIDI.

Chapter 4, *Program Structure and Design,* is a continuation of chapter 3, and delves into more general programming principles. The approach used in chapter 4 (and throughout the book in general) is designed to demonstrate fundamental computer science concepts through musical examples, so that musicians new to programming will learn directly by creating music rather than by writing programs unrelated to their interests.

Chapters 3 and 4 establish a baseline of understanding with which to proceed to more advanced topics, and equips composers with the minimal understanding of computer concepts needed to produce interactive work.

Chapter 5, *Interface Design,* covers principles of interface design and reviews Max's interface objects.

III   Core Components

Chapter 6, *Listener Objects,* shows techniques for analyzing and storing performance information.

Chapter 7, *Composer Objects,* introduces methods for generating and processing computer music.

IV   Advanced Techniques and Concepts

Chapter 8, *Sound Design,* explores the use of sound through synthesis, orchestration, mixing, and computer-controlled signal processing.

Chapter 9, *Performance Structures,* offers suggestions for compositional strategies to create larger works, and contains descriptions of score objects that can be used for coordinating events during a performance.

Chapter 10, *Multimedia Extensions and New Controllers,* focuses on multimedia applications of interactive composition, Max's QuickTime extensions, and new controllers.

Appendix A, contains an index of the examples used in the book, cross referenced with related topics in the Max manual. This provides a single source for all information regarding software examples. Also useful will be Max's on-line help files, a software feature that calls up a description and working example of an object when the option key is held down while any object is clicked.

Acknowledgements

I am deeply grateful to Miller Puckette, David Zicarelli, Cort Lippe, Alan Strange, Dale Stammen, and Jason Vantomme for their thorough feedback at various stages of this book. I would also like to thank the following reviewers: Michael Pelz-Sherman, John P. Lamar, Burton Beerman, and Julian Richards. Dale Stammen and Michael Pelz-Sherman helped to test and edit the examples for the book. Special thanks to my student research assistants, Alex Gottschalk, Jason Duva, Brian Lee, and Scott Pagano.

Funding for this project was provided by the Center for Computer Research in Music and Acoustics (CCRMA), a Stanford University Paris Scholarship, an Oberlin College Faculty Research Grant, and Brown University. Special thanks goes to Tim Self at Opcode for software support.

The single source that proved the most useful to me was Robert Rowe's *Interactive Computer Music Systems* (MIT Press). It summarizes much of the research related to the development of interactive music, and explains Rowe's *Cypher* program. In addition, Rowe lays out a conceptual framework that was the starting point for this text. It would be an ideal reference for readers seeking a more in-depth study of various types of interactive music systems.

Finally, I must acknowledge the help of my wife, Karina Lutz, whose unflagging support was not just moral, but tangible as the first editor of this book.

I   *Introduction, History, and Theory*

1   *Introduction and Background*

Interaction is a two-way street. Nothing is more interactive than a good conversation: two people sharing words and thoughts, both parties engaged. Ideas seem to fly. One thought spontaneously affects the next. Participants in conversation assume much past experience and find excitement in shared experience. Conversations stay within a consistent context that creates a feeling of mutual understanding without being predictable. On the other hand, when only one person does the talking it isn't interactive—it is a lecture, a soliloquy.

Computers simulate interaction. Computers continue to move into the home and workplace, not because they are capable of millions of calculations per second but because they are clever mimics, able to represent images, sounds, and actions from the real world and imagined worlds. Computers simulate interaction in this constructed world by allowing users to change aspects of their current state and behavior. This interactive loop is completed when the computers, in turn, affect the further actions of the users.

Interaction means action. Computer programs are more or less interactive, depending on how they respond to human actions and how they engage human response. Interactivity comes from a feeling of participation, where the range of possible actions is known or intuited, and the results have significant and obvious effects, yet there is enough mystery maintained to spark curiosity and exploration. Television is not very interactive (yet). The viewer does not have any way to change aspects of a show, except for switching channels, changing the volume, or altering the controls for color, tint, and horizontal hold. The medium will become more interactive when viewer actions have a meaningful impact on the content and structure of the work.

This book describes techniques for creating interactive computer music (hereafter referred to simply as interactive music). Interactive music is defined here as a music composition or improvisation where software interprets a live performance to affect music generated or modified by computers. Usually this involves a performer playing an instrument while a computer creates music that is in some way shaped by the performance. This is a broad definition that encompasses a wide range of techniques, from simple triggers of predetermined musical material, to highly interactive improvisational systems that change their behavior from one performance to the next. Interactive music may also have applications in commercial multimedia software and CD-ROM titles, such as educational or entertainment titles, where the user (the "performer") controls aspects of music selection and compositional processes using the computer keyboard and mouse.

Performers participate in the creation of an interactive work, in part, by the amount of freedom they have to produce significant results in the computer's response. For example, a fully notated, predetermined score could be made slightly interactive by allowing a performer to control a single parameter of the computer-generated music, such as tempo. In more sophisticated interactive pieces, performers control many significant musical parameters and the composition can change dramatically according to their interpretation. In the most extreme examples, a performer is free to play any kind of music, and the computer has enough "intelligence" to respond in a way that makes sense and naturally encourages the performer's continuation. Like good conversations, interactive compositions succeed by encouraging spontaneity while residing within the boundaries of a dynamic context that seems whole and engaging.

Interactive music is a natural extension of a long history of collaborations. Music has always been an interactive art in which musicians respond to each other as they play, whether it is a conductor with an orchestra, a lead singer with a rock band, or the members of a jazz combo or a string quartet. Performers listen to each other while they play, continuously altering and shaping their performance according to what they hear. Many traditional musical relationships can be simulated with the computer. These models can be valuable starting points for an interactive work. More importantly, interactive techniques may suggest a new musical genre, one where the computer's capabilities are used to create new musical relationships that may exist only between humans and computers in a digital world.

The adjective "virtual" is a current buzzword that describes computer simulations of things that behave like real-world objects, situations, and phenomena. Describing such a simulation, Brenda Laurel writes, "A virtual world may not look anything like the one we know, but the persuasiveness of its representation allows us to respond to it *as if it were real.*" (1993) Interactive music techniques can be used to model many of the key elements in making and listening to music: instruments, performers, composers, and listeners. *Virtual instruments* behave somewhat like real instruments, and can be played from the computer keyboard, a MIDI controller, or as an extension of a traditional instrument. *Virtual performers* may play with human performers, interacting with "musical intelligence" in a duet, combo, or accompaniment role. *Virtual composers* create original music based on flexible and sometimes unpredictable processes specified by a real composer. These processes might represent the same musical ideas that a composer may choose in order to create a piece for acoustic instruments. Other processes may be specifically designed to take advantage of the capabilities of the computer. Finally, a *virtual listener* or *virtual critic* may pass judgment by reacting to and altering the final outcome of a performance (Rowe 1993). Such a critic might be designed to analyze the accuracy of a performance, or steer the output of a composition away from too much repetition.

The behavior of these virtual entities must be described by the programmer, who must answer the questions: How are virtual instruments played? How does a virtual performer respond to musical input? How do virtual composers generate, process, and structure musical material? What are the criteria for a virtual critic to judge the success or failure of a performance or or a piece of music? The opinions of the programmer are impossible to separate from the final outcome. There is a compelling reason why composers and other artists need to become involved in the creation of software, and why programs like Max are needed to make software creation more accessible to artists. Among other things, artists are experts at creating vivid imaginary worlds that engage the mind and the senses. These talents are especially needed in creating rich and engaging computer environments. Computers are not intelligent. They derive their appearance of intelligence only from the knowledge and experience of the person who creates the software they run.

Components of an Interactive System

Broadly speaking, interactive music works by having a computer interpret a performer's actions in order to alter musical parameters, such as tempo, rhythm, or orchestration. These parameters are controlled by computer music processes immediately responsive to musical data (such as individual notes or dynamics) or gestural information (such as key pressure, foot pedals, or computer mouse movements). Interactive software simulates intelligent behavior by modeling human hearing, understanding, and response (Rowe 1993). The response must be believable in the sense that it seems appropriate for the action taken, and appropriate for the style of music. This process is somewhat analogous to the distinct activities that take place during a jazz improvisation or other musical dialogue: listening, interpreting, composing, and performing. Figure 1.1 describes five steps to creating an interactive piece:

1. Human input, instruments—Human activity is translated into digital information and sent to the computer.

2. Computer listening, performance analysis—The computer receives the human input and analyzes the performance information for timing, pitch, dynamics, or other musical characteristics.

3. Interpretation—The software interprets the computer listener information, generating data that will influence the composition.

4. Computer composition—Computer processes, responsible for all aspects of the computer generated music, are based on the results of the computer's interpretation of the performance.

5. Sound generation and output, performance—The computer plays the music, using sounds created internally, or by sending musical information to devices that generate sound.

The first two steps are very practical, and limited, and deal mainly with facts. The software should be accurate in its analysis and, therefore, must understand certain things about human performance. The last three steps are artistic decisions limited only by a composer's skill and imagination, since there are countless ways that performance information can be interpreted to create original music and sound.

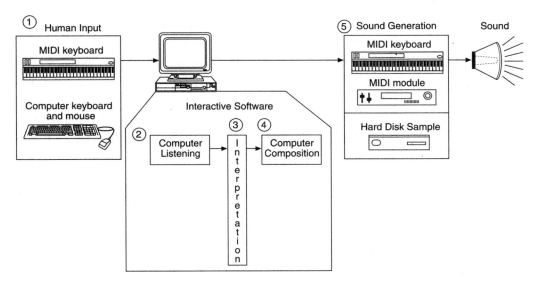

Figure 1.1
Basic components of an interactive composition

Enhancing the Roles of Performer and Composer

Another way of viewing the processes of interactive music is to examine the traditional roles of composer and performer, roles that often become blurred in interactive works. Performers may be asked to invent musical material that will become an integral part of a computer composition. Composers may perform their work during a concert by manipulating musical parameters using a computer keyboard and mouse. Even the "audience" may take on the role of composer and performer in works designed to be viewed on screen, by changing parameters and control processes from a computer terminal.

What makes a great musical performer? The notation system used for "Western art music" conveys specific information regarding pitch, somewhat less specific information regarding tempo and rhythm, and even less information regarding phrasing, vibrato, and dynamics—essentially a loose set of directions on how to create music. The performer's artistry supplies the nuances and subtleties missing in the score, bringing the music to life. Improvisers also bring music to life with the same expressive musical elements, while supplying pitch and rhythmic information used to create music within the boundaries of a particular style. These elements of interpretation impart the "feel" to music. Along with virtuosity, these are the qualities that are valued most highly in musicians, whether it is the aggressive punctuation of a jazz solo, a soprano's approach to the penultimate note of an aria, or the long, drawn-out climax of an electric guitar solo. While these qualities are assumed in all good players, it is precisely these elements that are most difficult for the computer to generate, since they come not only from the context of the music, but from an emotional experience as well as a lifetime of making music. Although researchers have discovered some rules that may impart musicality to computer music, no model has yet come close to the complex subtleties created by humans.

Using the techniques of interactive composition, elements of a live performance can be used to impart a human musical sense to a machine, forming a bridge to the musical traditions of the past through the interpretation of expressive information. At the same time, the computer opens up new possibilities for musicians to expand their abilities beyond the physical limitations of their instrument. These techniques invite our most highly esteemed musicians to continue using their greatest talents while participating in the process of making music in the computer age.

Many of the interactive methods for performance can also be used by composers to experiment with ideas while creating a new work. Composers have always used processes to generate large musical structures from simple musical material. A canon (round) is an example of a simple and widely used musical process: begin a melody with one singer, begin the same melody with a second singer while the first continues, and so on. Many types of musical processes can be easily represented in software by an algorithm, step-by-step instructions used to accomplish a specific task. Interactive techniques provide an intuitive platform for real-time exploration of musical processes. This immediacy in generating and manipulating musical materials provides the composer with an interactive laboratory where musical ideas and time-varying compositional processes are quickly realized and refined. The benefit of getting immediate aural feedback from this kind of experimentation cannot be overemphasized. Within this laboratory environment composers can generate scores for acoustic works, create situations for improvisation with other musicians, or compose solo pieces to be played directly from the computer. The same tools can help shape interactive pieces on-the-spot during rehearsals or performances and can even be used to control nonmusical aspects of a concert presentation, such as the video display or the control of lighting systems.

Audience Reception and Participation

Audience members, untrained in the intricacies of computers or composition, may not be interested in the complexities of software design, the sophistication of musical processes, or the amount of memory in a computer. They come to concerts for a variety of reasons, not the least being to enjoy the drama of a live performance. It is exciting to watch the musical skill of a great performer, to witness the interaction between members of an ensemble, and to take in the pageantry of costumes, ritual, lighting, and stage personalities (Wishart 1995).

Live interactive music contains an element of magic, since the computer music responds "invisibly" to a performer. The drama is heightened when the roles of the computer and performer are clearly defined, and when the actions of one has an observable impact on the actions of another, although an overly simplistic approach will quickly wear thin. On the other hand, complex responses that are more indirectly influenced by a performer may produce highly successful musical results, but without some observable connection the dramatic relationship will be lost to the audience.

Outside of the concert and studio setting, interactive techniques invite participants into the music-making process. Installations, computer games, and works on CD-ROM may require audience or user input to select and process music, allowing nonmusicians the feeling of actively participating in creating music. Computer users may be asked to become performers, playing music from a computer keyboard or other computer input device. They may also be asked to become composers, selecting, ordering, and generating computer music from on-screen controls. Amateurs and students may come to a better understanding of music by their direct involvement in making music. Interactive movies, games, web sites, and educational titles are all more compelling when the sound responds immediately to the user's actions. These recent inventions may be better understood by putting them in perspective with the pioneering work that led to their development.

A Brief History of Interactive Composition

Prior to the invention of recording, all music was interactive to some degree. That is, all music was performed live; musicians interacted with each other, with their instruments, and with their audience. Technical innovations in the twentieth century have reduced opportunities for musical interaction. Recording eliminated the rapport between audience members and performers; since music could be heard anywhere at any time, the focus of the moment, and the energy needed to create it, was lost. Multitrack tape techniques further eliminated interaction between musicians, making it possible for an engineer to record a band with each member appearing at the studio on separate occasions to record their part on separate tracks (although many bands prefer to capture the excitement of their live interaction in the studio). Studio musicians may respond or react to prerecorded music, rather than interacting with live players. Their primary interaction is through feedback with a producer or engineer. This mode of creating music has more recently spilled over into large pop music concerts that employ prerecorded tapes, with the musicians on stage playing a minimal role or even lip synching, so that the sound is as close to the original studio recording as possible.

Computer music, however, did not begin as an interactive art form. The first general-purpose computer music program was created by Max Mathews at Bell Laboratories in the early sixties (Dodge and Jerse 1985). The first computer music systems could not be designed for interaction since the primitive equipment was not capable of handling the immense number of calculations needed for a live performance. These systems required hours of programming and waiting before even a single short melody could be heard. Part of the attraction for some composers was to have absolute control over all aspects of a composition, specifying each and every detail to the computer, which would, in turn, implement them flawlessly. Interestingly, the limitations of these systems and the experimental nature of the software created unpredictable results that did lead to meaningful "interactions" between composers and computers; composers programmed what they thought they would hear; computers interpreted the data differently, and often composers were surprised to hear the results. Then they either adjusted the data to sound more like their original intention, or decided that they were delighted by their "mistake" and continued in that new direction. More than a few composers have remarked that some of their best work was discovered unintentionally through a flaw in the system or by entering erroneous data. The final result of early computer works was a tape, distributed as a recording, or played through loudspeakers for an audience.

Many composers continue to create tape pieces, preferring to work in an optimal studio environment to realize an ideal version of a work with great detail, complexity, and subtlety. Since interactive systems are often limited by the requirement to run in real time, some of the most advanced techniques in computer-generated music are only available on non-real-time systems (although faster computer processors are closing this gap).

To some people, the lack of visual stimulus may pose a problem for presenting tape music in a concert setting. The addition of a musician playing along with the tape adds an interesting human component to a concert presentation, but may limit the performer's interpretation of tempo and phrasing since, no matter how passionate or unusual the performer's interpretation, the tape always remains the same. For a large number of computer music compositions, however, tape remains the most viable, permanent, and dependable medium. Thus, interactive composition represents an interesting subset of the field of computer and electronic music.

Early Analog Experiments

During the sixties and early seventies, the first devices used for creating computer music were very expensive, and housed at only a few research facilities such as Columbia University, Stanford University, and Bell Labs. At the same time, analog electronics were being employed in concert settings to process the sound of instruments and to create synthetic sounds in real time. So-called live electronic systems began to be used in the early sixties and proliferated throughout the seventies. Many of these pieces used tape delay techniques or processed analog instruments through specially built electronic circuitry contained in "modules," with each module altering the sound in a specific way, such as adding distortion or reverberation. A few composers showed the promise of interactive systems, where the system behaved differently with different musical input, allowing a performer not just to trigger preset processes, but to shape them as well.

The early electronic works of John Cage influenced a number of composers experimenting with "live electronic" music in the sixties. Their interest in improvisation and indeterminacy naturally led to the first interactive electronic systems. Gordon Mumma's *Hornpipe* (1967) showed promising new ways of musical thought. Mumma describes *Hornpipe* as "an interactive live-electronic work for solo hornist, cybersonic console, and a performance space." He coined the term *cybersonic,* described as interactive electronic circuitry that alters and creates sound based on a performer's input. Mumma's "cybersonic console" contained microphones for "listening" to the sounds made by the horn as well as for analyzing the acoustical resonance of the space. During the course of the piece, the hornist freely chose pitches that affected the electronic processing in different ways. Thus, the hornist's performance and the resultant sound altered by the acoustics of the room created an interactive loop that was further processed by electronics (Cope 1977).

In the mid-sixties, the introduction of voltage-controlled synthesizers opened the way for interactive techniques. A control voltage is an electrical signal that can be used to automate analog synthesizer processes. Almost anything that can be changed on an analog synthesizer module can be controlled with voltages. The amount and duration of voltages becomes an abstraction that can be applied to numerous parameters. With control-voltage synthesizers, keyboards produce higher voltages for higher tones, and lower voltages for lower tones. Voltages from the keyboard can be redirected so that each pitch can produce a different vibrato rate, for example. Envelope followers turn any kind of analog signal, even acoustic sounds played via microphone, into voltages. In this way, changes in dynamic levels can be applied to any number of parameters, affecting the synthesizer. For example, in several of his tape compositions beginning with *Touch*, composer Morton Subotnick used his voice to control various parameters of synthesized sounds on a Buchla analog synthesizer by translating the amplitude of his arch-shaped phrases and short accented syllables into voltages via an envelope follower. Even though the final result was a studio composition that exists only on tape, the interactive techniques applied during the composing process imparted a human element that would otherwise be missing.

Subotnick later worked with long-term collaborator and electrical engineer, Donald Buchla, to develop an early digital/analog hybrid system that would handle control voltages from analog input signals. The result was an evening-length multimedia "opera," *Ascent Into Air*

(1983), featuring interactive computer processing of live instruments and computer-generated music, all under the control of two cellists who are part of a small ensemble of musicians on stage. In another large staged work, *Hungers* (1986), musicians controlled the playback and display of multiple video images in addition to musical processes. Subotnick worked with composer/programmer Marc Coniglio to create the software for *Hungers,* which eventually became *Interactor,* a large computer program for interactive composition.

Early Computer Experiments

Most of the computer music research and composition during the seventies centered on sound synthesis and processing methods using mainframe computers to produce tape pieces. One notable exception was the GROOVE system, a pioneering work in real-time computer systems developed by Max Mathews and F. Richard Moore at Bell Labs. The GROOVE system, in use at Bell Labs from 1968 to 1979, featured a conducting program that enabled a person to control the tempo, dynamic level, and balance of a computer ensemble that had knowledge of a predetermined musical score. The system was used by performers to investigate performance nuances in older music, as well as by composers, such as Emmanuel Ghent and Laurie Speigel, to conduct original compositions (Dodge and Jerse 1985).

David Behrman, another pioneer in interactive composition, spent much of his early career creating works featuring real-time processing of acoustic instruments. He was one of a few composers who began to use microcomputers when they first became available in the mid-seventies. In John Schaefers's book, *New Sounds,* Behrman explains: "I used the computer as an interface between some circuitry I had built that made electronic music, and a pitch-sensing device that listens for pitches made by acoustic instruments." He maintains that his pieces "are in the form of computer programs and hardware." In his work *Figure in a Clearing,* a cellist improvises on a set of notes, and the computer creates harmonies and timbres that depend on the order and choice of those notes. As the performer responds to the harmonies, the improvisation triggers a new set of computer sounds (Schaefer 1987).

Composer Joel Chadabe has employed concepts of interaction in his music since 1967, when he began creating works for a Moog analog system that involved the automated control of timbre and rhythm (Chadabe 1989). Ten years later, along with Roger Meyers, he developed interactive music software to power one of the first portable digital systems. In an article in 1983, "Interactive Composing: An Overview," Chadabe described his piece *Rhythms:*

In *Rhythms,* the computer automatically generates melodies and rhythmic patterns, articulated in sounds reminiscent of Indonesian, Caribbean, and African percussion instruments. I perform by pressing keys at the terminal keyboard, thereby transposing chords, changing pitch relationships within chords, triggering melodic variations, altering rhythmic patterns, overlapping voices, and introducing random notes. But although I trigger each set of changes to begin, I cannot foresee the details of each change. I must react to what I hear in deciding what to do next. It is a distinctive characteristic of interactive composing that a performer, in deciding each successive performance action, reacts to information automatically generated by the system.

Many of the early interactive computer systems built in the late seventies and early eighties were actually digital/analog hybrid systems that consisted of a simple computer sending voltages to an analog synthesizer. George Lewis, a well-known jazz trombonist, began building such a system in 1979, using a computer with 1 kilobyte of RAM to control a Moog synthesizer. His program evolved, and continues to evolve, into a more elaborate system that enables him to use his improvisational skills to create a true dialogue with the computer (Lewis 1994; see chap. 3) .

Early MIDI Systems

The rapid development of computer technology in the early eighties led to dramatically improved techniques for interactive composition. First, the availability of small, inexpensive, and sophisticated personal computers enabled numerous musicians and programmers to begin exploring interactive computer music on their own, without the need for support from large institutions. Companies began to make music software commercially available, and introduced the first computer music sequencers, editors, and notation programs. Second, a group of prominent musical instrument manufacturers agreed on a standard method for sending and receiving musical information digitally, establishing MIDI (Musical Instrument Digital Interface) as a universal standard. Third, researchers began to solve some of the central problems of interactive music that had previously eluded computer music programmers: how to schedule musical events in real time, how to get a computer to follow a score, and how to get a computer to recognize musical input (see chap. 9).

Many of the problems of score following were first solved independently by Barry Vercoe working at IRCAM and MIT and Roger Dannenberg working at Carnegie-Mellon University, who presented their findings at the 1984 International Computer Music Conference. Their work had a large impact on subsequent research in interactive music systems (leading two years later to the development of a number of interactive programs, including Max, Jam Factory, and Interactor). Other methods had already been tried for improvisation, where the computer responded immediately to any unknown pitch or dynamic information. Two influential symposiums held at the STEIM studios in Amsterdam in 1984 and 1986, STEIM Symposium on Interactive Composing and Live Electronic Music, brought together an influential group of researchers and composers to share and discuss their work. The talks focused on new computer techniques as well as on the design and performance of new electronic instruments (see chap. 10).

The development of MIDI had an immediate impact on the proliferation of portable interactive systems that could be used easily and dependably in concert situations. MIDI controllers provided a consistent way of expressing performance nuances and other physical gestures to the computer. The limited amount of data transferred via MIDI enabled common personal computers to handle music processing in real time. However, these same limitations meant that important musical information regarding timbre, vibrato, and other constantly changing subtleties of nuance was not well-represented.

Encouraged by the availability and new potential of personal computer systems, Chadabe founded a company, Intelligent Music, to provide an outlet for interactive composition software for Apple's Macintosh Computer. Joining Chadabe's company was David Zicarelli, a top Macintosh music programmer who had become well-known for his innovative interface design for other MIDI software. The company's first software packages, M and Jam Factory, were released in 1986 (Zicarelli 1987). Zicarelli created Jam Factory, and became one of Chadabe's collaborators for M . Both applications controlled MIDI systems with software that offered immediate feedback using graphic and gestural interfaces to modify ongoing musical processes. These programs relied on a performer's actions to create and manipulate musical patterns generated by the software. MIDI devices or a Macintosh keyboard and mouse could be used to influence musical parameters in real time while listening to the resulting changes. Zicarelli writes, "My motivation for writing Jam Factory was my interest in creating a program that would listen to MIDI input and 'improvise' immediately at some level of proficiency, while allowing me to improve its ability."

Mills College was also a center for the development of interactive systems in the mid-eighties. The Hierarchical Music Specification Language (HMSL), an object-oriented programming language developed at Mills, has been used extensively for interactive music composition and improvisation. Further additions have added sound synthesis capabilities using a Motorola 56000 processor on an Audiomedia or Sound-Tools card, enabling HMSL to control sound-generating circuits while also controlling MIDI devices (Polansky and Rosenboom 1987).

By 1990, numerous highly programmable interactive MIDI systems had proven successful in concert situations. Work in this area continued at MIT, producing Tod Machover's Hyperinstrument system and Robert Rowe's Cypher. Cypher, along with Daniel Oppenheim's Dmix, and Karla Scaletti's Kyma, feature graphical interfaces that encourage composers to realize musical ideas quickly, with many of the details and much of the complexity of the programming language (such as C or Lisp) hidden from the user. All of these programs generate MIDI data, but Kyma adds synthesis and sound processing capabilities as part of an integrated composition package. Max is, by far, the most widely used program of this nature.

History and Development of Max

Max was developed at the Institute de Recherche et Coordination Acoustique/Musique (IRCAM) in Paris, beginning in 1986. The principal author was Miller Puckette, an MIT graduate who originally designed Max to control IRCAM's powerful 4X synthesizer. The 4X was created by a team of engineers who spent several years to produce a costly digital synthesizer that could handle sophisticated sound synthesis in real time. Of the 4X Puckette (1991) writes:

Although the original idea was to build an oscillator bank [for sound synthesis], by 1985 most of the composers who tried to use the 4X were interested in "signal processing," using the term to mean transforming the sound of a live instrument in some way. This change of focus was the product of opportunity and necessity. Opportunity because "signal processing" is capable of a richer sonic result than pure synthesis, and since it is easier to create musical connections between a live player and electronics if the electronics are acting on the live sound itself. Necessity because it was clear that after eight years of refining the digital oscillator, we lacked the software to specify interesting real-time timbral control at the level of detail needed. Signal processing, by contrast, can often yield interesting results from only a small number of control parameters.

According to Puckette, the main challenge of synchronizing a live player and the computer had two components. First, the computer needed to obtain pitch information from the performer. Second, after the stream of notes was detected, the computer needed to use "score following" techniques to understand where the player was in a score and respond appropriately.

Puckette had worked several years earlier with Barry Vercoe at MIT on the problem of score following. Those years, 1982–1984, coincided with the introduction of the Macintosh computer and the development of MIDI. While the physical problems of note detection were easily solved for keyboard instruments, where each key was an actual switch, it was fairly difficult for other instruments. Hardware devices known as pitch detectors give an indication of pitches played on acoustic instruments via microphone, but since the nature of the attack and spectrum of each instrument is so varied, these devices have yet to be proven accurate. In 1984, Lawrence Beauregard, a flutist working at IRCAM in conjunction with Vercoe, took a standard flute and added switches to the keys so that a computer could detect the player's fingering. Since each fingering produces several pitches depending on how hard the instrument is blown, an acoustic pitch detector was added to deduce the correct pitch, making it reliable enough to use in concert.

It took approximately three years to produce the first concert works that demonstrated score-following techniques using the Beauregard flute and the 4X. The 1987 concert featured *Jupiter* by Philippe Manoury and *Aloni* by Thierry Lancino. Because of the difficulty of programming the 4X, Max was developed as control software for the 4X, running on a Macintosh computer. The 4X was set up as a MIDI device, with Max controlling the equivalent of hundreds of MIDI controllers, making productions easier and more efficient.

From there, Max grew into a versatile graphical programming language designed for real-time control of MIDI devices. Other programmers contributing to the early development of Max included Lee Boynton, Cort Lippe, and Zack Settel. In 1990, the continuing evolution of Max split into two distinct directions. One path led to David Zicarelli, who began working on a commercially available version of Max at Intelligent Music. Max was extended under Zicarelli's authorship, and eventually released by Opcode Systems, Inc., in 1991 as a full-featured Macintosh programming environment with improved screen graphics, playback of standard MIDI files, multimedia capabilities, and a large collection of new features. Because of its ease of use and availability, Max has been adopted by a large number of composers. It was especially welcomed by those who had been frustrated by the slow production time of non-real-time music systems, or who had been hampered by their inexperience with computer programming. Much of the success of Max can be attributed to contributions made from a community of programmers and composers who have greatly expanded the program's capabilities with custom libraries of additional functions that are distributed without cost by Opcode, and many more that are exchanged freely over the Internet.

Meanwhile, IRCAM continued developing new hardware systems as a response to composers' demands for interactive real-time signal processing. In 1990, the IRCAM Signal Processing Workstation (ISPW) was introduced to replace the 4X system. Puckette adapted Max for the ISPW, adding a library of signal-processing objects. In addition to controlling musical events, Max could now influence the production and processing of audio signals, controlling such things as sampling, oscillators, harmonizers, delay lines, filtering, and pitch tracking (Lindeman 1990). The ISPW represented a flexible and powerful hardware environment, replacing the need for MIDI devices, with Max as a single unified "front end" to control every aspect of music production (Lippe and Puckette 1991). The ISPW was a great advance for interactive composition, but was too costly to be affordable by most individuals. Unfortunately, the life span of the ISPW was brief, due to its dependence on the NeXT computer to run. NeXT stopped making computers just a few years after the ISPW was completed.

The primary software used for signal processing and synthesis on the ISPW is FTS ("faster than sound"). IRCAM has continued the development of FTS as a system that runs on multiple hardware and software platforms. Most recently, Miller Puckette's new software system, Pd (Pure Data), provides the main features of Max and FTS while addressing some of the shortcomings of the original Max paradigm. By taking advantage of faster processor speeds, Pd is able to integrate audio synthesis and signal processing with video processing and 3-D graphics in a single real-time software environment. The graphics program, GEM (Graphics Environment for Multimedia), was written by Mark Danks to operate within the Pd environment. This holds great promise for composers and visual artists to explore an interactive and unified audiovisual medium.

These new capabilities provide composers, using off-the-shelf equipment, with a sophisticated interactive system capable of handling not only MIDI data but also real-time sound synthesis, timbre analysis, pitch tracking, and signal processing (for more on this topic see chapter 8). Since much of this software is still in the development stages, the remainder of this text demonstrates concepts of interactive music using the Opcode version of Max and commonly available MIDI hardware. These techniques should remain viable in future incarnations of Max and in other interactive systems.

2   Interaction: Defining Relationships between Computers and Performers

Regardless of musical style or technique, a central issue that confronts all composers of interactive music is the drama of human-computer interaction. What is the *relationship* between humans and computers? Strong and clear musical ideas or an extramusical context will suggest the appropriate paradigm for this relationship. What role does the computer play? Is it an equal partner improvising with a "mind of its own"? Is it a slave, taking all its orders from the human performers by following or mimicking their every move? Is it a meta-composer, absorbing musical material and developing it with endless variations?

Since interactive relationships occur naturally between performers in traditional music ensembles, a study of traditional models of performance and composition will yield rich material for computer interaction. Hopefully, new modes of thought based on the computer's unique capabilities will evolve from a closer look at known performance models. This chapter will examine three types of models useful for interactive composition: performance models, instrument models, and composition models.

Performance Models

Music notation needs to be "interpreted," or made "musical," by a performer. While the general choice of pitch and rhythm are not open to interpretation in traditional classical music, much of the musical information is supplied by the performers. This multitude of continuously changing parameters, such as tempo, vibrato, or dynamics, necessitates interaction among several players. These parameters are frequently discussed by musicians in the process of rehearsing a piece: intonation, tempo, phrasing, timbre production, vibrato, and dynamic balance.

Active two-way listening informs each player of the current state of the music which suggests appropriate ways to proceed. Appropriateness is defined differently for each musical style and technique. The performer's awareness of the implied rules for a given style helps to create a musically satisfying result. Most improvised music, for example, gives the performer much wider freedom to act, since he or she can simultaneously play the roles of interpreter and composer to create a dialogue with other musicians. Usually this lies within a predetermined framework containing basic musical material presented in a known musical structure, along with variation techniques based on collectively held assumptions for the rules of style. The improviser's choices change the very fabric of the piece, with ensemble members listening and responding in kind. Interactive pieces are capable of improvisational responses because they create flexible structures that generate compositional material based on musical input. By relinquishing absolute control over certain musical parameters, a composer can hope to increase a performer's engagement and spontaneity.

Control issues cause contention even in the most staid of music traditions. Who is in charge? Who follows and who leads? How much of a "voice" do group members have? How much say does a composer have? What tasks and decisions are left up to the performer? Part of the interest and drama of a live performance lies in these balances of power. The roles adopted by each player imply a set of constraints for what they can or cannot do. Since computers are oblivious to protocol or personality, composers must define roles for the computer and the performer, giving the computer musical character by creating a power relationship between the two. The drama that ensues during the course of an interactive performance is shaped by the relationship between humans and computers, a relationship that is flexible and may change during the course of a piece.

Interactive schemes run the gamut from highly predictable, carefully crafted structures, to open, free, and spontaneous expressions. Similar relationships exist in all types of music and can be clearly seen in the traditions of Western art music (classical music) and jazz. While many twentieth century innovations show promising new ideas for redesigning performance relationships, jazz improvisation offers the most complete working model for interactive music, since it encompasses such a wide variety of performance techniques: notated music, improvisation based on a harmonic or melodic framework, free improvisation, and quotation. But no traditional model is either complete or entirely appropriate for the computer, and all types of music suggest various relationships that may prove useful to composers. Simulation of real-world models is only a stepping stone for original designs idiomatic to the digital medium. The following models look at control issues in three traditions: symphony orchestra, string quartet, and jazz combo, with suggestions for control design for computer pieces.

The Conductor Model—Symphony Orchestra

The paradigm of the symphony orchestra is one where the conductor is the master controller, a personality acting as a conduit for musical expression. The conductor follows and interprets a score, acting as the single source for coordinating players' actions by directing the time flow, shaping the dynamics, and adjusting the acoustical balance. The symbiotic relationship between conductor and orchestra places all the large, global decisions regarding interpretation in the hands of the conductor, who relies on the players' skills and judgment for further interpretation. Feedback from the orchestra, in the form of musical production and facial expressions, continually informs the conductor's current and future actions.

Timing and dynamic balance are especially crucial in an orchestral setting. With so many people to coordinate, it is important that all participants have a good sense of time and a good set of ears. It is not enough for a conductor's method of communication to be clear and unambiguous. To command the authority needed to influence players, a conductor must prove reliable by demonstrating skill, and believable by demonstrating knowledge. Inferior conductors are largely ignored by players, who decide that their own interpretation of the piece will be more successful. Good orchestras are interactive when orchestra members are responsive to a conductor's gestures, when they listen to each other, and when the conductor listens to the orchestra as a collection of individuals.

The conductor model has been used extensively for interactive composition. In fact, one line of the early research in interactive techniques was dedicated to one goal: finding a method to allow a musician real-time control over the tempo of a predetermined computer music "score." With the conductor model, musical material is predetermined with the performer acting as the conductor. A performer supplies the beat (tempo) to the computer. A conducting pulse could come from any MIDI device, such as tapping a foot pedal or playing simple quarter notes with one hand, or from a performer using beat-tracking algorithms, which derive the beat from a real-time analysis of a performance. (See Timing Analysis in chapter 6.) One method uses *score-following* techniques, where the computer contains both the performer's score and the computer score in its memory. The computer follows the score by matching the performer's notes to the same part stored in memory. The matched notes orient the computer in the piece and trigger the notes stored in the computer score (see chap. 9). Minimally, this method requires that the performer control the tempo of the computer music in real time. More developed systems include control of additional parameters, such as dynamics, vibrato, and timbre. In Tod Machover's *Bug Mudra,* for example, a specially designed glove allows a conductor to control the mix levels, reverb, and panning of the computer music while simultaneously conducting three performers (Machover 1991).

Other specially designed conducting devices, such as Max Mathews's Radio Baton, enable a musician to use one or two sticks (batons) to control tempo and other musical aspects of a score stored in the computer (Mathews and Schloss 1989). More recently, Guy Garnett's *Flute Fantasy,* originally written for flute and tape, was redesigned using Max to make the music more flexible and responsive to the performer, adding a role for a conductor using a MIDI baton based on Donald Buchla's *Lightning* device to control the computer's tempo, phrasing, and dynamics (Garnett 1992).

In interactive works for orchestra or large ensemble, the actual "conductor" of the computer music may be a keyboard player or other member of the ensemble. In a revised version of Pierre Boulez's *Explosante Fixe,* a conductor directs a large ensemble, while a single flute is tracked by a computer using score-following techniques to trigger all the electronic events on an ISPW and on MIDI samplers.

(For a simple demonstration of how the conductor model works, see the example on CD-ROM, *Conduct Chopin,* in the Tempo Follower section for chapter 6. It allows a performer to control the tempo of a

Chopin Prelude stored in the computer's memory, by tapping the foot pedal while the modulation wheel controls the dynamic level.)

The Chamber Music Model—String Quartet

The interaction in the chamber music model is more complex since several musicians reciprocally influence each others' performance. In a string quartet, for example, even though the first violinist is often considered the effective "leader" (i.e., conductor) of the group, in reality the interplay between musicians demonstrates shared control. Intonation, phrasing, and tempo are constantly in flux, with control often passed around to the musician with the most prominent musical material. This taking and yielding of control, which makes the string quartet so dynamic, is a strong feature built into the composition itself. It is a drama about the relationship of four musicians, each one capable of exhibiting character and independence by adding their musical personality to the score. These relationships are displayed even more vividly in improvised performances.

Examples of the chamber music model in interactive composition are numerous. For example, the first movement of *Snake Charmer,* for clarinet and computer (Winkler 1991), begins with a computer introduction set at a fixed dynamic level. When the clarinet enters, it is able to influence the dynamic level of the computer part for a short time, after which the computer stops "listening" to the performer and continues on its own. This give and take occurs many times during a performance, with occasional outbursts from the computer that cause the clarinetist to increase his dynamic level to match the computer. Similar methods have been used to give or take away control of the tempo and other parameters from the computer (Rowe 1993).

The Improvisation Model—Jazz Combo

The jazz combo provides abundant examples of interaction ripe for computer simulation. Traditional jazz pieces provide a structure and a shared conceptual framework in which musicians interact with each other, influencing both the interpretation of written music (the head), and the improvisation of primary compositional material (solos). Even the basic harmonic structure of a tune is open to unlimited interpretation by a performer, who selects voicing and variants of the harmony to suit the immediate mood of the piece. A favorite trick of the jazz bassist, for example, is to play a third below the root of the established chord, thus turning, say, an E half-diminished chord into a C9 chord. Musicians trade off taking control of the music, fashioning their solos into spontaneous personal statements that alter and influence the surrounding accompaniment. Relationships change frequently as two members trade riffs, or a third jumps momentarily to the conversational foreground.

What makes this relationship function to produce music that does not sound like random babbling is that there are a huge number of shared assumptions and implied rules based on years of collective experience. This kind of musical intelligence can be simulated with interactive software on a very simple level. Computers can recognize patterns, identifying such things as scale types, chord progressions, rhythmic and melodic patterns, and tempo. Using this information, sets of rules and assumptions can be coded into computer algorithms made to generate new music that seems natural and responsive to the performer's material. Just as a jazz combo responds naturally to a soloist's changing moods, so too can an interactive piece respond to a performer; each performance is a unique and unpredictable event, held within more or less scripted boundaries. The limitation of the range of possible parameter changes focuses the music, giving it a distinct character.

Free Improvisation

The free jazz movement of the sixties produced performances that were highly interactive, spontaneous, expressive, and unpredictable. Such music offers a complex model of the highest level of interactivity. The computer may interact subtly or cryptically with the performer, creating listenable music on its own, seemingly independent from the live performer. Neither the performer nor the computer may be "in control," but each one will have some influence on how the other responds. The free improvisation model poses artistic and technical challenges that may yield new musical forms idiomatic to the techniques of interactive composition.

A good example of this idea of a "virtual" performer can be seen in the work of composer and improviser George Lewis, who describes his early experiences creating and performing with an interactive system written in the Forth programming language in the late seventies:

Coming from a tradition (African-American) that emphasizes collective improvised expression in music, this way of doing music with computers seemed quite natural. The computer was regarded as "just another musician in the band." Hours were spent in the tweaking stage, listening to and adjusting the real-time output of the computer, searching for a range of behavior that was compatible with human musicians. By compatible, I mean that music transmits information about its source. An improvisor (anyone, really) takes the presence or absence of certain sonic activities as a guide to what is going on (Lewis 1994).

Lewis's strategy allows for a great deal of independence between a computer and a performer, establishing musical personalities that do not directly control each other, but rather have mutual influence that contributes to the final outcome of an improvisation. His goal is to make the computer's "playing" listenable as music on its own by viewing its behavior as separate from and independent of the performer. He explains:

For me this independence is necessary in order to give the improvising musician something to think about. Later, when I speak of musical "interaction" with some of the later models of this computer program, I mean that the interaction takes place in the manner of two improvisors that have their own "personalities." The program's extraction of important features from my activity is not reintroduced directly, but used to condition and guide a separate process of real-time algorithmic composition.

The performer interacts with the audible results of this process, just as the program interacts with the audible results of what I am thinking about musically; neither party to the communication has final authority to force a certain outcome—no one is "in charge." I communicate with such programs only by means of my own musical behavior.

Thus, performance features recognized by the software are applied indirectly to the computer music causing responses that are not always obvious but are still influenced by a performer's actions. To deal successfully with such a free form requires great skill on the part of the performer who is, to a large extent, the composer as well. More often, a composer will create a more or less rigid framework or structure in which the interaction will unfold.

Musical Form and Structure

Music is a temporal art, an art whose primary medium is time. Most composers, hopefully, are gifted at generating interesting musical materials. It is in the *composing* of these materials that the deeper art is revealed. Composing, in this case, is about musical structure, musical form, and especially time. This is how dramatic situations are created and unfold: What is the music about (characters, scene, plot)? What changes? How does it change (dramatic action)? When does it change (dramatic timing)? Taking away some performer control might result in a precisely crafted piece, with structure and timing essential to the realization of a work. Adding more performer control will increase the opportunity for spontaneous expression and serendipitous results. It is possible to contain a performance within a carefully described structure, while still allowing performer freedom within those confines. Popular rock songs, for instance, may feature an improvised guitar solo within a tightly structured performance. While a performer might experience great freedom and connection in a freely improvised performance, a conceptual or structural framework gives the music a coherent shape and stylistic consistency that provides a road map for the performers and the audience. Thus, one of the new challenges facing composers of interactive works is to create malleable forms based on flexible musical structures that respond to human input.

Levels of Indeterminacy

When beginning to form a conceptual basis for understanding interactive relationships, traditional models can be useful. However, since the virtue of the computer is that it can do things human performers cannot do, it is essential to break free from the limitations of traditional models and develop new forms that take advantage of the computer's capabilities. Of primary concern is differentiating between predetermined and indeterminate actions.

Predetermined actions are known before the performance begins, represented to the performer as a notated score, and to the computer as a sequence (or an algorithm producing fixed results). Predetermined actions are usually easier to implement, are very dependable, can be created with great attention to detail, and can represent the composer's idealized vision of a work—a polished, finished version. Even within a traditional performer's score, however, there are many indeterminate elements open to interpretation (such as subtleties of intonation, timing, phrasing, and articulation). Thus, *indeterminacy* exists on several levels, based on the ability to predict the final outcome of a performance. However, it is usually a term denoting significant musical features that are not precisely fixed or determined in advance.

Composers interested in process, relationships, action, and dialogue may prefer highly indeterminate actions that are improvisational or based on processes where the specific outcome is unknown. The outcome may vary from completely surprising results to a range of known possibilities. Compared to predetermined actions, indeterminate actions tend to be more spontaneous, expressive, and interactive. They also can be more difficult to implement, harder to control, and less reliable. When a performer improvises, for example, the input is *unexpected* to the system, whereas with a notated score the computer may contain a version of the performer's score and look for *expected* input. (See score following, chapter 9.) Improvisational works need software that recognizes performance features or conditions to trigger events. Similarly, the computer output may be indeterminate, ranging from a highly constrained process that produces variations with minute differences to wildly random results that will continually surprise the performer. Indeterminacy often results from surrendering some control to unpredictable processes with widely changing behavior.

Improvisational processes have a high degree of *indeterminacy* since musical features are not precisely fixed or determined in advance. The concept of indeterminacy is ideally suited for computer music since the degree of randomness and the range of random parameters can be specified precisely (see chap. 7). Compositional techniques of indeterminacy were pioneered in the forties and fifties by composer John Cage, who created very strict rules (algorithms) to generate large scores for both acoustic ensembles and electronic tape pieces. To create some of his pieces, he used random procedures to pick one of many compositional options or to set musical parameters. He also experimented with indeterminacy in performance, offering verbal instructions or graphic images to performers in place of traditional scores. Many of the pieces used "chance operations," such as throwing coins, to create everything from the smallest details to the larger musical structures (Nyman 1980).

Many composers were influenced by Cage's work and implemented some of his ideas in different and imaginative ways. Of particular note is the work of Earle Brown, whose "open form" compositions were inspired by Alexander Calder's mobiles. Whereas Cage used random procedures to be free of his own influence over musical materials, Brown used his compositional skills to create all his musical material beforehand, allowing musicians to choose from this material within an intentionally ambiguous form. Two works for orchestra, entitled *Available Forms* (1962–63), consist of many short passages of music labeled with large numbers. During a performance, the conductor improvises the selection and order of the musical material, selecting passages of music and instruments by holding up the number of fingers representing the musical excerpts and cuing in a soloist, section, or the whole orchestra. In *Available Forms,* the score segments are entirely written out, but the selection of instrumentation, density, timing, and prewritten material is left entirely in the hands of the conductor. In this way the music was represented in changeable form, like Calder's mobiles, whose materials never changed but whose form was constantly in flux as the various sections spun around (Griffith 1981).

European composers, most notably Karlheinz Stockhausen, also created works in mobile form that used elaborate indeterminate processes to create musical material and form. The orchestral works of Witold Lutoslawski features short quasi-improvisational moments surrounded by larger, carefully notated sections that define the form on the large scale. Thus, there are indeterminate events within a predetermined structure. The groundbreaking experimental works from the fifties and sixties are worthy of study as models of interaction and indeterminacy that may be useful to computer musicians.

Linear vs. Nonlinear Structures

The structure of a finished work is most often comprised of multiple sections, with local events determining the connection of one note or sound to the next. Both local events and larger compositional structures may be more or less predetermined or indeterminate. The design of interactive software will depend on the types of interaction and the amount of freedom desired in the larger structure and in the smaller events.

Compositional structures may be considered *linear,* with sections of music ordered sequentially as in a traditional score, or *nonlinear,* with sections ordered differently for each performance, determined by performer input or computer processes (see fig. 2.1). Within each large section, smaller "local" events may be predetermined and ordered as in a traditional score, or they may contain aspects of indeterminacy.

Nonlinear structures have sections whose order is not determined before a performance, with several parts of a composition available at any given time. For example, a score might contain five measures of music that can be performed in any order. Thus, the way that sections are chosen, or the method for navigating large collections of material, will have an essential impact on the form of a work. The timing and ordering of musical sections in response to user input requires new modes of compositional thought that challenge traditional notions of form and cohesion. Structure, form, timing, order, development, and transition: These are some of the issues that are of primary concern to composers of a traditional score. A composer employing nonlinear structures must be willing to give up total control of these important compositional decisions, delegating them to a performer or to improvisational computer processes. If sections seem to pop up without connection or purpose, there is a danger of losing the feeling of the work as a completed whole, and losing the connected, forward-propelling impetus that gives some music a coherent dramatic structure. What is gained is a malleable form, full of spontaneity and invention, given shape by a skillful performer. Similar concepts of nonlinear structure may be viewed in CD-ROM titles, hypertext, and multimedia works where issues of navigation affect cohesion and experience.

A single large computer program with many highly interactive parameters could also serve as a nonlinear structure without specifying sections, since such a complex system could be always "on" and responsive to a performer's input in a number of unpredictable ways. This model assumes that the computer's response will be rich and varied, a virtual entity capable of making informed musical decisions. Such a program structure would seem to suggest free improvisation as the input, but that is by no means the only option. In fact, a performer playing a traditional written score within a very free interactive computer environment may produce compelling results, with the subtleties

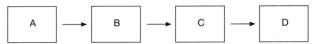

Linear Structures. Each section of music is sequentially ordered.

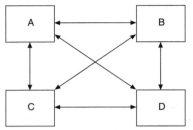

Nonlinear Structures. Any one section of music may be preordered or followed by another section.

Figure 2.1
Linear and nonlinear structures

of score interpretation reflected in the computer music, and the computer, in turn, influencing the performer's interpretation of the score.

Predetermined vs. Improvisational Events

Notes, phrases, rhythms, sounds, dynamics, and articulation make up the smaller musical events that form larger sections. Like the structures that they create, musical events for both the performer and the computer can be predetermined or improvisational. (*Improvisational* is a better term than *nonlinear* for indeterminate note-to-note events, since music at this micro level usually appears to be linear.) Written scores for the performer have their counterpart as fixed sequences for the computer. A sequence may be considered here not only as a prerecorded performance, but also as any computer process that produces identical musical results each time it is run. For example, pitch sets and rhythmic values or mathematical functions stored in the computer could be used as input to generate the same musical passage for each performance.

Improvisation is a huge subject that is beyond the scope of this book. The extensive body of literature available on jazz improvisation is worthy of study for concepts applicable to interactive works. A performer's improvisation may work in conjunction with improvisational computer processes, simulating dialogue between two or more performers. An improvisation may also trigger predetermined event data stored in the computer by specifying target notes that could be used to trigger such things as short sequences of predetermined grace notes or to supply a stored harmonic accompaniment.

The computer can be in an improvisational "state," awaiting any input without expectations from the performer, and containing randomized variables that produce continuous variations or other unpredictable results. A highly improvisational work could have several sections, with each section's behavior static in the sense that it would always be "on" and continuously responsive to performer input. Thus, there could be great activity and variety within a section, but the character of each section would be different, based on selected computer processes. Thus, each performance would be familiar, yet different. Improvisational sections may also evolve, with musical parameters changing gradually over time.

Between strictly predetermined music and "free" improvisation lie strategies that combine both these techniques. Often a composer may wish to have sections well-delineated and structured linearly to control the sense of timing, pacing, or harmonic motion, with the smaller events within this larger structure open to improvisation and surprise. One thing to keep in mind is that a very high level of improvisational skill and artistry is needed to create an entirely "free" performance successfully. When using performers untrained in the art of improvisation, it might be best to use either a written score or a guided improvisation that offers musical models or instructions that constrain choices of material. A few "free" sections, where musicians respond purely to the computer music to create a dialogue, could be mixed with more predetermined sections.

These issues of control and expectation, and the drama they create, are ripe for exploration, suggesting many types of relationships uniquely idiomatic to the interactive medium. For example, a performer may be controlling the tempo of the computer, when suddenly the tempo is taken over by the computer, forcing the performer to "keep up" with it, the resultant struggle creating audible tension. Or part of a performer's improvisation may become the basis of computer variations as they are sent to various transformative algorithms. These techniques hold great promise for interactive composition, suggesting a new paradigm for creating music. What is intriguing is that a player must work to learn the personality of the computer algorithms in order to engage in a dialogue with the computer, and the computer music may, in turn, "learn" the musical personality of the performer, incorporating his or her human idiosyncrasies and the subtleties of playing style.

Instrument Design and Limitations

Control can also be viewed on a more immediate level between performers and their instruments. The physical limitations of each instrument's unique sound-producing mechanism requires physical skills that make an instrument difficult to control. This helps create the idiosyncratic qualities associated with that instrument, the qualities that give it *character.* Many twentieth century composers, in their quest for new sounds, challenged the physical limitations of instruments by breaking free of their normal playing methods. John Cage, for example, created pieces for *prepared piano,* which required the performer to insert metal bolts, rubber bands, and pieces of paper into the piano strings to alter the sounds of the instrument. Other composers used such extended techniques to play brass mouthpieces, place gongs in tubs of water, or tap the wooden body of a string instrument.

Ironically, computer music, with its unlimited capacity for creating new sounds, lacks the very physical limitations of playing techniques and sound producing mechanisms that are responsible for producing such richness and character in acoustic music. Thus, performance gestures shaped by a particular instrumental technique become valuable data when applied to sound and computer music processes that reflect their idiosyncratic nature. Furthermore, it is possible to *simulate* some aspects of these physical restrictions by limiting a computer's response to range or dynamic level, changing articulations, or creating a tempo that is slightly uneven. Chapter 7 will cover ideas for defining instruments and "humanizing" techniques.

Human-machine interaction begins with the study the physical actions that produce music and the acoustic properties of instruments that respond to these actions. Using the arm to bow a cello is an entirely different physical activity from blowing into a saxophone, and these gestures help produce the characteristic sound of a particular instrument. Orchestration utilizes the strengths and weaknesses of various instruments by taking into consideration the subtleties that arise with each instrument's unique method of sound production and playing technique.

MIDI devices fall into several categories. Most dedicated MIDI controllers are modeled after acoustic instruments, such as keyboard synthesizers, electronic drum pads, or wind controllers. These devices take advantage of a musician's expertise with an instrument. They act as a familiar interface to digital sound modules, which may be an integrated part of the instrument, as in the case of most MIDI keyboards, or may be a self-contained rack-mounted unit accessed by an external controller.

While most MIDI instruments do not produce acoustic sounds, hybrid MIDI/acoustic instruments, such as the Zeta MIDI violin or Yamaha MIDI Grand Piano, try to have the best of both worlds: real acoustic sound produced from a traditional instrument, and an accurate and dependable MIDI controller. This enables performers to play with all the subtle variations of tone production and interpretation developed over years of practice, while also sending digital information. Many of these instruments have specially designed hardware switches that determine MIDI information from the physical aspects of a performance, such as the hand position on the neck of a string instrument or the valve position of a wind instrument.

Pitch-to-MIDI converters are also used in hybrid MIDI/acoustic instruments to track pitch and dynamics, but their primary use is to add MIDI capabilities to a traditional acoustic instrument by transforming its audio signal, received via microphone, into MIDI data. While this might seem ideal, the complexity of sound and the variety of playing techniques available on an acoustic instrument makes the translation from the acoustic realm to the digital realm difficult. So far, stand alone pitch-to-MIDI converters have proven less accurate than specially designed MIDI instruments.

Continuous controller devices augment the performance capabilities of MIDI instruments by adding foot pedals, data sliders, aftertouch, and modulation wheels. Continuous controllers add physical hooks to synthesizer parameters that shape aspects of the sound and should be considered important and expressive additions to models of traditional instruments. Max can follow each controller as it sends continuous values between 0 and 127. Some controllers can even offer clues to Max about how a tone module will produce changes in timbre and vibrato, since the control of these parameters is often assigned to aftertouch, breath control, and the modulation wheel.

Several unconventional MIDI devices have been developed that promise new ways for humans to interact with computers. Most of these devices are designed to turn physical motion and body position into MIDI data. (See the last part of chapter 10 for details.) These dedicated MIDI controllers open up exciting artistic possibilities for nonmusicians to interact with a composition. Thus, music may be generated based on the motions of a dancer, taking advantage of expert physical control and expressive use of the body. Motion detectors, which respond to a person's presence in a location, allow people to "walk through" active sound installation, triggering sounds via MIDI.

The typing keyboard and mouse should not be underestimated as devices for shaping and generating music, since they have the advantage of having a large number of expert users. Typists can already execute lightning fast keystrokes; even children quickly gain expertise playing computer games that challenge hand-to-eye coordination. While the keypad provides an easy layout for entering accurate and discrete data, the mouse represents motions made by the hand, smoothly describing a continuum of data with familiar gestures. This technique should not be compared with a musician's years of experience shaping musical phrases on a traditional instrument, since many of the expressive qualities of a musical instrument would be lost using the keyboard and mouse. Besides, the theatrical aspect of an onstage performer effortlessly typing on a computer keyboard lacks the visual interest and drama of a musician's effort and elegance in playing an instrument. Nevertheless, the computer's controls open up creation and performance to many people who might never otherwise actively participate in making music. It also forces trained musicians into new territory by making it impossible for them to fall back on ingrained habits associated with an instrument. Many composers practice with these standard computer input devices in order to control software during performances, where the computer may stand in as a solo instrument or be part of an ensemble of other musical instruments (or other computers).

The numerous types of input devices described here all have their merits; the needs of the composer will determine which devices will work best. Thought should be given to the kinds of physical gestures used to send data to the computer, and to how specific human movements can best serve a composition. With models based on acoustic instruments come not only the benefits of prior musical experience and training, but also all the old habits and attitudes associated with that particular instrument. Playing new sounds with old instruments only makes sense if the old technique is valid for the composition.

The history of music shows that new technology has always influenced instrument design and sparked new musical thought. The piano music of Chopin and Liszt was inspired by the huge dramatic sound of a new piano design. The brilliance and loudness of the thicker strings was made possible by the development of the one-piece cast-iron frame around 1825. The phonograph record and magnetic tape inspired the experiments in Musique Concrete by Pierre Schaeffer, beginning in the late 1940s. The invention of the guitar pickup in the 1930s was central to the later development of rock and roll. So it makes sense today, as digital technology provides new sounds and performance capabilities, that old instruments are evolving and new instruments are being built to fully realize this new potential. New compositional ideas demand new technical resources, with many technical innovations fueled by a composer's musical vision.

II *Programming Foundation*

3 *Graphic Programming with Max*

This chapter is designed to provide a technical foundation for readers new to programming and unfamiliar with Max. Part I presents an overview of programming languages and some computer science concepts that are pertinent to gaining a better understanding of interactive programming using Max. Part II is designed to familiarize the reader with the basic Max concepts and operations needed to understand the examples in this book. Some of this introductory information is also covered in Opcode's *Max Tutorial*. While an effort has been made to make this book readable without programming in Max, it is ideally suited for those who have worked through the Max tutorial and are eager to apply their knowledge to create interactive works.

Brief Overview of Programming Languages

Computer hardware operates on a *binary* level, only understanding sequences of 0s and 1s. Each digit represents a *bit*, a single location in computer memory. A bit is a simple switch set to be either on (1) or off (0). Numbers are represented in memory as groups of bits, or *bytes*. Memory capacity is usually expressed in thousands of bytes (kilobytes), millions of bytes (megabytes), or billions of bytes (gigabytes).

Inside the computer, the lowest-level codes are the built-in instruction sets for doing simple arithmetic, comparing values, and storing and retrieving data. The lowest-level programming language, which describes the position of each bit, is called *machine language*. The programmer's typed-in program directly reflects the hardware structure of the computer. A single eight-bit byte allows 256 different instructions—that is, there are 256 different possible combinations of 0s and 1s, starting with 00000000 and ending with 11111111. Each digit in the binary system represents powers of 2, whereas in the commonly used decimal system, each digit represents powers of 10 (the one's place, the ten's place, the one hundred's place, etc). For example, in binary the number 10 represents 2 (2^1), the number 100 represents 4 (2^2), and the number 1000 represents 8 (2^3). Thus, decimal number 60 would be 00111100—that is (from left to right), $32 + 16 + 8 + 4 = 60$.

Since most people find staring at a long series of eight-digit numbers counterproductive and counterintuitive, *assembly language* was developed to give meaning to the machine-language code by representing each instruction by a short word or abbreviation. For instance, ADD R3, R4 means "add the number stored in memory location R3 to the number in R4." Because assembly commands are direct commands to the processor or memory of the computer, each type of computer has its own unique assembly language (Cooper 1987).

Unlike assembly language, *high-level* languages have the benefit of being machine independent, allowing programmers to solve complex problems in software without having to be concerned with the hardware structure of the target computer. High-level languages, like Pascal and C, were designed to aid programmers by providing commands that are concise yet easier to understand than machine or assembly language. Such languages use a *compiler* to translate a single line of code into many machine-level instructions without the programmer having to be concerned about the details of memory locations and bits. High-level languages often contain commands resembling English. For example, Pascal contains commands such as *repeat . . . until* for executing a "conditional loop." A conditional loop will *repeat* a task, such as adding one to increment a number, *until* a condition is met, such as the number finally equals 100. Then the process stops. This makes programming conceptually closer to everyday ways of thinking.

Even though high-level languages resemble English, their extensive rules can be unforgiving. A simple error in typing, such as a forgotten semicolon or misplaced parentheses, will effectively halt the program; such software errors are commonly known as *bugs*. The process of *debugging* software (searching for and fixing errors) usually accounts for the vast majority of time spent to complete an application written in a high-level language.

Object-Oriented Programming

Many high-level languages are slowly incorporating aspects of *object-oriented* programming techniques. Object-oriented languages allow programmers to "build software systems as collections of interacting objects, each of which models the behavior of some real-world entity." (Pope 1991) A model of real-world behavior is achieved by breaking down a complex entity or process into its constituent parts. One advantage of this concept is that large sections of code can be written, debugged, and reused for a variety of purposes. Each self-contained object has a clearly stated function, and communicates with other objects by passing *messages*. Messages pass data between objects, or send instructions to begin processes. Many small objects can be linked together to form a single larger object.

Since the early eighties, numerous interactive music systems have contained object-oriented features. *Smalltalk* is probably the most prominent representative of a true object-oriented language. It has been used to design a number of interactive music systems such as DMIX (Oppenheim 1990) and Kyma (Scaletti 1987). Object-oriented features have also been added to commonly used languages such as Pascal and C.

Max's basic concept and design share a number of attributes associated with object-oriented programming, such as message passing, although Max lacks some of the elements common to fully developed object-oriented languages. Max offers the numerous benefits of *modular programming,* where large complex programs are constructed of many smaller modules (this is also a feature found in most "structured" languages, such as C, that create large programs out of collections of smaller subroutines). By debugging small modules and making sure that each one works in and of itself, it is easier to locate problem spots and verify that a program functions properly as it grows larger and larger. For example, a complex Max program could be designed to generate melodic variations based on a live performance. Ideally, this process would be divided into smaller identifiable tasks, each one represented by a module designed for one purpose. By putting together small, fully tested objects, programs are easier to test and debug, and components are reusable in other contexts.

Figure 3.1 shows the structure of primary modules and submodules in an imaginary program called *Melodic Variation.* The program would capture melodic input from a performer and generate variations.

Module 1. "Listen" to an incoming performance via MIDI input

Module 2. Analyze the melody

        Submodule a. Analyze for pitch

        Submodule b. Analyze for interval

        Submodule c. Analyze for scale

                Subsubmodule a. Analyze for key

        Submodule d. Analyze for tempo

        Submodule e. Analyze for rhythm

Module 3. Record or otherwise store information from #2

Module 4. Send stored information to variation objects

Module 5. Generate variations by processing original material

        Submodule a. Variation technique #1

        Submodule b Variation technique #2

        Submodule c.....Variation technique #3

Figure 3.1
Modules and submodules

Example 3.1 shows that Max objects can be arranged hierarchically, much like files on a computer. More specialized objects can be saved as separate files and "nested" inside other objects. This example also shows how complex problems are more easily solved by breaking them down into manageable components. Rather than searching a large program for bugs, the programmer is able to pinpoint a problem. If the program doesn't receive MIDI data, check Module 1. If all the information was stored correctly, but there were unexpected results, check Module 4 or 5. The structure of Module 2 shows how objects can be further broken down. A module placed inside of another is said to be "nested." The purpose of a nested module is always to solve a small part of a problem for the main module. Max uses nested objects to increase the readability and clarity of a program.

An important aspect of object-oriented programming is the *reusability* of objects. In general, an object performs a specific task or several related tasks. Once an object is created, that object can be called upon as often as needed and can be modified to perform in a variety of situations. This is much more efficient than having to rewrite the object over and over again for each similar function. For example, a single object that is used to transpose a melody could be called upon to transpose many different melodies, or could be used to transpose chords. Reuse is not limited to a single program; the object could also be used in completely different programs that need the function that the object performs. Object-oriented programs are easier to debug and modify than other language types, since fixing a bug in one object or otherwise changing that object will not interfere with other parts of the program (Pope 1991).

Each object is given a descriptive name and stored as part of a collection or *library*. Libraries can be swapped, exchanged, and reused by many different people. The task of creating software then becomes a collective experience—each individual being able to use the expertise and experience of others. Drawing upon a collection of previously tested objects, programs can be pieced together with minimal time spent writing new code. Collections of Max objects are available at numerous Internet sites.

Messages, Variables, and Algorithms

Communication between objects is done by sending and receiving *messages*. Objects output data in reply to receiving a message. Once an object is completed, the programmer is concerned primarily with the information sent to the object, and what the object will do to that information. Data within an object and the complex internal workings of the process are purposefully hidden from the outside world, because there is no need to know exactly *how* an object works. *What* becomes more important than *how*.

As an example, consider a radio as an object in a box. It has a simple two-knob user interface that controls two values, one for station and the other for volume. These values are *variable;* they represent data inside the box that can change. The volume dial (the input device) controls the process of amplification, sending an electrical "message" to the inside of the box to increase or decrease loudness. The tuner dial selects which radio frequency "message" it will process into sound, and displays the frequency in the interface. The actual processes (wires, circuits, transistors) are hidden from the user; they are *encapsulated* within the object.

A variable is a value or other data (information) used by the computer that can change. Just as the physical circuitry of a radio does

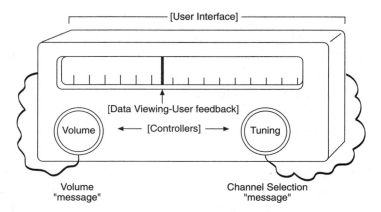

Figure 3.2
Encapsulation: radio "object"

not change when using a radio, the computer processes themselves do not change when running a program. These processes, known as *algorithms,* represent the implementation of a plan of action for completing a task. Encapsulation results when the data used by an object are bundled together with the method or process for completing a task.

Computers are used to solve problems. An algorithm is a step-by-step description for solving a problem. Examples of algorithms abound in everyday life. A cooking recipe is a classic case; it carefully describes the ingredients (data types), quantity (values), and step-by-step cooking procedure (algorithm or method). Algorithms usually solve a single problem or a related group of problems. Large algorithms often contain smaller ones. For example, a recipe for baking bread would have a "sub-algorithm" describing the process for kneading the dough.

Fourth-Generation Programming Languages

Some new programming languages come with specialized packages of pretested algorithms, enabling programmers and nonprogrammers to develop and test software more quickly. In general, so-called Fourth-Generation Languages (4GLs) are not only languages, but interactive programming environments (Teufel 1991). The 4GL philosophy is to insulate programmers from all the details of writing code. These languages provide packages of well-defined tools designed to build specific types of applications, complemented by an intuitive interface that allows the user to manipulate data through sensible screen graphics rather than writing lines of code. 4GLs automatically generate computer code based on the graphical configurations. Productivity is increased because a far greater percentage of time is spent building applications rather than testing and debugging software.

Some common software packages, like spreadsheets and database systems, use 4GL techniques to create custom-made applications. They ask the user to describe *what* needs to be specified to solve a problem, rather than *how* to solve it. 4GLs are narrowly defined to solve a specific type of problem easily. However, what is gained in ease of use is sacrificed in flexibility. One drawback is that computer code generated by a 4GL is usually unavailable to the programmer, making it difficult to do something that the 4GL can't generate by default. Whereas more flexible languages like C take longer to create applications, they often have the advantage of faster run times and cross-platform compatibility, which means that a program in C can run on a variety of computers, although as computer processors speed up, these differences may become less significant.

Max is a high-level graphic programming language, written in C, that incorporates many aspects of 4GLs. When a Max patch is opened, the text file stored on disk is interpreted to create its graphic representation on the computer screen. When Max is operating, each of the Max objects calls upon functions written in C without the user needing to program in C, since that level of programming complexity is hidden from the user. To get around the problem of limited flexibility associated with many fourth-generation languages, C programmers are able to write customized external objects that can be used like any of the objects that are shipped with the Max program. Since C code runs faster than Max, these external objects may also be a way to speed up complex processes. For more information on external objects, see the Max Software Developers Kit.

Since fourth-generation languages are often equipped with easy to use graphical interfaces, the distinction between 4GLs and computer applications is sometimes fuzzy. The primary distinction lies in software packages used to create applications, versus those that are used primarily for editing data. A word processor, for instance, is an application designed specifically for editing text; the output is a file to print rather than a useful set of tools or instructions for producing documents. (However, the ability to create templates and to save formatting gives it some ability to produce documents.) A 4GL, on the other hand, provides an intuitive interface to generate the code for a useful custom-designed application.

A more apt comparison would be between Max and a music-sequencing program, like Opcode's Vision. Music sequencers are applications optimally designed to edit MIDI data. The file is the unique work of a composer and the output is a musical composition. While Max may also be used to edit MIDI data, its main purpose is to create objects for manipulating, generating, processing, and storing MIDI data. In fact, Max can be used to create stand-alone applications, such as editors for synthesizers. Even though Max is often used to produce music that is personal and unique to a composer, the tools created for such a purpose are reusable and portable, which means they may be used by the same composer or other musicians in a variety of situations.

Graphical Programming

Humans are oriented to the world primarily through sight. Computer screen graphics and other elements of graphical user interfaces, or GUI (pronounced *gooey*), allow people to interact with their computers in an easier, more intuitive way, by modeling interaction with physical objects. GUI is slowly replacing older *command-line* interfaces, which require typing in somewhat cryptic commands to get the computer to do something. The popularity of the Apple Macintosh computer and Microsoft's Windows operating system is testimony to the power of intuitive graphic interfaces. By manipulating objects on the screen that mimic a real-world function, a Macintosh file folder, for instance, the user is able to execute a large number of high-level commands without experience or knowledge of programming.

Because interactive applications require a large investment of time to produce a usable GUI, many languages have added tools for speeding up the programming process. With a GUI builder, much of the interface can be created automatically, with the programmer selecting premade graphics from a menu or palette, which decreases the total programming effort. Programmers may begin by specifying how the program will look based on what they want it to do. Max comes equipped with a collection of intuitive, user-friendly screen objects designed specifically for building interfaces for interactive composition. This helps shift the focus away from programming and back to music, since actions related to music can be specified before they are fully implemented.

The evolution of programming languages has produced more and more *abstraction,* a process that allows the general pattern or "the big picture" to be observed while ignoring inessential details (Teufel 1991). Complexities of computer implementation and irrelevant details are hidden, allowing humans to interact with computers on a broad level that is conceptually closer to everyday life. This enables programmers to focus on the essential knowledge from the real world that is needed to achieve the desired results. For musicians and other artists, this means they can spend more time pondering the intricacies of creativity, aesthetics, and artistic thought. Abstraction and metaphor encourage connections made within a larger conceptual framework.

Introduction to Max

Max borrows some of the best aspects of other programming languages and combines them into a package geared specifically to real-time computer music applications: it has an intuitive graphical user interface, it comes with a collection of graphical objects for building custom interfaces, it can create stand-alone applications, and it allows unlimited expandability by breaking out of the Max environment to include external objects written in C. While Max is by no means perfect (its imperfections stemming mostly from the limitation of MIDI rather than flaws in the program design), it is an excellent programming language with which to discuss the techniques of interactive composition. Its user interface is relatively easy to understand; its visual appearance is easy to follow since it resembles flow charts; it allows the composer to focus on developing musical ideas; and it comes with a standard library of objects specially designed for interactive composition.

Objects

Max programs are created by connecting *objects* on the computer screen graphically. Objects are algorithms that precipitate actions. They *do* something. Max comes with a large library of standard objects. *Custom* objects are created by grouping together any number of the standard objects, and *external* objects are new objects programmed in C. Max programs are *modular,* consisting of many of these self-contained algorithms, each one solving a specific problem to achieve a desired musical result. Building larger and more complex programs is a process of adding and connecting together more and more small modules.

Objects receive *messages* from the computer keyboard and mouse, from MIDI instruments, or from other Max objects. A message is *data* (numbers) sent to an object to be processed, or *instructions* (words) sent to an object to describe how it will function. Each object is designed to perform a well-defined task.

Connections between objects are drawn graphically by using the mouse to connect the output of one object to the input of another. These lines allow messages to be sent and received between objects. Because the lines connecting objects resemble wiring, a Max program is often referred to as a Max *patch,* a term borrowed from the wiring systems used to control analog synthesizers. One patch can be placed within another patch to create a custom-made object, known as a *subpatch* (or an embedded object). Thus, the terms "program" and "patch" usually refer to the entire collection of smaller objects and subpatches.

Figure 3.3 shows the anatomy of a simple Max program. This example creates a minor chord for each single note played, adding the third and the fifth of the chord at a lower dynamic level. Each box is an object designed for a specific task. The **notein** object allows notes from the keyboard to enter into Max. The **noteout** object sends a MIDI

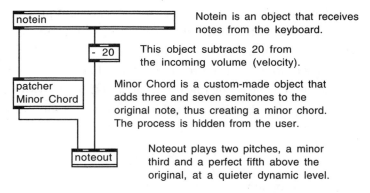

Figure 3.3
Anatomy of a simple Max program

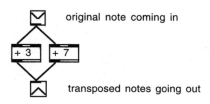

original note coming in

transposed notes going out

Figure 3.4
An embedded object, **patcher MinorChord**

message containing note and dynamic information to a synthesizer. The − object (minus) subtracts twenty from the original dynamic level, and uses that number as the new dynamic level for a chord. All connections are made between the short black bars above and below each object. These are the object's inlets and outlets.

The object **patcher Minor Chord** is an example of a custom object. It is a subpatch designed to add three and seven semitones to the original note. The process inside **patcher Minor Chord** can be viewed by double clicking on the object (fig. 3.4). The square boxes with the triangle, above and below the + objects (add), create inlets and outlets for data. The original pitch enters the object, gets processed, and then is passed through the outlet.

Programs are created in a patcher window, where standard objects are chosen from a palette located at the top of the screen and connected together. Each type of object is represented in the palette by an icon and is selected by clicking on the icon and then clicking in the window at the desired location to place the object, a process familiar to anyone who has used a paint program. The palette is visible only in *edit mode.* Clicking on the lock icon in the upper left corner of the screen toggles between edit mode (unlocked) and run mode (locked). Holding down the command key and clicking anywhere in the window also toggles between edit mode and run mode.

Figure 3.5 shows the patcher window in edit mode, including the palette containing icons of various standard Max objects. The first three, starting from the left are the object box, the message box, and the comment box. Notice that all three are differentiated visually, the object box has double lines on top and bottom, the message box has single lines, and the comment box has dotted lines. *Object boxes* do something. *Message boxes* send data to objects. *Comment boxes* simply display text on the screen, without affecting the program.

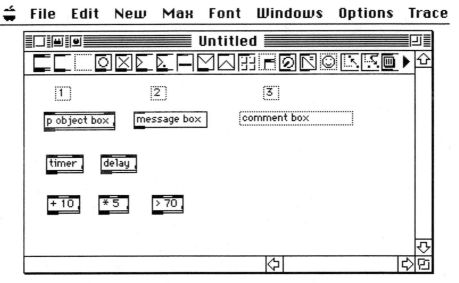

Figure 3.5
The **patcher** window

A descriptive name typed into the object box describes its function, such as **timer** or **delay.** The user doesn't need to know exactly how **delay** works, only that it will delay a specific type of data entering it by a specified amount of time. An object box can also contain symbols for simple math or comparisons, such as **+ 10** (add 10), **∗ 5** (times 5), or **> 70** (greater than 70). An object may be thought of as a "black box," with data entry, processing, and output occurring without any of the "insides" known to the user. All that needs to be known is what kind of action takes place inside each box, and what type of information is expected. This simplifies matters tremendously, allowing musicians to deal with higher levels of programming more closely related to musical concepts.

Once an object receives data at its inputs, all the parameters and variables that define the process are put into action. After the process is completed and a result has been computed the data will be sent to any object that it is connected to one of its outlets. If there are no more objects connected, then the program will search for the next process to begin.

Another group of objects, called user **interface objects** (fig. 3.6), use graphic icons to represent their function. Their appearance suggests

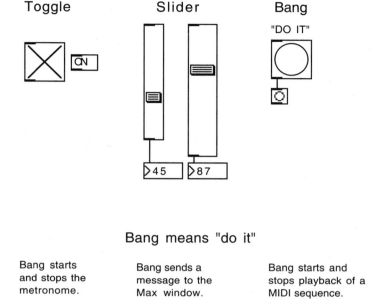

Figure 3.6
Examples of user interface objects

the way they operate, as well as the results they will produce. These are the objects used to create the user interface, and they all operate in real time. For example, various types of **sliders** (analogous to mixing-board faders) increase or decrease values as they are moved up and down. **Toggle switches** may be used to switch between one of two inputs, or to start and stop processes, sending out a one for on, and a zero for off. A special interface object, the **bang button**, outputs a *bang* message, which means "do it." The **bang button** can be thought of as an "on" switch, starting the process of whatever object it is connected to. The **bang button** and the **toggle switch** are available as the fourth and fifth items in the palette (fig. 3.5). The eighth item is the slider.

The number box passes a number
message to the plus object,
adding 10 to the number.

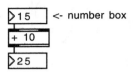
<- number box

<- slider object

The message box passes the message
start to the seq object, starting the
playback of a MIDI sequencer file.

The slider object passes a
number to the number box.

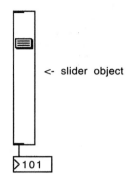

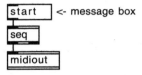
<- message box

Figure 3.7
How objects pass messages

Passing Messages

The double black bars above and below the object name have points
where lines connect the output of one object to the input of another.
These lines represent the connections that enable messages to pass between objects. Object *outlets* (processed data) are always located at the
bottom bars; object *inlets* (data to be processed) are always at the top
bars. Objects have varying numbers of inlets and outlets depending on
their function. In figure 3.7, a data message (the number 15) is passed
from a number box to the **+** object (configured to add 10). The results
of the calculation are then passed to a second number box for display.
In another example, a *control message* (the word *start*) is passed to the
seq object, which starts a sequencer. [Control messages and parameter
names are shown in *italics* throughout this book. Object names appear
in **bold**.] Since control messages may send commands to an object,
they are sometimes referred to as "command" messages.

Each inlet and outlet has a specific purpose, as specified in the Max
manual. With the Assistance Option selected in the options menu, a
brief description of an inlet or outlet will appear at the bottom of the
patcher window by pointing to it with the mouse. Extensive on-line

random
Generate a random number

When it receives a bang, random will generate a
number between 0 and one less than its range.

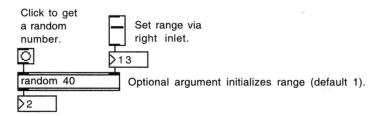

Click to get
a random
number.

Set range via
right inlet.

Optional argument initializes range (default 1).

Figure 3.8
Help file: **random**.help

help files are available explaining each Max object (fig. 3.8). New help
files can be created to describe custom objects. Simply holding down
the Option key and clicking on an object will bring up an operating
example with text explaining inlets, outlets, arguments, and other aspects of the object's operation.

Parameters and Arguments

Each object has a limited number of *parameters,* which are set to determine its behavior. Parameters are the elements in each object that define its function. Most often, they are variables, changing during a
performance according to a score or improvisation. For example, the
delay object has one parameter: delay time (fig. 3.10). The number
2000, representing 2000 milliseconds (two seconds), sent directly to
the delay object's right inlet, will set the object so that a *bang* message
entering the left inlet will be output two seconds later.

Other objects have more controllable parameters. The **noteout** object creates a single MIDI note with the parameters of pitch, velocity,
and MIDI channel. Velocity and pitch messages must be sent to **noteout** before it will play a note on a synthesizer. Some parameters will
use a logical default value if a message is not received in the right inlets.
The parameter for a MIDI channel number, for instance, if not specified
will always default to MIDI channel 1. In figure 3.9, a MIDI instrument

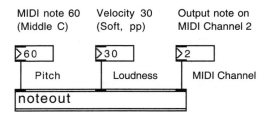

Figure 3.9
Object parameters

These two examples are identical, delaying the bang message by two seconds.

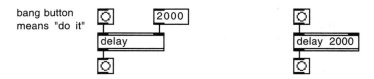

The number 2000 entering the right inlet, sets the delay time parameter to 2000 milliseconds (two seconds).

The argument, 2000, sets the value for the delay time parameter without using the inlet. Any number received by the right inlet will override the typed in argument.

Figure 3.10
Changing object parameters with object inlets and arguments

set to receive on MIDI channel 2 will play middle C at a low dynamic level.

Some parameters can be typed directly into an object box as *arguments,* rather than sending data through an inlet. Any new data entering the inlets will override (replace) the written arguments (fig. 3.10). The list of possible arguments for each object is specified in the reference manual. For most objects, using arguments is optional, while a few require arguments to work. Arguments may be useful in avoiding hidden errors by *initializing* parameters; setting reasonable parameter values each time the program is started up. Arguments should always be used when parameter values are *constants,* meaning that they will never change during the course of running the program; while inlets should be used to change parameter variables while the program is running.

Objects that offer multiple parameter settings can sometimes take lists of data representing values sent to the various parameters. Figure

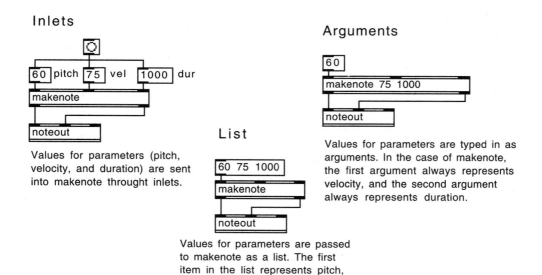

Inlets

Values for parameters (pitch, velocity, and duration) are sent into makenote throught inlets.

Arguments

Values for parameters are typed in as arguments. In the case of makenote, the first argument always represents velocity, and the second argument always represents duration.

List

Values for parameters are passed to makenote as a list. The first item in the list represents pitch, the second represents velocity, and the third represents duration.

Figure 3.11
Three ways to set parameters

3.11 shows three different ways to set parameters for **makenote;** the results for all three are identical. Each example passes the message 60 75 100 to a **makenote** object, creating a single note (60 = C) at a medium dynamic level (velocity 75) lasting one second (1000 milliseconds). The first example uses individual values sent to three inlets, the second uses a list of value (lists are always sent to the left inlet), and the third uses two arguments for velocity and duration with just the note value entering the left inlet.

Message Types

A message is any information passed from one object to another. A message can be sent from the output of an object, a user interface object, or a **message box.** A message box stores and displays any type of message. It sends its message out with a *bang* or a mouse click.

The types of messages Max understands are the following:

1. Numbers—Numbers in Max are either integer numbers (type *int*) or decimal numbers (type *float*).

Figure 3.12
Symbols

2. Words—Words are called "symbols" in Max. Many objects receive symbols that are *control messages,* messages used to describe the operation of the object. For example, when the **delay** object receives the message *stop*, it will immediately stop the delay process, preventing any further output.

3. Lists—A list always begins with a number, and consists of two or more numbers or symbols separated by spaces (for example, [33 stop 2.25]). The order of items in a list is significant, usually representing the order and parameters of the inlets for the object that will receive the list. For example, if the list [60 25 2] is sent to **noteout** it will interpret the first item as pitch, the second item as velocity, and the third item as MIDI channel. This is the identical order and parameters associated with **noteout's** three inlets.

4. *Bangs*—As mentioned before, a *bang* is a special message that means "do it." A *bang* message can be sent by clicking on the **bang button,** or by clicking on the word *bang* in a **message box.** Either way, it sends the same message.

To clarify these concepts, consider the audio signal path in a typical MIDI studio as an analogy to a Max program (fig. 3.13). Three "objects" are needed to produce sound: a keyboard, an amplifier, and speakers. These devices do something: all are connected by wires that transmit electrical "messages" between one object and the next. Thus, to hear a sound from a keyboard, the **synthesizer** object sends a message (of *type* electrical signal) to the **amplifier** object. The amplifier object processes the data, multiplying it to increase the signal. It then sends a new message consisting of the processed data to the **speaker** object. The speaker object processes the data by translating electrical current into mechanical motion, creating sound waves by moving the speaker cone back and forth. Notice that all these "objects" receive the same type of message (electrical signal) and all have one carefully defined but different function or thing that they do with the data: the keyboard handles audio

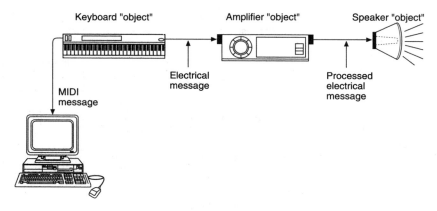

Figure 3.13
Objects and messages: MIDI studio

input to the system, translating physical gestures via the synthesizer module into electrical signals, the amplifier processes the data by multiplication, and the speakers handle output, moving the speaker cones by translating electrical energy into mechanical energy. In addition, the keyboard can send and receive a different message type, MIDI, to and from a computer.

Sometimes the distinction between messages, message boxes, and interface objects can be confusing. Just remember that, in Max programming, *anything that is sent or received is a message.* Almost everything else is some kind of object. Interface objects are optimized for real-time control of messages from the Macintosh keyboard or mouse. For example, **number box** displays the numbers that it sends and receives. It can be controlled physically by clicking and dragging the mouse, which sends out a continuous stream of numbers, or by typing in a single number and hitting return. A **message box**, by comparison, is an object used to display a single message. Whereas a message box always displays an actual message, most other user interface objects are more active, graphically showing how messages are sent (fig. 3.14). Many interface objects hide the details of message passing, providing more intuitive tools for programming.

There are often multiple ways of sending a message in Max. If a number is a constant, a message box may be used, since message boxes retain their value each time the program is used. The **int** object, however, is optimally designed to store a single number (an integer). When

The user interface objects on top send out the
messages printed in the message boxes below.

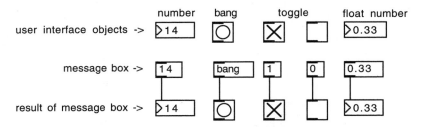

Figure 3.14
Interface objects and message equivalence

values need to be selected to change the behavior of the program in real-time, then a number box is ideal. Number boxes do not save their values after quitting the program. They are initialized (beginning value) automatically with a default value of zero (unless a minimum value is specified). Figure 3.15 shows multiple ways to send the same message. In the first example, the **metro** (metronome) object starts with a *bang* message or with a nonzero number, it will provide continuous *bangs*, representing a tempo of 500 milliseconds (or quarter note = 120), until it receives a *stop* message or the number zero. Each of these methods has its merits, depending on the context of the program. However, because of its obvious on/off function, the toggle switch is best suited to control **metro** from the user interface. The second example shows three different ways to send a single number.

Get Info

Many objects can be customized by selecting them while in edit mode and then choosing GET INFO from the Max menu; command-i is the keyboard shortcut. In figure 3.16, a number box is configured to have a minimum value of 60 and a maximum value of 72. The display output is set to show familiar note names rather than MIDI note numbers. It is a good idea to limit values to filter out unacceptable data or to describe a desired range. For example, number boxes used to send note and velocity information should be limited to a minimum of 0 and a maximum of 127, since these are the only valid values for pitch and velocity.

Different ways to start/stop a metronome.
Bang or one to start, stop or zero to stop.

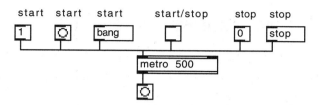

All these patches send the message 25 to be added to 50.
The number box on the left and the slider are changable
anytime the program is running. The message box on the
right must be typed in in edit mode.

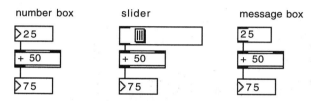

Figure 3.15
Multiple ways to send the same message

Sliders can set a range, as well as automatically offset or multiply values to scale them to a desired range using GET INFO. Using a slider to control the speed of a metronome (in milliseconds) would possibly require that the typical range, from 0 to 127, be first offset by 50 (to avoid impossibly fast tempi) and then multiplied by 20 to provide a reasonable range of metronome speeds between 50 and 2590 milliseconds (in increments of 20 milliseconds). These features help to limit information to values appropriate for a specific purpose.

Order of execution

Even though Max is fast enough to give the appearance that many things happen at once, in reality, a Max patch executes only one step at a time. Max schedules the order of events from right-to-left: objects appearing to the right of other objects will be executed first (fig. 3.17). Max objects with more than one inlet also expect to receive data in

display note names

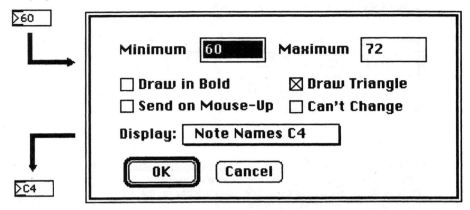

specify offset and multiplier

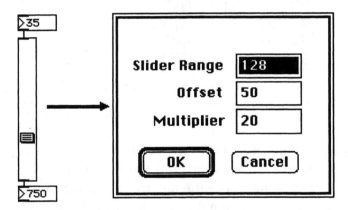

Figure 3.16
Get Info

right-to-left order. Almost all objects will do something when a message is received in the leftmost inlet. Messages received in the other inlets are data used to set parameters in preparation for receiving a message in the left inlet, which triggers an action.

If a single outlet sends data to more than one object, it will do so in a right-to-left order. In the rare instance where the inlets of two or more such objects are perfectly aligned vertically, the bottom object will be executed first (bottom-to-top order). (See the section on debugging in the Max manual).

Notein messages are sent out
from right to left.

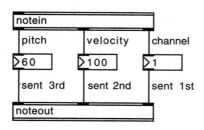

sent 3rd | sent 2nd | sent 1st

Multiple "bang" messages are
sent out from right to left.

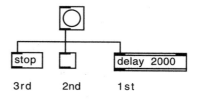

3rd   2nd   1st

Channel and velocity set the
parameters;
pitch triggers a noteout.

Figure 3.17
Right-to-left order

How Max Handles MIDI

MIDI is a standardized way of sending musical information between digital instruments and computers. MIDI is made up of binary messages, consisting of a series of zeros (off) and ones (on) that are the signals used to control computer hardware. Each MIDI message is comprised of two or more bytes of data. Each byte is made up of eight bits. MIDI transmits data one bit at a time in a series (serially), but the bits are transmitted so fast, 31,250 bits each second, that many events are perceived as occurring simultaneously.

Most MIDI messages are composed of two or three bytes (fig. 3.18). The first byte is called the *status* byte. It is actually divided into two parts. The first part tells the receiving device what type of MIDI data to expect; the second part determines on which channel the message will be sent. Any subsequent bytes are *data* bytes representing values for a particular type of message. A status byte always begins with 1; a data byte always begins with 0. The first bit is sent out first to inform the computer to expect a status byte or a data byte. This leaves seven digits to store MIDI information. The maximum number represented by seven binary digits is 127, which also corresponds to the maximum range of most MIDI data, including pitch, velocity, continuous controller data, patch change, and so on.

Anatomy of a MIDI Message:

Status Byte   _____ Data Bytes _____

1001   0000   00111100   01000000

Type/ Channel (1-16)   Note Number (pitch)   Velocity Number (loudness)

NoteOn/ 1   60 = middle C   64 = mp

Figure 3.18
Anatomy of a MIDI message

The most common message, ***NoteOn,*** sends three bytes: a status byte (type of data and channel), a note number byte (pitch), and a velocity byte (loudness). Figure 3.18 shows the three-byte MIDI message received by Max when middle C is played on a keyboard: [1001000 00111100 01000000]. Fortunately, Max displays this as three integers: 1 for MIDI channel, 60 for pitch, and 64 for velocity. The process of transposing that note by a major second would involve simply adding the number 2 to the pitch, to make D (62). Imagine how time consuming it would be to have to program in binary by taking 00111100 (decimal 60) and adding 00000010 (decimal 2) to create 00111110 (decimal 62)!

Max translates all the essential data from complex MIDI messages and presents it to the user as simple integers that use specialized MIDI objects. These objects handle input and output from Max and separate specific types of data from the entire MIDI stream, such as note data or pitch bend data. From there, it is quite easy to manipulate and process the numbers, using algorithms to create music. After the processing is completed, Max repackages the final output in the form of complete MIDI messages before sending the data out to a MIDI device which automates the confusing task of interpreting and assembling binary messages. In between input and output, Max is busy processing the data received.

Most MIDI devices *receive* data on at least sixteen channels, while they usually *send* data on only one channel. Each MIDI channel can have a different sound assigned to it. MIDI objects in Max can specify on what channels they will send and receive data. In figure 3.19, the

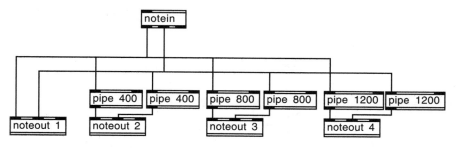

Figure 3.19
MIDI channels

original note (pitch and velocity) is immediately sent to channel 1, and then delayed three times using the **pipe** object, each time playing on a different MIDI channel. The first delayed note is sent to channel 2 after a 400 millisecond delay. The next note is delayed 800 milliseconds and sent to channel 3. The final note is delayed 1200 milliseconds and sent to channel 4. This enables the original note to be repeated three times, each time with a different sound.

Sending and Receiving Notes

Many Max programs use **notein** for input, and **noteout** for output (fig. 3.20). **Notein** does not take note messages through its inlet, since it receives messages directly from the computer's serial port, which is connected to a synthesizer via the MIDI interface. (The inlet on *notein* may be used to specify the input device.) Likewise, **noteout** does not have an outlet at all, since it never passes data to other objects within Max. **Notein** separates a MIDI *Note-On* message, sent via a MIDI controller, into its three parts: pitch, velocity, and MIDI channel. Note number 60, middle C, may be used as a reference to calculate the note names and the register for other note numbers, or a number box may be set to display note numbers as more familiar note names, such as D3 or B5, using Get Info.

When a keyboard note is released, a *Note-Off* message is sent, beginning with a *Note-Off* status byte (1000), and otherwise identical to its corresponding *Note-On* message. Max interprets this as a second event, receiving the same note number and MIDI channel, with velocity 0. Since a single keystroke is usually thought of as a single event, a special

Notein receives MIDI data
from any MIDI device,
representing pitch, velocity,
and MIDI channel.

Noteout sends MIDI note data to a MIDI device.

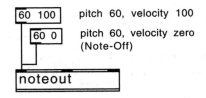

pitch 60, velocity 100

pitch 60, velocity zero
(Note-Off)

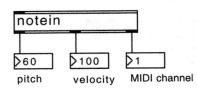

pitch   velocity   MIDI channel

Stripnote removes Note-Off
messages from incoming
MIDI data.

Makenote simplifies programming by adding
a Note-Off message to a note after a given
duration. Without makenote, a note would
continue forever.

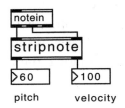

pitch   velocity

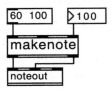

Figure 3.20
notein and **noteout**

object, **stripnote**, is often paired with **notein. Stripnote** ignores *Note-Off* messages which allows a one-to-one correspondence between each note played and each note input to Max. (**Stripnote** works by simply filtering out the number zero.)

On the other end, **noteout** takes three integers, representing pitch, velocity, and MIDI channel, and packages them into a complete three-byte MIDI message (fig. 3.20). **Makenote** usually precedes **noteout**, restoring the *Note-Off* messages that were removed by stripnote, so that a note can end. **Makenote's** right inlet determines the duration of each note. When a note begins, **makenote** sends velocity and pitch data to **noteout**. At the end of the specified duration time, **makenote** sends a second message to **noteout** with velocity zero (*Note-Off*). Without **makenote** to provide a *Note-Off* message, a note could continue indefinitely. Since **noteout** communicates directly with the computer's serial port, it does not pass any data to other objects within Max, and so it does not contain an outlet.

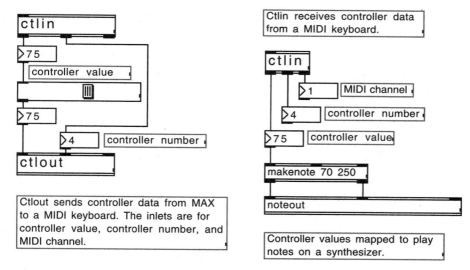

Figure 3.21
MIDI controllers

Continuous Controller Data

Max also handles all types of MIDI data not directly related to notes. *Continuous controllers* (fig. 3.21) are MIDI controller devices that include the modulation wheels, foot pedals, data sliders, and aftertouch that are present on many MIDI keyboard instruments. Each controller is identified by a corresponding controller number, and outputs values between 0 and 127. These data can be interpreted by the computer in a variety of ways. The modulation wheel, for example, is continuous controller number 1. It often controls vibrato and timbre changes on a synthesizer, but it can be used to control computer processes, such as changing tempo or delay time. **Ctlin** and **ctlout** handle continuous controller input and output from Max. The object's parameters, from left to right, correspond to controller value (data), controller number (identifies type of controller), and MIDI channel. Many control numbers are reserved for common functions found on synthesizers, such as controller number 7, which is used to control the overall volume of each MIDI channel. This is similar to moving a volume slider, and is different from a velocity value, which represents the dynamic level of a single note.

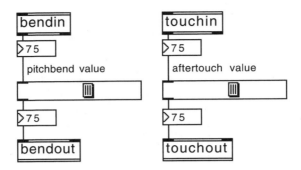

Figure 3.22
Pitchbend and aftertouch

Continuous controller data can be *remapped* in Max, using the incoming numbers to control a host of functions within the program or on a synthesizer. For example, a modulation wheel could be used to influence the computer's tempo or alter synthesis parameters, or the data could be remapped directly to control the main volume or play pitches (fig. 3.21). In this way, MIDI controllers can be used as valuable physical input for computer processes.

Two MIDI controllers are not covered by **ctlin** and **ctlout**: pitchbend and aftertouch (fig. 3.22). These controllers have their own special objects. Pitchbend messages have two data bytes, as opposed to one for continuous controllers, which gives them thousands of numbers to represent pitch in fine increments to assure continuous, smooth pitch glides. These numbers are scaled (divided) as they enter Max, using **bendin**, to fall within a 0 to 127 range, with 64 being the middle resting place for the pitchbend wheel. (Two related objects, **xbendin** and **xbendout**, will maintain the finer resolution of pitchbend values.) Pitchbend response can be set on each instrument to determine how a particular sound will respond to the pitchbend data sent from **bendout**. Similarly, aftertouch uses **touchin** and **touchout** to transmit continuous pressure applied to the keyboard.

Program Change Messages

Each sound or "voice" that is selectable from a synthesizer's front panel may be assigned a specific program change number. A computer can send a program change message to select sounds or "banks" (groups)

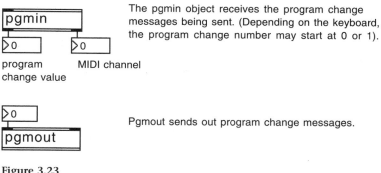

Figure 3.23
Program change messages

of sounds from a synthesizer automatically. This message can be used to automate timbre changes and create orchestrations in Max. A separate program change message can be sent on each MIDI channel (fig. 3.23). **Pgmin** and **pgmout** receive and send program change messages with the right inlet/outlet representing MIDI channel, and the left inlet/outlet representing data (program selection number).

Sending and Receiving Complete MIDI Messages

Max also has provisions for sending and receiving the entire stream of MIDI data, which could include messages for notes, continuous controllers, MIDI channels, and program changes—in other words, everything sent to the serial port via MIDI. **Midiin** accepts the entire MIDI stream, and is often paired with **midiparse**, which separates all the data into its various types (fig. 3.24). If only pitch and velocity are required for input, **notein** is a much more efficient choice than **midiin**. However, it is sometimes useful to have the entire MIDI stream available. On the output side, **midiformat** packs the various types of data into a message that is sent out as a MIDI stream by **midiout**. **Midiin** and **midiout** are often used in conjunction with the **seq** object, which can record and play back a performance (sequence), and which writes and reads standard MIDI files saved to disk. Seq can also play standard MIDI files created with another software application, such as a sequencer or a notation program. A MIDI overview and specification can be found in the Max manual.

Midiin is an object that receives all MIDI data being sent to Max.

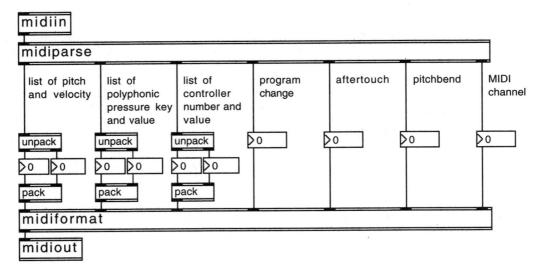

Figure 3.24
midiin and **midiout**

Chapter Summary

Max is a full-featured programming environment for interactive composition that borrows some of the best features from current trends in programming languages:

1. It has an intuitive GUI with interface building tools.

2. It uses elements of object-oriented design.

3. It can create stand-alone applications.

4. It can be customized and expanded with external objects written in C.

This chapter completes the basic foundation for Max programming. Chapters 4 and 5 will investigate more advanced programming topics, such as data structures and interface design. Subsequent chapters will focus on the specific use of various objects to produce interactive compositions.

4   *Program Structure and Design*

Composers creating interactive works must be simultaneously aware of both musical and programming concepts. Although similarities and overlap exist in writing software and in writing music, it may be helpful to separated the two conceptually since each may have a different goal. Viewed one way, programming provides the necessary *tools* (algorithms) for a composer to create a finished *work of art* (sound). Since these two tasks are intricately connected, it is important to remember not to mistake the paintbrush for the painting. The composition is based on a decision-making process that involves how sounds are presented over time; this has always been a central concern for composers. Viewed another way, software *is* a composition (as much as a traditional musical score is a composition) that embodies musical potential through logic and imagination. It contains all of the possibilities that may occur and is more like a musical entity whose behavior can change than like a fixed work of art.

Max is seductive; it is easy to develop an endless variety of inventive ways to produce and process music, but much more difficult to meld these capabilities together to form a coherent work of art. Composers may lose sight of their music by creating more and more modules that add functionality to their programs, only to realize that, after months of work, there is no *composition,* only a great collection of tools. Composing deals with the difficult aesthetic decisions needed to create musical form by selecting and developing the materials best suited to express certain musical concepts, inventing musical processes, unfolding a dramatic shape, painting a mood, and forming a tangible sense of the passing of time. Programming allows the composer to realize this artistic vision in a way that is, sometimes but not always, conducive to the creative process.

Both composers and software developers work in an abstract world to create something that is convincingly whole and complete. Both create form by organizing a multitude of parts using logic, strategy, and aesthetic reasoning. Musicians often speak about the "organic" quality of a work; by which they mean that all the parts are essential and related, grown out of the same substance to create musical entities, characters, or feelings. Small moments create small sections that are defined by their function within a piece—for example, an opening statement or a transition. These are in turn grouped together, forming larger meaningful sections, with all the parts related to a unified whole. Successful computer applications, like successful music compositions, are also much more than the sum of their parts.

Writing a computer program involves purpose and creativity. Beauty and elegance emerge from the structure and design of the multiple components that go into a large computer program. A problem may be solved with a solution that is graceful in its simplicity and efficiency. Max programming encourages *organic thinking* by using completely independent modular parts to create larger integrated wholes. Modules also have the benefit of reusability; they may be used in other programs, or they may be modified to take on new functions. Finally, the user interface design (discussed in the next chapter) shows more striking aesthetic parallels, such as how to choose images that best represent program functions, or how to navigate between the various components of a program.

Approaches to Programming

Max encourages spontaneous experimentation. Tinkering and hacking seem to be the essential experience shared by all beginners. More substantial work requires some planning. Defining the nature and scope of the project will shorten the time devoted to software development by focusing on a clear purpose. Is the software going to be used to create a single piece? If so, what will be the computer requirements? Should the software be flexible enough to be used for many pieces? Will the software be an application that other people may use? Will it be small or large, general or specific?

Decisions regarding software and music design can be based on two approaches that are mutually beneficial: bottom-up design and top-down design. Bottom-up design can be thought of as a working strategy that starts with detail, making small working components that are intuitively linked together to create a larger structure through exploration and experimentation. Top-down design begins with the big picture, the overview, describing the purpose, actions, and structure before any of the details are written.

Bottom-Up Design

Max's intuitive user interface encourages bottom-up design because it quickly turns ideas into working programs. Most composers who are new to Max will begin by writing a simple patch, later thinking up ways to add to it and modify it. That, in turn, will lead to other ideas for patches that might work well with the previous one. Experimentation will lead to discovery and invention. The program will spontaneously grow as each new module or function suggests new possibilities. This programming process is highly interactive. Eventually, the program will reveal its final form. Immediacy, serendipity, and play are all characteristics of a bottom-up approach. Composers may interact freely with their inventions, programming by rehearsal and exploration of the program's capabilities. Ongoing work may be "auditioned" during each step of the process, with the musical results suggesting new programming ideas.

Top-Down Design

Large creative projects require pre-thought and planning, while still maintaining the flexibility needed for discovery. The level of organization is usually proportional to the size and complexity of the project. Top-down design begins with the stated purpose or goal of the finished product. It begins with the largest view, imagining the whole, and proceeds from there by breaking it into increasingly smaller component parts.

Many experienced composers work using a top-down approach when writing acoustic music, sketching out and planning an entire piece before writing a single note. This kind of precomposition is the epitome of top-down design; it is essentially a process that first defines *what it is about,* then continues by sketching a map of the form and large structure, and by identifying the primary elements and processes that will be used. Like writing from a detailed outline, top-down design provides a coherent conceptual map of a large complex form.

Similarly, large computer programs may begin as sketches, key words, and diagrams on paper. Max programming lends itself to top-down design by its ability to create a finished interface before any details are completed. This can act as a guide to help define the capabilities of a program. The completed interface can then be broken down into large objects whose connected appearance is a visual diagram of the program. Thus, the program's actions and purposes are first graphically represented. The ensuing work makes the interface functional by breaking down each large object into smaller coordinated modules.

Figure 4.1 shows a prototype of the interface for a new version of the author's FollowPlay program. The original version of FollowPlay is a large collection of objects, which grew bottom-up as new modules added functionality with each new composition. Eventually, the large number of controls for the various parameters became unmanageable from a single interface. In this attempt at conceptualizing a unified interface, all the necessary controls and visual feedback for a performance were placed in a front panel, and editing subpatches were readily available in a categorical listing. This shows how a program's functions can be defined in the interface, before all the subpatches have been written. The next chapter takes an in-depth look at techniques and concepts for building user interfaces in Max.

Both large and small programs will benefit from a clear idea of purpose and a strategy for implementation. Most likely, the large picture and the details will evolve together. The overview suggests a starting point and general direction; as the reality of the details that emerge suggest structural changes, the overview can be updated to represent the new form. Always during this process, the concept of live musical input will influence programming decisions. Rigid plans are not usually effective because the actual outcome of a program and new discoveries made along the way can never be fully anticipated. Plans are best for maintaining continuity from the initial idea to the final creation. A top-down design helps give the finished piece a viable structure with parts integrated into a coherent whole.

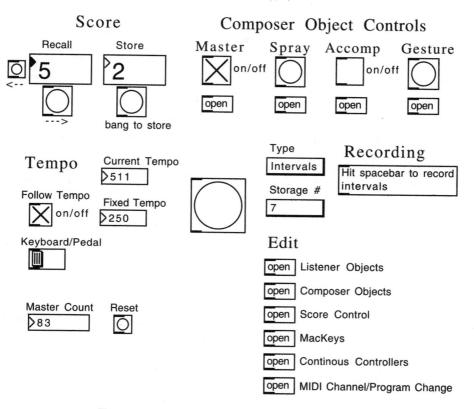

Figure 4.1
Top-down design: followplay interface prototype

Using this "precompositional" approach with Max, one might begin
by defining the overall musical idea—what the piece will be about—
and then creating an interface that will exemplify the actions needed
to produce the music. Having top-level elements in place, the composer may make a series of sketches, building the bottom objects and
experimenting with musical materials and musical processes. Periodically, the maps of the musical and software structure may be modified
as needed or desired, with the interface evolving along with musical
changes.

Suggestions for Max Programming

One of the exciting yet potentially maddening things about Max is that there are so many different ways to do the same thing. Max does not suggest, as do some programming languages, a specific syntax or procedure to structure programs. Programmers are free to develop their own ways to build, organize, and link objects, so that their thought process is reflected in the very design of the software. With this freedom of design comes the increased potential for confusion and undue complication. Here are a few general Max programming suggestions:

1. *Keep it simple.* Try to find simple solutions to complex problems. Choose the objects designed for a specific task that use the fewest number of steps. Make patches do a limited number of things. Eliminate redundant objects and variables. Don't use complex objects to do simple jobs.

2. *Make it modular.* Write many small, modular patches, rather than one large one. Each module can be created and tested separately, so that debugging and updating is easier. Small modules with just a few parameters are more reliable than larger modules. Also, self-contained modules can be easily lifted out of existing programs and reused for other purposes.

3. *Make it readable.* Readability stems from clearly written programs which are logically laid out, use obvious names for objects and variables, and are well-documented. Max programs and patches should have a description at the top of the page explaining their function and features, and additional comments to describe any parts of the program that are not self-explicit. Ideally, a clear graphic depiction of the function of the software should be made obvious by the user interface and by the language's flowchart design. Make important connections visible and unimportant ones invisible. Give objects names that describe their functions, with clearly marked inlets and outlets. Group together objects related by their function.

Often ideas strike quickly, and this is where Max excels as a programming language, enabling the programmer to connect objects rapidly, even while the program is running. The down side is that this can leave a program messy and unreadable. Keep data flow uncluttered by creating logical downward progressions, using right-to-left order, and by avoiding multiple crossed or overlapping wires (unless the overlapping wires all come from or go to the same place). Max requires constant "cleaning up" to make connections clear by segmenting cords and spacing objects so that they are visible and show important connections.

The readability of programs will be greatly improved by "commenting": writing on-screen comments as a way of annotating processes, parameter functions, inlets and outlets, and complicated solutions to problems. Too often someone returns to a program and stares in utter amazement at the incomprehensible mess that previously seemed so simple to understand. Commenting not only acts as an important memory aid for the programmer, but helps others who will use the program or who want to alter objects for their own use. Good commenting strategies include placing comments on the sides of a mostly vertical patch, writing a brief description above a self-contained algorithm, and placing objects far enough apart to accommodate comment boxes. Patcher inlets and outlets may also be commented on to describe the expected input and output using GET INFO. This is an especially helpful way to remember the function of various parameters in custom-made objects.

4. *Encapsulate and hide programming complexities.* Many objects with a complex relationship can be grouped together and encapsulated into a larger patch. Encapsulation embeds and masks complexity, and will help keep the overall program structure simple and greatly improve readability. Ideally, an encapsulated algorithm should perform a single function only, no matter how complex that function is, such as generating varying rhythm from a steady metronome pulse.

5. *Make it generalized and reusable.* Try to give an object variables that make it flexible in many contexts, not just for a specific piece. If a particular variable is never used, eliminate or disable it. A small, general-purpose object will be more useful in a greater number of contexts than a larger special-purpose object. On the other hand, some pieces will demand "custom built" objects with unique capabilities specially designed for that composition.

Keep important values in one place, especially if many objects use those values. Several objects can share values stored in the same **table** or **collection,** for instance. Changing the contents of such a **table** will change the values of all the objects that use that file.

6. *Keep it consistent.* Use similar fonts, standard placement of comments, and patcher-embedding schemes. Be consistent in all aspects of the program. For large projects, a personal style sheet may be helpful, to document in advance the size, fonts, layout, and conventions that will be followed. Capitalizing the names of custom-made objects will help distinguish them from the lower-cased standard objects. Consistency should also follow already established practices within Max itself. For example, when making new objects with multiple inlets, the left inlet should always be the one to trigger the operation performed by the object.

7. *Make it foolproof (complete).* Make the program work for all possible situations. This includes accepting *any* kind of information that a user may send to a program, especially errors. Have variables default to numbers that allow the program to work normally. This can be done by writing arguments into object boxes, or by initializing variables at startup using **loadbang**, which automatically sends a *bang* when a program is loaded. Limit **number boxes** and **sliders** to acceptable values by assigning ranges using Get Info. For instance, the **number box** controlling transposition should never send out values greater than 127, since this will produce illogical values beyond the range of MIDI. To avoid this situation, constrain the possible choices by setting the **number box** to reasonable minimum and maximum values. The **split** object may also be used to filter out numbers outside of a desirable range. A "reset" function is helpful to return variables to their proper state at the beginning of a work, and at each large section. Also, have a clear way to start and stop processes. A "panic" button is helpful to stop all output. A useful object to include in a panic button is **flush** because it is specially designed to shut off all notes currently playing, while avoiding "stuck" MIDI notes (notes that play indefinitely because they have not received a corresponding *Note-Off* message). **Flush** keeps track of every *Note-On* message on every MIDI channel, and supplies an appropriate *Note-Off* message when it receives a *bang*. Inserting **flush** between **makenote** and **noteout**, and sending a *bang* to **flush** when channels and programs are changed will insure that all notes receive a timely *Note-Off* command.

Handling Data in Max

While the previous section aimed at concepts for improving overall programming skills, the remainder of this chapter deals with the nuts and bolts of Max programming: data storage, data flow, algorithms, and debugging. All computer programs require data input, data processing, data storage, and data output.

Data from the outside world usually comes to Max from either a MIDI instrument or from the computer keyboard and mouse. (Other types of input devices are discussed in chapter 10). Once data have been received, Max will either process the information with an algorithm or store the information in a data storage object, or both. Max also produces computer-generated data, using algorithms and pre-stored values that do not necessarily require user input.

Data storage objects are designed to hold information in computer memory in a format that makes it readily available to the program. "Data types" are the various types of information understood by the program. "Data flow" is a general term used to describe the pathways and procedures for moving data or sending messages from one object to another.

Max outputs MIDI data to any MIDI controllable device. It can also output text, graphics, and video to the computer screen, control devices from the computer's serial port, such as a laser disk player, and play sounds internally through the computer's sound output.

Data Storage Objects: Storing and Recalling Information

Max data storage objects are specially built to receive, store, and send information. This could be as simple as storing the last note played on a synthesizer, or as complex as storing the entire score for a large piece. As was mentioned in the previous chapter, Max has several data types. Some data storage objects store only one type of data, such as integers, and others may store several types. A comparison of three commonly used storage objects will show the diversity of size and functionality: **int** (integer) stores a single number, **table** stores many integers in a graphical format, and **coll** has the capacity for large amounts of storage of all of the data types available in Max.

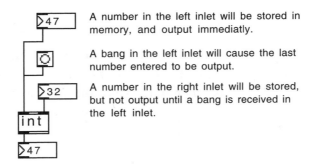

> A number in the left inlet will be stored in memory, and output immediatly.

> A bang in the left inlet will cause the last number entered to be output.

> A number in the right inlet will be stored, but not output until a bang is received in the left inlet.

An optional argument is output when a bang is received in the left inlet.

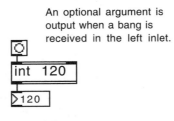

Figure 4.2
int

Int

Int is the simplest data storage object; it holds a single integer in memory (fig. 4.2). A number entering the left inlet is stored and also immediately sent out. A number entering the right inlet is just stored. **Int** only remembers the last number it received; each new number replaces the old one. A *bang* entering the left inlet will output the stored number. An optional argument following **int** may be used to set an initial value. **Int** is an efficient way to store a constant number, a value that will never change while running a program, as opposed to a variable number. In the second example, a *bang* to **int** will always send the number 120.

Figure 4.3 shows how an **int** can be used to delay either the note being played, or the previous note played, using Max's right-to-left ordering principle. A **gate** object is used to show two scenarios. A 1 sent to **gate** allows data to pass through; a 0 closes the **gate** and stops the flow of information. With the left **gate** open (which will close the right **gate**), the incoming note number, 69 (A above middle C), is first stored in the **int**'s right inlet; then it goes through the **gate** triggering a *bang*. (A number in the left inlet of **int** would do the same thing.) The num-

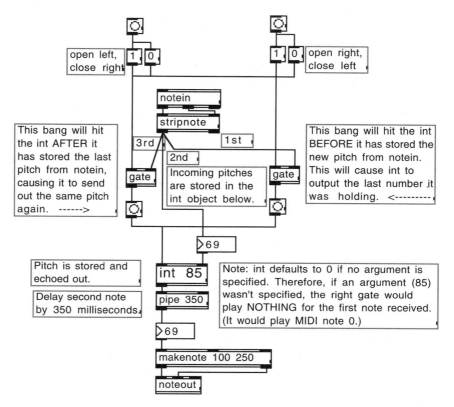

Figure 4.3
int and order of operation

ber is then delayed 350 milliseconds using **pipe**, an object that delays numbers. The result is an echo, or repeat, of the same note.

With the right **gate** open, the incoming note number first triggers a *bang*, which outputs the previously played number stored in **int**. (The very first value from a **notein** will trigger the argument 85.) After the old note is output, the new note is stored. The result is that the note played will trigger the previous note 350 milliseconds later.

Table

A **table** stores a list of integers in a structure called an "array" (fig. 4.4). Think of a simple array like a single row of post office mailboxes, where each mailbox has an address (represented by the index number) and each box contains one item (a single data number). An address is a

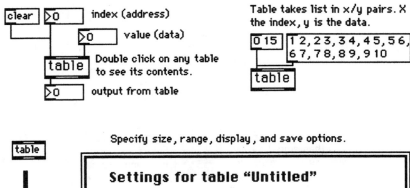

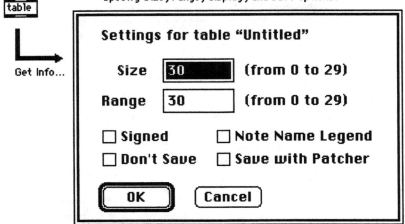

Figure 4.4
table

location inside the computer's memory where data is stored. When an index number is sent to **table**'s left inlet, out pops the number stored in that location. To store numbers, a data number is first sent to the right inlet, followed by the address in the left inlet. Numbers may also be sent as a list, in *x/y* pairs: the *x* is the address, the *y* is the data. The number of addresses that a **table** contains determines its size. The default size is 127, although the user can change the size and other settings for **table** by highlighting the object in edit mode and selecting GET INFO under the Max menu.

Double-clicking on **table** brings up a graphical editing window that displays the array (fig. 4.5). The left side contains tools for editing, selecting, and viewing the data. This example holds values that show a series of small ascending curves. This data could represent the shape of a melody or changes in velocity, for example, depending on how the values are interpreted by the composer.

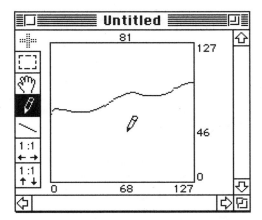

Figure 4.5
table graphic editing window

Figure 4.6 shows how a **metro** object may be used in conjunction with a **counter** to create a melody by continuously scrolling through note data stored in **table**. The data is then transposed up, so that the lowest note will be 48 (one octave below middle C). This avoids MIDI notes that are too low to hear. Most computer music programs work by storing and playing back lists of numbers, representing the basic musical parameters of pitches, dynamics, timing, and duration. **Table** does an excellent job of storing and editing lists of numbers, but because it can only store a single value for each index, it is inconvenient for storing multiple messages that may need to be sent out together, such as several notes for producing chords; for this purpose **coll** is used.

Coll

The **coll** object, short for "collection," is Max's most complete and complex data storage object (fig. 4.7). It stores and organizes most of Max's data types, including numbers, symbols, and lists. It can modify the entire collection with such useful operations as sorting, swapping, and inserting data. At each address, **coll** stores single items or a list of items. The first item at each address is the index, which can be a number or a word. When **coll** receives a number or word that matches the first item, it sends the remaining information listed after the index out the left outlet, and the index number itself out the right outlet.

Table Music uses a metro to access notes stored in a table.

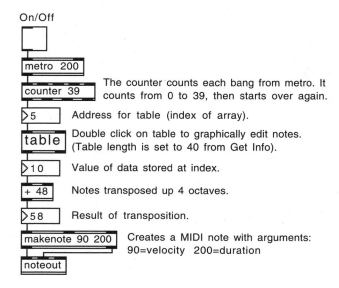

On/Off

metro 200

counter 39   The counter counts each bang from metro. It counts from 0 to 39, then starts over again.

▷5   Address for table (index of array).

table   Double click on table to graphically edit notes. (Table length is set to 40 from Get Info).

▷10   Value of data stored at index.

+ 48   Notes transposed up 4 octaves.

▷58   Result of transposition.

makenote 90 200   Creates a MIDI note with arguments: 90=velocity 200=duration

noteout

Figure 4.6
table music

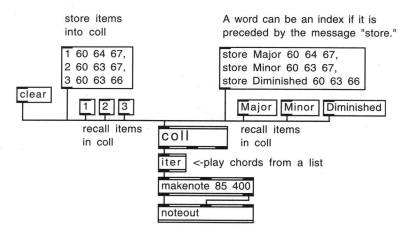

store items
into coll

A word can be an index if it is
preceded by the message "store."

1 60 64 67,
2 60 63 67,
3 60 63 66

store Major 60 64 67,
store Minor 60 63 67,
store Diminished 60 63 66

clear

1 2 3

Major Minor Diminished

recall items
in coll

coll

recall items
in coll

iter   <-play chords from a list

makenote 85 400

noteout

Figure 4.7
coll

```
1, 60 64 67;
2, 60 63 67;
3, 60 63 66;
Major, 60 64 67;
Minor, 60 63 67;
Diminished, 60 63 66;
```

Figure 4.8
Contents of **coll**—lists

Figure 4.7 shows how **coll** stores and recalls lists. The same messages can be stored and recalled using numbers or words as indexes. The message store preceding a word informs **coll** that a word will be used for the index and is not necessary if the index is a number. The messages grouped on the left will have results identical to the corresponding messages grouped on the right: The large lists above will store the information containing the notes for C major, minor, and diminished chords; the single messages below are indexes that will play the chords. **Iter** takes a list and automatically outputs the items in sequential order. In this case, the three notes are played in such quick succession that a chord will be produced. (Remember that MIDI is a serial protocol that can only receive one message at a time.)

Double clicking on **coll** will reveal its contents, where the first item is the index, separated by a comma from the data, and a semicolon marks the end of each address (fig. 4.8).

Similarly, **coll** can store and output words. For example, a line in a **coll** reading [*1, record;*] would output the command message *record* whenever a 1 is received. A series of such messages could be used to control the *record, stop,* and *start* functions of a **sequencer** object.

Unlike a **table**, the size of a **coll** does not need to be specified before storing information. In fact, except for graphic editing, **coll** can do everything **table** does, plus all its other capabilities. However, **table** is more efficient (faster) at storing and retrieving single integers.

Coll and **table** share a number of features used to save and recall data. Both can be named using an argument and can save data as a separate file. Multiple copies of objects with the same name will always share the same data (even if a separate file has not been saved). For example, a **table** named Intervals may contain a list of intervals for creating melodies and harmonies that appear in several locations in a program, and each copy will always contain identical information: when one of them changes, the others will change as well. **Coll** and

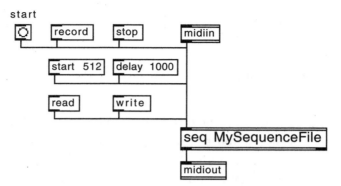

Seq records and plays back a standard MIDI sequence file.

Figure 4.9
seq

table files without arguments can be stored automatically as part of a program by checking SAVE WITH PATCHER in the GET INFO window. Data files can also be loaded with the *read* message (which brings up a Macintosh "OPEN" window), and saved with the *write* message (which brings up a Macintosh "SAVE" window).

Seq and Detonate

Seq (fig. 4.9) is an object that records and plays back MIDI files. **Midiin** allows the entire MIDI stream to enter Max—all information regarding notes, velocities, pitch bend, continuous controllers, and so on comes in on sixteen MIDI channels. **Seq** records this information after receiving a *record* message. Using the *write* message, **seq** can save a recording as a standard MIDI file, which can be read by many other sequencer and notation programs. Similarly, **seq** can read in any standard MIDI file with the message *read*. This allows Max to import and play back complex musical arrangements created with a full-featured sequencer application, such as Opcode's StudioVision. **Seq** takes as an argument the name of a MIDI file, stored on disk, and will automatically load that file when the program is started.

The **seq** in figure 4.10 will automatically load a file called My-Sequence. (The file needs to be placed with the program on the disk so that Max will know where to find it.) A *bang* or *start* message to **seq** plays back the file at the original tempo. A number following *start*

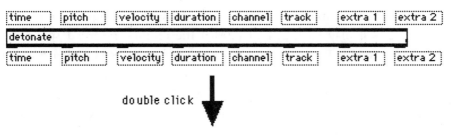

double click

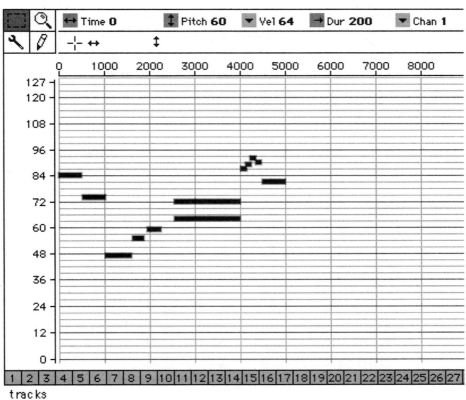

Figure 4.10
detonate

scales the tempo; *start 1024* will play back at the original tempo, *start 512* will play back at half (50%) the original recorded speed, and *start 2048* will play back at twice the recorded speed. Other numbers can be used to produce a desirable tempo. **Seq** output can be sent directly to **midiout**, which sends the MIDI stream to a MIDI device. Data from **seq** can also be separated into individual parameters using **midiparse** (see fig. 3.24).

A related object, **detonate,** is a graphic editor for MIDI sequence data, and has features like **seq's** for reading and writing MIDI files (fig. 4.10). Multiple tracks of MIDI data can be viewed and edited in a piano-roll type view, with note durations proportional to their length (a feature common to most sequencer applications). Data may be viewed in a variety of other ways. Unlike **seq, detonate** does not record timing information automatically, but must have information regarding rhythm and tempo sent to it from another source in Max. This allows for the original tempo and rhythm to be altered in ways that are not possible with **seq.** (See the Max manual for details about using **detonate**).

Other Max Data Storage Objects

Int, table, coll, seq, and **detonate** are data storage objects often used in Max, and other specialized storage objects will be covered in the next two chapters. Here we will mention briefly two versions of array-type objects that store numbers: **funbuff** and **bag.**

Funbuff stores x/y pairs of numbers together the same way **table** does. However, unlike **table, funbuff** has no graphic editing and no predetermined size or ordering. **Funbuff** stores data at any address. For instance, it is able to store numbers at locations 2 and 200 only, without having data stored in between. Only specified locations contain data. This saves memory and accommodates situations in which the range of incoming data varies widely. **Funbuff** also has analysis capabilities, responding to *min* and *max* commands by sending out the minimum and maximum *y* values. This might be useful in determining the highest or lowest notes played in a piece, or looking at the dynamic range.

Bag stores one or more numbers without addresses. A one in the right inlet will add numbers entering the left inlet to the collection. A zero in the right inlet removes any previously entered numbers match-

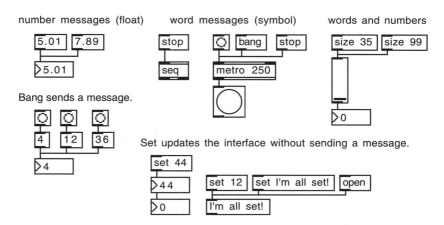

Figure 4.11
Message types and display

ing the numbers entering the left inlet. A *bang* outputs all of the numbers in the order received, starting with the most recent. **Bag** could be used to grab pitches from a soloist's improvisation, remove pitches outside a specified scale, and, finally, play the notes back in reverse order with a *bang*.

Messages: Data Types and Display

Whereas objects embody the processes, capabilities, and potential of a program, messages provide the information that is the lifeblood of the system. Max objects communicate to each other by sending messages. Messages consist of a single word, a single number, or a list of any combination of words and numbers. Max has two main message types: control messages and data messages. Control messages are special commands that control objects. They tell objects to begin or end processes or actions, or change an object's variables or settings. For instance, sending the message *stop* to a **metro** object will cause it to stop. Data messages are usually numbers representing musical information that will be processed, stored, or output. MIDI and number boxes are two common ways that data messages are sent in Max.

Interface objects are designed to send and receive messages, both control and data types (fig. 4.11). A **slider,** for example, selects data messages (integers) using a mouse. A mouse may also be used to select command messages from a familiar Macintosh-style **menu. Message**

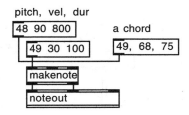

Figure 4.12
Message lists

box is used to display and edit messages. Clicking on a **message box**, or sending it a *bang* will output its contents. The word set, preceding a message will cause a message to be displayed without triggering any output. The open command will bring up a dialog box in which to type a new message. When the word open is followed by a one, it will output the message when the user clicks OK. Otherwise, the message will simply be displayed.

Many Max objects accept lists in the left inlet, representing multiple parameters. If items in a list are separated by a space, all the elements will be sent out together as one message. If items in a list are separated by a comma, each item will be sent out consecutively as a separate message. In figure 4.12, the lists on the left represent the values for each inlet to **makenote**, maintaining the original order, from right to left: pitch, velocity, and duration. (Please note that not all objects accept lists corresponding exactly to their inlets.) All three numbers are sent as a list, creating a single note. The message to the right, with values separated by commas, sends out three numbers consecutively. Each single number entering the left inlet represents pitch. The three pitches are sent out in series so close together that a chord is heard. The last values sent for the other parameters, velocity and duration, remain current until new ones are received.

Figure 4.13 shows various ways to handle lists sent to a **table** object. Clicking on the list [2 9] will store the number 9 at index 2 (the same as sending a 9 to the right inlet followed by a 2 to the left). A list of numbered pairs separated by commas will send out each pair sequentially, loading up the **table**. A list of four single values separated by comas will index four values in the **table**, creating a chord. The control message *clear* sets all values in the **table** to 0. When the toggle switch is turned on to the subpatch, **A Little List Tune**, a message of twelve

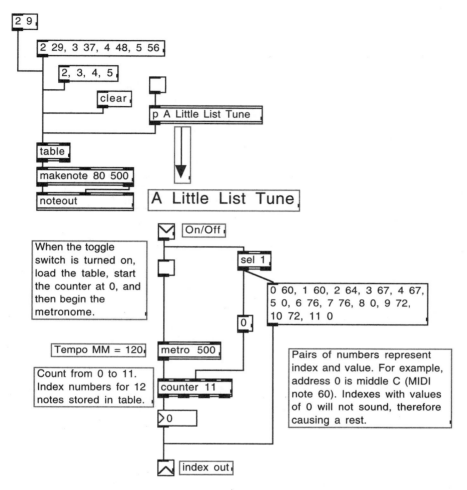

Figure 4.13
Message lists to **table:** a little list tune

paired numbers representing a melody is sent to **table,** a **counter** is reset to 0, and a **metro** object begins playing the melody by increasing the values on a **counter** that is indexed to the **table,** cycling continuously through the twelve notes at the rate of two per second.

Message Arguments

Messages can accept variables. A dollar sign, followed by a number, holds a place in the message that can be changed by an incoming message or list (fig. 4.14). The number represents the order of the item in

Message argument $1 represents pitch values in the
left message list and velocity values in the right list.

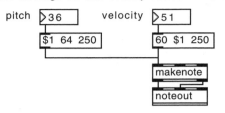

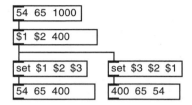

Only the first and second items in the
list are variable (1000 is ignored).

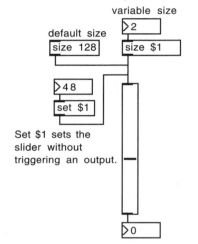

Here, message arguments are being used to
allow variation in the range (size) of a slider.

Set $1 sets the
slider without
triggering an output.

In this example, the three numbers in
the addition problem are packed into a
list that is sent to a message box.

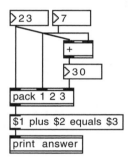

Figure 4.14
Message arguments

the list. *$1* will be replaced by any single item or the first item of a list,
$2 will be replaced by the second item in a list, and so on. The first
example on the left uses *$1* to hold a place in one list representing
pitch and in another list representing velocity. Incoming values from
the **number box** will create and send out a new list to create a complete **makenote** message with variable pitch or velocity. The example
on the right shows that a list [*$1 $2 4000*] will take the first two values
in another list that is passed to it. The third item in the passed list,
1000, is ignored because there is no corresponding *$3* for it to go to.
Instead, the first two items become the new list, along with the fixed
value, 400. The *set* command displays the message. Since each variable
represents the order of the list, when they are reversed [*set $3 $2 $1*],
the list is displayed backwards. The example below, showing a **slider,**

Pack combines individual numbers into a list. Unpack separates
lists into individual numbers. Both objects default to lists of two.

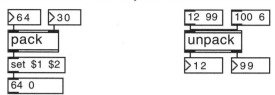

Arguments to pack specify the number and   The number of outlets is determined by the
types (float, int) of inputs. Any input to   number of arguments, and the type of outlet (int
the first inlet causes the output of a list.   or float) is determined by the type of argument.

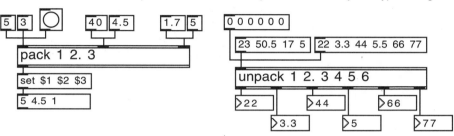

Figure 4.15
pack and **unpack**

uses the *size* message followed by a *$1* to alter the range of the **slider.**
Sending *set* $1 to the **slider** will display a new **slider** position without
sending out a number. The last example, on the bottom right, packs
three numbers into a list that is then used to display a sentence in the
print window.

Forming and Changing Messages

Max includes control messages and objects for manipulating messages.
The most commonly used are **pack** and **unpack**. **Pack** combines individual numbers into a list (fig. 4.15). **Unpack** separates lists into individual numbers. It is often used to separate lists stored in a **coll**. Both
objects default to lists of two. Optional arguments can specify larger
sized lists and data type (*int* or *float*).

Additional items can be added to the beginning or ending of a message using **prepend** or **append** (which have two forms: an object form
and a message form) (fig. 4.16). **Iter** separates a list, sending out each
individual item in order. **Thresh** packs everything received within a
specified amount of time into a list. **Sort** sorts a list from low to high

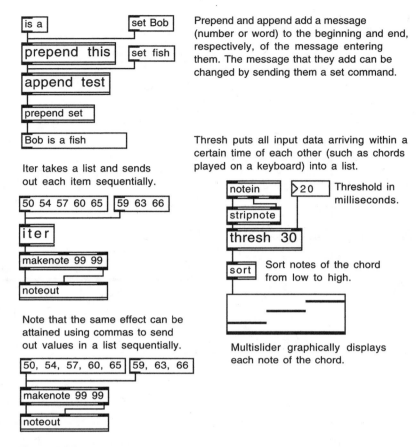

Prepend and append add a message (number or word) to the beginning and end, respectively, of the message entering them. The message that they add can be changed by sending them a set command.

Thresh puts all input data arriving within a certain time of each other (such as chords played on a keyboard) into a list.

Threshold in milliseconds.

Sort notes of the chord from low to high.

Iter takes a list and sends out each item sequentially.

Note that the same effect can be attained using commas to send out values in a list sequentially.

Multislider graphically displays each note of the chord.

Figure 4.16
Manipulating messages

and the results are graphically displayed with multiSlider. (**Sort** created by James McCartney, is not a standard Max object. MultiSlider was written by Michael Lee and Adrian Freed.) A **coll** can also sort items it contains from low to high with the command, *sort 0.*

Data Flow: Moving Information through the System

Max has a variety of ways to send and receive data and control messages. Message flow describes the pipes and pathways by which information travels. The speed, direction, and amount of information sent and processed are crucial to the success of a live computer music piece, especially when many split-second calculations are involved. In Max, this comes down to several basic functions. *Order of operation* deals with the precise ordering of events. *Data routing* is like information "faucets," turning on and off the flow of information and changing its destination. *Remote messages* send and receive any type of data without using connecting cords. Finally, messages may move by *data selection,* creating a pathway dependent on the content of the data. Data selection and identification are two primary ways that decisions are made in Max.

Order of Operation

It is important to reemphasize that the chronological order of events in Max is generally from *right to left.* When a single output has multiple destinations, any operation graphically situated to the right of another will be executed first. Many software problems arise from the general confusion caused by the improper order of execution, exasperated by our well-ingrained habits of reading from left to right. Figure 4.17 shows the number 6, added to three different numbers. One at a time, the 6 is added to 10, then 30, then 50. The results go to a single number box, which displays the results of the leftmost operation, 56, since that was the last one executed.

The ordering of operations can get very confusing with complex patches. During editing and rewriting, an act as simple as moving a single object box may inadvertently change the order of execution and introduce a bug into the program that could take hours to track down. To avoid such pitfalls, two objects, **bangbang** and **trigger,** are used to ensure a chosen order when a single item is sent out to multiple places (fig. 4.18). **Bangbang** outputs one or more *bangs* each time it receives any message. Two or more *bangs* are sent sequentially, from right to

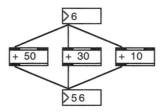

Figure 4.17
Order of operation

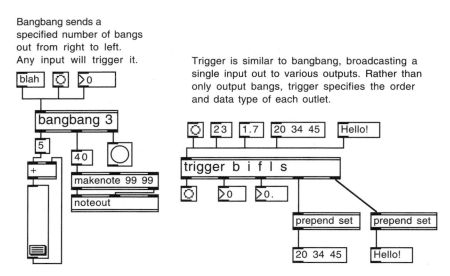

Figure 4.18
Order control: **bangbang** and **trigger**

left, out separate outlets. (**Bangbang** defaults to two *bangs* out, but an argument can specify the exact number of outlets.)

Trigger can be used in the same way as **bangbang**, but it is able to route numbers, lists, and symbols, as well as *bangs*. Any single message sent to **trigger** causes multiple outputs, with the order (right to left) and data type of each outlet specified in the argument list. The data types for each outlet in figure 4.18, from right to left, are symbol (s), list (l), float (f), integer (i), and *bang* (b). **Trigger** is an essential object for scheduling the order of messages. To avoid potential problems, use **bangbang** and **trigger** often to permanently build in the essential order needed for a program to run properly.

Sometimes the right-to-left ordering of Max prevents the successful execution of an algorithm. To get around this, **swap** reverses the order of its two inlets, effectively turning the execution into left-to-right ordering. Figure 4.19 produces a mixed-up keyboard by swapping incoming velocity and pitch. The louder the note, the higher the pitch. Low notes on the keyboard will be quiet, while higher notes will be loud.

Data Routing

Data in Max can be thought of as traveling through pipelines comprised of the connections to and from objects. Objects for data routing

Swap is useful in changing the order of events. It takes two input values, each of which goes out the opposite outlet. In this example, pitch and velocity parameters are swapped, so that notes played harder will sound higher, and lower pitches will sound softer.

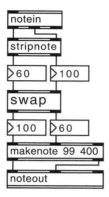

Figure 4.19
swap

direct incoming streams of data to appropriate outlets, and also open and close data pipelines. The two most useful objects for this are **gate** and **switch.**

Input is said to be "gated" when the data flow can be turned on or off; when the gate is open the data flows, and when the gate is closed the data stream is shut off. **Gate** accepts any data in the right inlet (fig. 4.20). In the left inlet, **gate** is open with a one and closed with a zero. The **toggle switch** is often coupled with **gate**, since it outputs a one in the on position and a zero in the off position. **Gate** can also "route" data. It takes an optional argument that expands its number of outlets, allowing for a single data path to be routed to one of several outlets. A number in the left inlet specifies which outlet the data will be routed to.

Switch is the opposite of **gate** (fig. 4.21). It selects one of several inlets and directs the data flow to a single outlet. Like **gate**, **switch** can also open and close data flow connections. The argument sets the number of inlets, with two as the default. The leftmost inlet is reserved as the control mechanism. A zero will shut down all data connections, a nonzero number will select between two or more inlets.

Ggate and **Gswitch**, user interface objects, that are animated graphic versions of **gate** and **switch** (fig. 4.22). **Ggate** takes one input and

Gate is a simple object that is closed by a 0 and opened by any other number received in the left inlet. When the gate is open, information received in the right inlet will pass through. When the gate is closed, all information will be blocked.

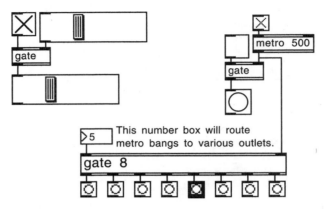

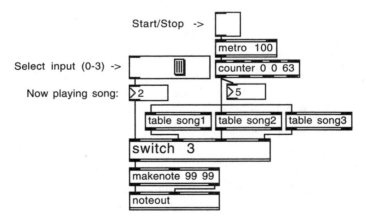

This number box will route metro bangs to various outlets.

Figure 4.20
gate

Switch selects between a number of inlets.

Figure 4.21
switch

from the Max Ggate help file:

Switches the right inlet between two outputs.

A bang at the control (left) input toggles the switch. A click on the switch also toggles it. A zero at the control input sets the switch to the left input while values > 0 sets the right input.

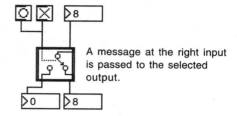

A message at the right input is passed to the selected output.

from the Max Gswitch help file:

Switches the output between two input streams.

A bang at the control (left) input toggles the switch. A click on the switch also toggles it. A zero at the control input sets the switch to the left input; greater than zero sets the right input.

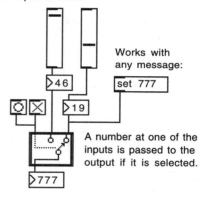

Works with any message:

A number at one of the inputs is passed to the output if it is selected.

Figure 4.22
Ggate and **Gswitch**

selects between one of two outlets. **Gswitch** selects between one of two inlets and has one outlet. These simplified objects have no ability to turn on and off data flow, or expand beyond two inputs or outputs.

Like **gate**, **route** takes one input and routes it to one of several outlets. It is specially designed to route lists (fig. 4.23). The arguments typed into **route** represent each outlet. If the first item in a list matches any of **route**'s arguments, then the first item is stripped from the list, and the remainder of the list is sent out the specified outlet. If the first item in a list does not match any of **route**'s arguments, the entire message is sent out the right outlet. In figure 4.23, the list on the right [*2 61 100 500*] is sent to **route**. The first item, 2, matches **route**'s third argument, which will cause the remainder of the list [*61 100 500*] to

Route takes any list or message as input, and uses the first item in it as an address for the output. For example, a list whose first item is the number 2 would get sent out of the third outlet, since outlets are numbered starting at 0.

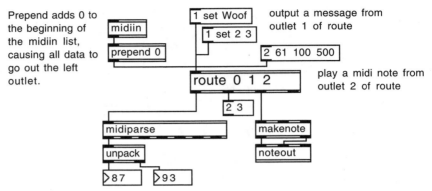

Prepend adds 0 to the beginning of the midiin list, causing all data to go out the left outlet.

output a message from outlet 1 of route

play a midi note from outlet 2 of route

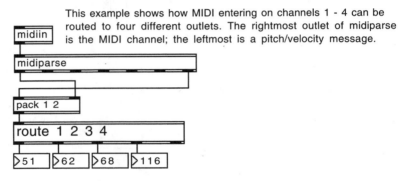

This example shows how MIDI entering on channels 1 - 4 can be routed to four different outlets. The rightmost outlet of midiparse is the MIDI channel; the leftmost is a pitch/velocity message.

Figure 4.23
route

be sent to **noteout** and play C♯ at velocity 100 for half a second. Note that the 2 does not get passed through with the rest of the list once it has been identified as one of **route**'s outlets.

Remote Messages

Max contains two extremely useful objects, **send** and **receive** (abbreviated **s** and **r**), that send messages remotely, that is, without using connecting lines. **Send** and **receive** objects must have descriptive names as arguments. *Any* data entering a **send** object will appear at the outlet of a **receive** object with the same name. Remote messages help to clear up the tangle of cords that often results from Max programming, al-

The most common objects used to remotely send and receive data are the send and receive objects (abbreviated s and r). Any send object will send its data to any receive object of the same name.

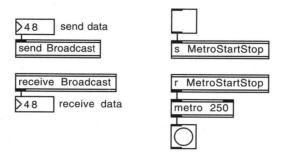

Remote messages can also be sent by the message object by using a semicolon followed by a receiver name. In the first example, Broadcast is the name of the receive object, and 55 is the data to be sent.

Figure 4.24
Remote messages

though they can be confusing to keep track of since they break the graphic connection between ins and outs. Since they can send information anywhere, it is possible to send messages to embedded patches or to entirely separate programs. Any loaded patch can share messages using **send** and **receive**.

Think of remote **sends** and **receives** like radio transmitters and receivers, broadcasting the data flow. Any message can be broadcast through a **send**. Any **receive** with the same name will pick up that signal, receiving exactly the same message. Remote messages may also be sent by the **message box** by using a semicolon, followed by the name of a receiver, followed by the data being sent. In figure 4.24, 55 sent to **send Broadcast** is identical to clicking on the **message box** containing *[; Broadcast 55]*. Multiple remote messages may be sent out by a single **message box** using semicolons as separators between messages.

Another object for remote messages, **value** (abbreviated **v**), stores a single value (or any type of message) and outputs the value with a *bang* (fig. 4.25). Like **send** and **receive**, **value** takes an obligatory argument

Value is like a combination of send, receive, and int. Once a number is set into it, all value objects with the same name have the same number set into them.

Figure 4.25
value

Table and coll are related to value, because two or more objects with the same name will share the same contents.

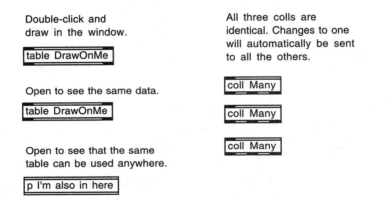

| Double-click and draw in the window. | All three colls are identical. Changes to one will automatically be sent to all the others. |

Double-click and
draw in the window.

table DrawOnMe

Open to see the same data.

table DrawOnMe

Open to see that the same
table can be used anywhere.

p I'm also in here

All three colls are
identical. Changes to one
will automatically be sent
to all the others.

coll Many

coll Many

coll Many

Figure 4.26
Remote **table** and **coll**

for its name and any **value** object with the same name will contain the same data. Changing the contents of one **value** object will change all of the **value** objects with the same name. Additional arguments, following the name, can be used to initialize the contents of **value** and to store any type of constant message.

Table and **coll** are related to **value**, because two or more objects with the same name will share the same contents, no matter where they appear in the program (fig. 4.26). As mentioned earlier, each **table** or **coll** with the same name will access the same data file. This means that **tables** and **colls** can record data in one part of a program and be used to create music in another part of a program.

Split selects a specified range of values and sends input within that range to the left outlet, and input outside of that range to the right. In this example, notes in the octave of middle C are sent to a different MIDI channel than other notes.

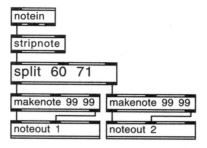

Figure 4.27
split

Data Selection

Max makes musical decisions by selecting and identifying specific values and ranges of values. **Split** identifies a range of values, specifying the upper and lower limits. If numbers passing through **split** fall within the prescribed range, the data will flow out the left outlet. All values outside the range will be sent out the right outlet. Thus, **split** routes data based on whether or not it fits in the range. In figure 4.27, **split** chooses notes between middle C and the B above it to play on MIDI channel 1, while all other notes play on MIDI channel 2. With two different sounds on MIDI channel 1 and 2, it is possible to orchestrate a piece according to the **split** range. A series of **split** objects can be used to identify several specific regions within a broad range of values by sending the right outlet of one **split** object into the left inlet of another **split** object with a different range.

Select (sel)is a very useful object since it can be used to look for specific numbers related to performance information. **Select** identifies numbers that are specified in its argument list and outputs a *bang* through a corresponding outlet whenever one of its arguments is matched. Like **route**, **select** passes anything that does not match an argument out the rightmost outlet. When used to match a single item, **select** can specify a changeable matching number through its right inlet. Figure 4.28 uses mod 12 (%12) to reduce all incoming notes to pitch class numbers, that is, numbers between 0 and 11 with 0

Select sends bangs out of specific outlets when it receives
a number matching one of its arguments. The order of the
arguments determines which outlet they are linked to.

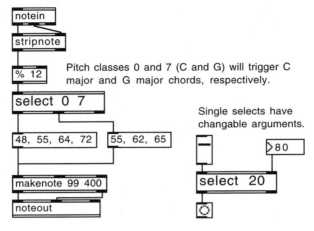

Pitch classes 0 and 7 (C and G) will trigger C
major and G major chords, respectively.

Single selects have
changable arguments.

Figure 4.28
sel (select)

representing C, 1 representing C♯, all the way to 11 representing B.
Select is then used to identify any note C (**select** 0) or G (**select** 7)
played anywhere on the keyboard and accompanies it with a chord.

C Programming Objects

Max is written in the C programming language, and many of the terms
and object names in Max are borrowed from C (as well as many concepts from the programming language Lisp). Some C-like objects have
been included in Max for people who are familiar with C programming. Relational operators are simple objects used to make decisions
and comparisons similar to those of **split** and **select**. Relational operators, such as > (greater than), < (less than), == (is equal to), and !=
(is not equal to) compare two numbers, sending out a 1 if the statement
is true, and a 0 if the statement is false.

Several relational operators can be combined in a single **if** statement.
The **if** object uses a condition to decide whether a statement should be
executed. If a condition is true, then a message is sent out; if it is not
true, then a different message or no message is sent out. These types
of conditional statements, which are the mainstay of musical feature

recognition, are used to trigger computer actions during a performance. For example, if the velocity is above 72 send a program change message to the synthesizer to play loud percussion sounds; if it is 72 or below, play quiet string sounds.

If is a conditional statement in the form of if/then/else; it reads *if* (something is true) *then* (do something) *else* (if it is not true, then do something else). An **if** statement can have the same results as numerous simpler objects, improving program efficiency and reducing the amount of clutter and complex wiring needed to make a program work. A series of **if** objects may be "cascaded," passing values through a series of conditional statements, to choose one of several actions. (See fig. 6.33 for an example.)

On the other hand, the function of an **if** statement may not be as obvious as functions represented graphically. For example, the **split** object in figure 4.27 is, in fact, a conditional statement. It reads: *if* the note number is within range, *then* send the number out the left outlet, *else* send the number out the right outlet. The example can be written like this using an **if** statement: [if $i1 >= 60 && $i1 <= 71 then $i1 else out2 $i1]. It says: *if* the value of the first inlet is greater than or equal to 60, *and* if it is less than or equal to 71, *then* send the number out the first outlet, *else* (if the condition is not true) send it out the second outlet. (out2 creates a second outlet, the default is one outlet.) Certainly, the function of the **split** object is more immediately understandable. An **if** statement equivalent to the **maximum** object can be seen in figure 4.29.

The **expr** (expression) object is like the **if** object, except that it evaluates a mathematical expression rather than making conditional decisions. **Expr** has a long list of available functions, such as *pow* (power) or *sqrt* (square root). Both **if** and **expr** take three types of variables. Unlike the $1 convention used in messages, **if** and **expr** must have the variable type specified using *$i1* for integers, *$f1* for floats, and *$s1* for symbols. The number 1 specifies the number and order of inlets, it stands as a place holder for values entering the first inlet. Each subsequent argument is also assigned a number, which automatically creates a corresponding inlet.

Thus, the expression in figure 4.30, expr (2 * $i1) + (5 * $i2) − 3, will create two inlets; the value entering the first inlet will be multiplied times two, the value entering the second inlet will be multiplied times

This example outputs the largest of two values.

Figure 4.29
if

Expr evaluates a mathematical expression.

The single expression on the left is equivalent to the four objects on the right.

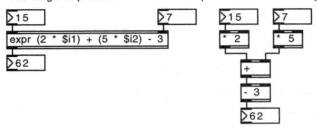

Figure 4.30
expr

five, and the results of both multiplications will be added together and three subtracted from the sum. The answer is sent out the outlet. As with other Max objects, the leftmost inlet triggers a calculation. Although **if** and **expr** may not be as immediately understandable as other graphic objects, their ability to do comparisons and evaluate complex expressions using C functions enables them to create processes that are very difficult to implement, or simply unavailable using groups of other objects. Figure 4.30 shows how a single **expr** statement can perform the same task as many combined objects.

Efficiency and Memory Management (adapted from the Opcode manual)

As Max programs get larger and more complex, issues of efficiency and programming style become more important. Try to develop consistent program usage for all patches. Here are some suggestions for improving the efficiency of Max programs.

1. Since there are so many different message types in Max, some objects have to "look up" the meaning of each message that they send and receive. This message look-up takes computer time and can slow down the program. Usually there are several ways to implement an idea in Max. Choosing objects that don't require message look-ups will speed up the program. In general, objects whose inputs and outputs can only be numbers will not require a message look-up, since only one kind of information will be processed. These speedy objects include **number boxes, select, ==,** and **int.** Message lookup is always performed on **message box** output, **gate, switch, send,** and **receive.**

2. If a constant value is needed, store it in an **int box** rather than a **message box.** Both will need a *bang* at the right time to send the number to its destination.

3. Use **notein** rather than **midiin** in whenever possible. Use **midiin** only if the program requires the entire MIDI stream, such as information on continuous controllers, pitchbend, and after touch. If there are several channels of MIDI input, it is most efficient to separate the MIDI streams using several **notein** objects with arguments to specify MIDI channels. Separating all **noteins** later on, or using **midiin + midiparse,** uses much more computation time.

4. Avoid using **pipe** and **delay** to solve problems of messages arriving too early. Instead, whenever possible use **trigger, bangbang, route, swap,** and so on, so that the right-to-left ordering of events solves the problem. These objects can be used wherever right-to-left ordering is critical, because the right-to-left organization of objects on the screen may be inadvertently rearranged when programs are cleaned up or rewritten.

5. Don't use a complex object to do a simple job. Large objects with lots of features also take more computer time. For instance, storing two numbers in a large **table** would be less efficient than using two **ints.**

6. Every visible box on the screen uses a minimum of 100 bytes of memory. Create a user interface for a program, where the only visible items on screen are those that control functions or variables. Hide all the wiring and patches that are doing most of the work. The next chapter offers suggestions for efficient interface design.

Debugging

Programming is never as simple as hooking objects together. A large part of the programming process entails tracking down programming problems, or bugs, that prevent the software from working as intended. Creating small, self-contained modules, and testing them as they are created, will help isolate problems. Most important, it is essential to view data going into a process, and to check the results. Number boxes are perhaps the most useful tool in this regard. They may be attached at any location to check numbers that are entering and leaving objects or patches. By simply taking a tap off a line, rather than placing them in the signal path, they may be deleted after the debugging process is completed.

Any message may be viewed in the Max window (command-m) by sending it to a **print** object. **Capture** can be used to capture numbers for both viewing and editing. Since it may be difficult to find the specific location of a problem in a complex patch, finding the source of a problem is not always easy, Max has a tracing feature that allows a programmer to step through each message sent while running a program. Data can be viewed each step of the way, and the specific problem spot identified. When Trace is enabled (one of the standard window menus), the patch chord through which a message will be sent will start blinking, and the message itself will be displayed in the Max window, along with its place of origin and destination. Each subsequent Step command will go on to the next message to send. If the location of problematic points are unknown, then a *breakpoint* may be set, allowing the computer to run at full speed until it encounters the *breakpoint* location. This insures that all previous messages are sent, up to a specific location, and the results up to that point can be reviewed. Stepping through a patch in this way also helps to understand how and in what order Max sends messages. (See the debugging section in the Max Manual.)

All the points mentioned in this chapter will help to produce a program that is reliable, readable, and efficient. The design of a program, of a composition, and of a user interface may be mutually influential. However, the real strength of a program will come from a foundation inspired by compelling musical ideas, coupled with the ability to use them in a convincing musical form.

5   *Interface Design*

The user interface influences the way people think and act while using a program. A broad view of the interface includes all of the points where humans interact with the computer, sending and receiving tactile, visual, or auditory information. Here, "interface" refers to graphical user interface (GUI), which is the graphical information viewed on a computer screen, as well as the physical devices, such as the computer keyboard and mouse, designed to send computer data in response to physical gestures. Most of these *tactile* interface devices map physical gestures onto the computer screen. Other devices are designed for specific functions. The MIDI keyboard, for example, allows keyboardists to communicate musical gestures to a computer.

Many composers enjoy programming in Max because it is intuitive, responsive, easy to use, and designed specifically for their needs. A constant challenge when programming in Max is to create a user interface that simplifies the complexities of programming and gives a visual representation of the actions needed to run the software. Understanding basic principles of interface design will help to utilize the large collection of sophisticated objects and options for creating user interfaces in Max.

Basic Principles of Interface Design

Interfaces are optimally designed for the activities of the user. Max programs are most often used for composing and performing music but have also been used to create stand-alone music applications and to build complex multimedia art work designed to be viewed on screen or projected in an art gallery or theater. Creating a software "product" with an optimal interface for others to use might not result in the best design for the programmer to use, since hiding programming details makes it more difficult to write software. Similarly, an interface for composing music that encourages experimentation with musical materials and ideas may not be the best interface for performance. In the heat of a performance, the performer or composer needs only the controls required to guide a piece in real-time and could be distracted by the availability of all the possibilities.

One model for a performance interface uses software to automate the controls based strictly on the music that is played, so that a musician can focus on the computer's musical response without being distracted by the computer's interface. The interface, then, could be totally "invisible"; the musician would just play, and the music would somehow guide the entire performance. This seamless approach may come closest to simulating musical "intelligence" and artistic creation in an environment in which humans physically and intuitively interact with computers.

On the other extreme, a composer might want to build an elaborate graphical interface with such responsive capabilities that it could be played as a versatile instrument on its own in a concert setting using the computer keyboard and mouse. This approach treats the computer interface as a musical instrument. It could be designed with limitations and idiosyncrasies that give real instruments their character, and suggest a playing style or technique for physically creating the sounds. A well-designed interface "feels right" to the end user.

At various stages of building a piece, the interface will often change from one suited to testing and rapid prototyping, to one more suitable for performance. Refining the interface at various stages helps the programmer clarify the "big picture" by organizing the most important activities and controls in one spot. A return to a top-down design approach can offer an overview of the program by focusing on the essential functions needed for the work. Part of the process of writing an interactive composition looks at what a performer will be doing, the actions required at the interface level, and the actions taken by the computer in response.

Two main areas of interface design are isolating and displaying relevant information, and allowing input devices control of information via intuitive and logical graphics. Displaying relevant information means that all aspects of the program are hidden from the user except the essential controls. The user must have easy access to these controls, and the computer must be able to display information in reply. Graphics are intuitive and logical if their function and mode of operation can be easily understood and if they appear in an order that makes sense with the things that surround them. By using images that make guessing their purpose easy, a new user can sit down without instructions and figure out how a program works. Ideally, a user interface should take commands that require obvious human gestures or logical text. The interface further clarifies actions by anticipating needed information, querying the user, and answering common questions that arise from using the software.

How will the interface reflect the activity of the user? How will it display the computer's response? How will the computer's response change the musician's input?

To summarize, the following basic principles of interface design are relevant to most types of programs (and are related to the programming principles outlined in chapter 4):

1. Design for the activity of the user (not the capability of the machine).

2. Isolate and display relevant information.

3. Have easy and logical access to controls needed at the moment.

4. Hide undue complexity; show only what counts.

5. Make it intuitive, using obvious gestures, images, or words.

6. The computer should respond naturally to user input.

7. Know the user. Think of the user's experience while running a program, considering background, experience, training, and psychology.

Building Interfaces in Max

There are so many ways to create user interfaces in Max that it is difficult to suggest one style. Some of the general ideas listed above, applied to Max, will not only help create a usable interface, but will also aid the readability and clarity of the program. Some suggestions, specific to Max and interactive composition, follow.

Hide anything that is not essential to running the program. Small patches are usable with all their information visible, if controls are located in an easy to reach place. While this isn't the most aesthetically pleasing approach, it is an essential step in building a program and in learning how modules will eventually work together. The next step in clarifying the interface is to create descriptive subpatches and to hide all extraneous graphic elements by selecting objects and patch cords and pressing command-K to hide or command-L to show. Holding down the option key while dragging a selection will highlight the patch cords as well. Finally, showing only graphic elements relevant to running the program clarifies the actions that will take place.

Make important controls and objects obvious and easily accessible. Place the main controls in an obvious location, such as the top of the page, the lefthand side, or the center, but always surrounded by space. Size fonts and graphic objects so that titles and directions are easy to read, and pertinent performance information is displayed. Make sure that the controls needed during a performance are not buried inside other objects. If you use various types of messages to display the contents of several patcher windows, it is possible to have controls appear only when they are needed, and disappear when a new section requires different actions.

Group related activities together. Lay out controls and objects so that they are grouped logically, not just according to function, but also according to how they will be used. For example, try to place controls for the next most likely task near the previous one. Also, place displays showing the results of an action, such as a large **bang button** from **metro,** close to where the action takes place, such as a tempo control **slider.**

Automate things that do not need human control. Routine, repetitive, and inconsequential tasks should be relegated to the computer so that humans may concentrate on other tasks. Performers have a difficult enough job playing a composition in front of an audience. Try to automate tasks, such as mouse or button clicks, that are not directly related to the music. Automation may occur in response to the musical information received, physical gestures, or elapsed time. (See chap. 9 for automated score objects.)

Encapsulate numerous interfaces and objects into a master interface. For large programs, create a separate master interface that will contain the essential controls for all the other objects. Once a program reaches the point where all the controls cannot be accessed from a single screen, a unifying interface may be needed to perform the necessary functions.

Max's Interface Objects

An interface usually evolves naturally with the creation of a program. As the number of modules grows, so does the complexity of accessing and controlling all the parameters, and it becomes increasingly important to have a well-designed interface. Periodically, it is necessary to reevaluate the interface, and occasionally redesign the whole thing. In some instances, it might be more useful to begin writing programs by first creating a user interface representing the tasks that need to be accomplished by the computer. Such a top-down approach would include a series of object boxes with nothing more than descriptive names along with their graphic controls. Programming time could then be focused on filling in this "empty shell" to eventually make all the objects functional.

Max comes with a rich palette of interface objects and graphic capabilities. **Sliders**, **dials**, and other interface objects generate and display data in an obvious way. The library of interface objects comes equipped with menus, windows, buttons, and items common to other Macintosh programs. Although Max's interface objects are adequate for most tasks, it usually requires writing external objects in C to expand beyond the limited capabilities of interface objects that come with the program.

Importing Graphics

Max's ability to import pictures from most graphics applications can help create an interface with clarity and visual interest, giving it a "custom" look without external programming. An image (in the form of a PICT file) may be copied from one application and pasted into Max using PASTE PICTURE from the edit window. (See the grid in fig. 5.12.) The image will be saved with the program, sometimes making the program slow to save and load. Better yet, a file or group of files containing images may be referenced from disk using **fpic**, a user interface object available in the middle section of the tools palette. Highlighting **fpic** and selecting GET INFO will call up a dialog box creating a link to a stored file. The message *pict* followed by a file name will also display a picture. As with all external files, Max needs to have the PICT file in one of the folders that it looks at when it starts up. The files comprising the search path are listed under FILE PREFERENCES in the EDIT menu. (See chap. 10 for more information on graphics.)

Pictures and words become interactive by using **ubuttons**, invisible buttons placed on an image, creating "hot spots" that will trigger with a click of a mouse. The **ubutton** can be any size, and it can be set up to act as an on/off switch (like **toggle**), or as a button (like **bang**). The default is button mode; when the mouse is clicked on the **ubutton** it sends a *bang* out the right outlet; when the mouse is released it sends a *bang* out the left outlet. (For a very well-developed example of **ubuttons**, graphics, and imbedded editing controls, study Charles Maynes *DMP11 Panel* on disk for chap. 8, and see fig. 8.9.)

Controlling Numbers

Number boxes, sliders, and **dials** are designed to send out number messages by clicking and dragging (fig. 5.1). These objects will animate with continuous input, giving instant visual feedback based on incoming information; this allows the user to monitor the status of changes made by the program. **Sliders** should have ranges constrained to select realistic values which they will send and receive. As always, the question to ask is what the user will be doing with these **sliders.** The answer to this question should lead to clues regarding their physical size, range, and placement on the screen.

IncDec is a very obvious interface object used to increment and decrement a number (fig. 5.2). **MultiSlider** is a collection of sliders most often used as a graphic display for lists of data. Moving any one slider with a mouse will send out a list representing all slider values.

User Interface Data Storage Objects

Max has important user interface objects that are used for data storage. One very useful object is **preset** (fig. 5.3). **Preset** remembers the settings of all the interface objects displayed in a single window, and recalls them with a single mouse click. **Preset** stores "screen snapshots," re-

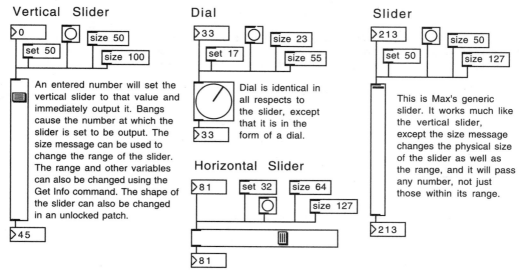

Vertical Slider

An entered number will set the vertical slider to that value and immediately output it. Bangs cause the number at which the slider is set to be output. The size message can be used to change the range of the slider. The range and other variables can also be changed using the Get Info command. The shape of the slider can also be changed in an unlocked patch.

Dial

Dial is identical in all respects to the slider, except that it is in the form of a dial.

Horizontal Slider

The horizontal slider is identical in all respects to the vertical slider, except that it slides horizontally.

Slider

This is Max's generic slider. It works much like the vertical slider, except the size message changes the physical size of the slider as well as the range, and it will pass any number, not just those within its range.

Figure 5.1
Controlling numbers

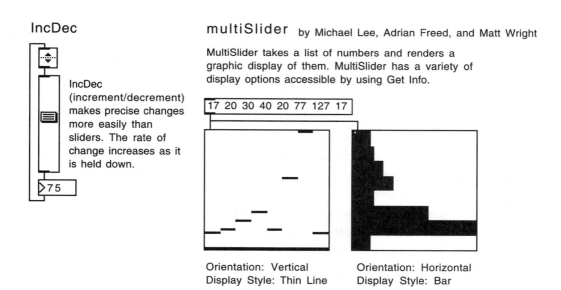

IncDec

IncDec (increment/decrement) makes precise changes more easily than sliders. The rate of change increases as it is held down.

multiSlider by Michael Lee, Adrian Freed, and Matt Wright

MultiSlider takes a list of numbers and renders a graphic display of them. MultiSlider has a variety of display options accessible by using Get Info.

17 20 30 40 20 77 127 17

Orientation: Vertical   Orientation: Horizontal
Display Style: Thin Line   Display Style: Bar

Figure 5.2
More number control: **IncDec** and **multiSlider**

The preset object takes "screen snapshots," storing the settings of other objects in the patch, and recalling them with a single click. Each address of the preset can store all or some of the values pictured on the screen. If a preset object is not connected to any other objects, it will store all the values in the patch. If the preset object is connected to one or more objects, it will only remember those settings.

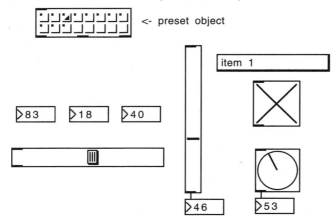

<- preset object

Figure 5.3
preset

cording every **number box, slider** position, **menu** selection, and other changeable interface objects visible on the screen. **Preset** can also store only some of the values pictured on the screen. If **preset** is connected to one or more objects, it will remember only those settings of the attached objects. If a **preset** object is not connected to any other objects, it will store all values displayed in the window.

Preset is essential for configuring a large program instantaneously during a performance. **Preset** can be thought of as a type of computer score, containing the directions needed for the computer to perform a piece. This makes it invaluable since it can send out numerous parameter changes in response to performance information or a mouse click. Like **table** and **coll**, Max can read and write **preset** files saved separately from the program, so that multiple **presets** with descriptive names can be stored on disk.

In figure 5.4, the **preset** is attached to a **table**, so it will store data only from the **table** and not from any other objects on the screen. The **table** can be opened, reconfigured, and the contents stored with **preset**. In this way, a single **table** can be used in multiple situations, with different files stored in one **preset**. (Otherwise, the **table** would have

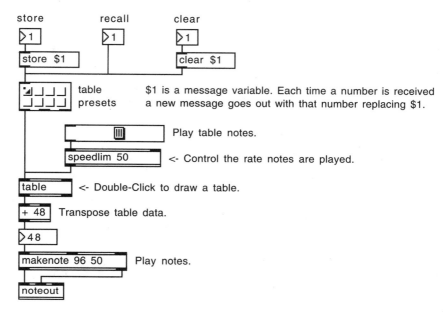

Figure 5.4
preset messages

to read in information from multiple lists, a **coll**, or a **table** file stored on disk.)

The **menu** object creates familiar Macintosh pulldown menus, which can be used to store numerous messages in a compact space. It is a data structure, like **table**, but the data it stores at a particular address are usually words, not numbers. An index number sent to the **menu**'s left inlet can output the message stored at that address. More commonly, messages are selected with a mouse.

In figure 5.5, example 1 and example 2 perform exactly the same function. Notice how much less screen space example 2 takes. Various commands for the **table** object have been condensed into a pulldown **menu.** To see how the **menu** works, select the **menu** object in example 2, and choose GET INFO from the Max menu (fig. 5.6). Listed in the dialog window are all the **menu** items separated by commas. To make a new **menu**, simply enter the new items, separated by commas. When an item is selected, a number is sent out the left outlet that represents the position of that item in the list (its index number). The index numbers are "off by one," so that the first item is index 0, the second item is index 1, the third item is index 2, and so on. The text itself will be

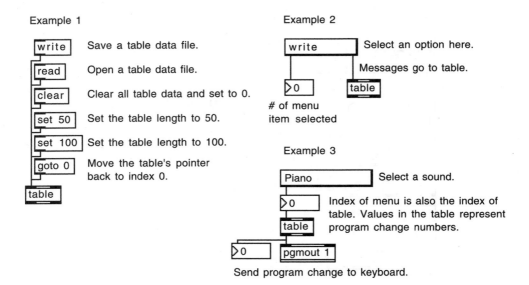

Example 1

write — Save a table data file.

read — Open a table data file.

clear — Clear all table data and set to 0.

set 50 — Set the table length to 50.

set 100 — Set the table length to 100.

goto 0 — Move the table's pointer back to index 0.

table

Example 2

write — Select an option here.

— Messages go to table.

▷ 0   table

# of menu item selected

Example 3

Piano — Select a sound.

▷ 0 — Index of menu is also the index of table. Values in the table represent program change numbers.

table

▷ 0   pgmout 1

Send program change to keyboard.

Figure 5.5
menu

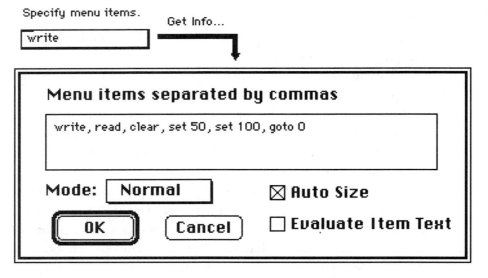

Specify menu items.

Get Info...

write

Menu items separated by commas

write, read, clear, set 50, set 100, goto 0

Mode: Normal   ☒ **Auto Size**

OK   Cancel   ☐ **Evaluate Item Text**

Figure 5.6
menu: Get Info

sent out the right outlet as a message by selecting the EVALUATE ITEM TEXT option in the dialog window. This option is checked in example 2, so that those messages will be sent to the **table** object in the same way that they are sent in example 1.

In the third example in figure 5.5, a **menu** selects a keyboard sound by name rather than by a program change number. The text displayed is for the benefit of the user and is not a message intended for Max. Instead, the order number from **menu's** left outlet is used as the index to a **table** containing corresponding program change numbers. An index number sent to the **table** will select the message at that address. In example 3, a descriptive word, "organ," selects the corresponding sound on a synthesizer when its index number is remapped to a **table**, sending out program change number 49.

User Feedback

The importance of using comment boxes for instructions and program clarification has already been emphasized. Text plays a central role in providing directions and feedback for the user, especially when the user is not the programmer. Text may be used interactively in response to user input—requesting information, selecting from a list, or offering feedback describing the results of the user's actions. Any task can send out a display message. The most frequently used objects for interactive text display are the **message** object and the **menu** object. The **message** box is most often a single message that is sent on a mouse click or when it receives a *bang*. It can also receive and display words and numbers. Figures 5.7 to 5.11 demonstrate three simple interfaces; each example responds to the user's input with descriptive text or graphics.

Figure 5.7 is very simple; it uses a **menu** to display messages in response to the request not to press the button. All the messages are items contained within the **menu** object. (Select GET INFO on **menu** to see the list.) The first selection is always presented when the program begins. Each press of the **button** sends the next number on a **counter** to the **menu**, cycling through index numbers 1 to 4. (The first argument, 0, sets the direction of the **counter** to up.) When the **menu** object receives a number, it displays the **menu** item corresponding to that number.

The second example (fig. 5.8) shows how the **message box** may be used to display one of several messages remotely. First, a **menu** is used

Please be sure to read the above directions.

unhidden:

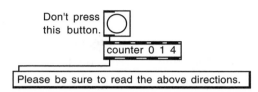

Please be sure to read the above directions.

Figure 5.7
menu displaying message

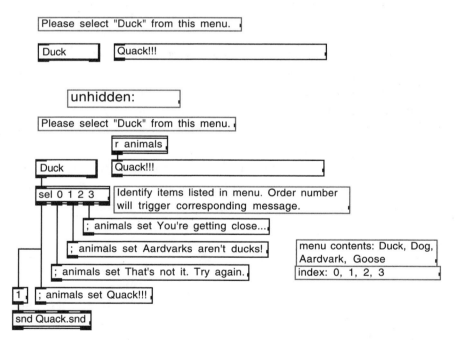

Figure 5.8
menu displaying remote messages

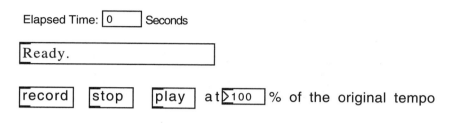

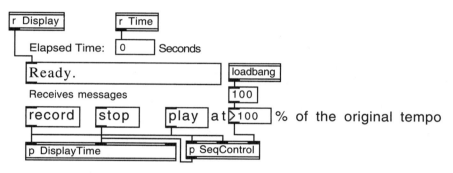

Figure 5.9
Timing feedback

to display one of four choices, with each index number triggering a remote message in response. A semicolon is followed by the descriptive name of the intended receive object, **animals.** The *set* command causes the remainder of the message object to be displayed in a **message box.** Two **menu** objects could also be used: the one on the screen with the names of animals could serve as the index to another **menu** with the responses. Depending on the task being performed, feedback other than words might be useful, such as spoken directions, animated graphics, or sound cues. When the word "duck" is selected from the **menu,** the responding text "Quack!!!" could be accompanied by a duck sound (stored on disk). Sending 1 to the **snd** object plays the soundfile Quack.snd. (See chap. 8 for more on the **snd** object.)

The third example (fig. 5.9) reports elapsed time during sequence recording and playback. A message indicates when a **sequence** is

DisplayTime sends directions to the interface on how to use the seq object for recording and playing back sequences. Recording and playback time are shown in seconds, and represented as dots.

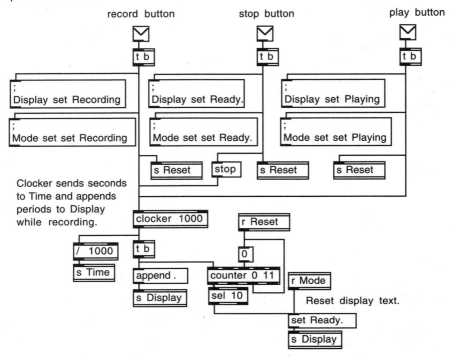

Figure 5.10
DisplayTime (subpatch of fig. 5.9)

recording, playing back, or ready (waiting). While recording or playing the **sequence**, a **clocker** counts off the seconds, displaying the numbers to show elapsed time, and adding a dot for each second to the end of the message. The tasks for displaying updated information and those for controlling **seq** functions are separated into two objects. **Display-Time** contains the instructions and displays that are sent remotely to the interface (fig. 5.10). **SeqControl** contains **seq** and related objects, as well as a mechanism to change the playback tempo (fig. 5.11).

DisplayTime reports the current status of the **seq** object to the user, showing one of three modes: ready, recording, and playing. The message [*append.*] adds a dot each second to the displayed message. Time, in seconds, is also displayed. The **receive** and **send** objects, **"Reset"** and **"Mode,"** are used within the subpatch to reset the display periodically.

SeqControl records and plays back performances using the seq object.

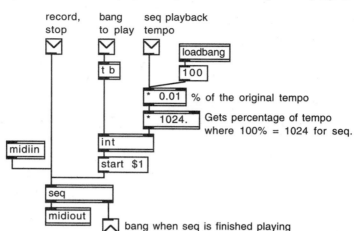

Figure 5.11
SeqControl (subpatch of fig. 5.9)

Users may enter messages from the user interface using the **dialog** object to call up a standard Macintosh dialog box (fig. 5.12). A *bang* to **dialog** opens up a window prompting the user to enter text. After the text is entered, the message will be sent out when the user clicks on the OKAY button. An optional argument will appear at the top of the dialog box and may include instructions or a description of the text to enter.

Computer Input Devices

Although the computer keyboard and mouse are usually used in conjunction with screen graphics to control some aspect of the interface, such as typing in numbers or moving **sliders**, Max has several objects that translate mouse motions and keystrokes directly into usable data for controlling musical processes. **MouseState** is Max's mouse interface object. **MouseState** tracks the position of the mouse, sending out information regarding the mouse's coordinates and button clicks. When a *bang* is received, **MouseState** sends out a report of the mouse's coordinates and the change in its location since the last report. Since mouse reports usually need to be fairly continuous, a metronome set to a very

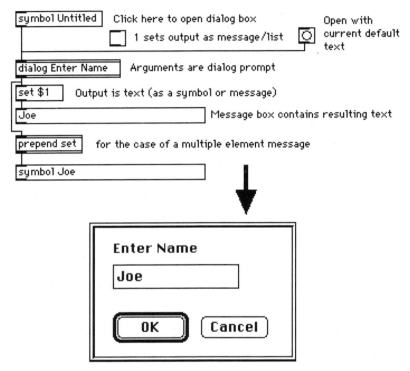

dialog Opcode help file

Open a dialog box for text entry

Dialog makes a symbol out of the text you type in (or a message if you set the right
inlet to 1) and sends it out the outlet when you click on the OK button in the dialog
box. (Note that the output of a dialog object is not directly "caused" by sending
object a message, so you can't count on it happening by a certain time.)

Figure 5.12
dialog (Opcode's help file)

fast rate is used to send *bangs* to **MouseState.** The state of the mouse
button (up or down) is always reported, so it does not need a *bang.*

Figure 5.13 uses the mouse as a multicontroller, sending *pitchbend,*
modulation wheel, and *sustain pedal* messages. In this case, a graphic
file has been imported, showing a control grid representing the various
values (fig. 5.14). With the keyboard's modulation wheel set to control
vibrato speed, moving the mouse to the right (along the X axis) increases the vibrato speed, and moving the mouse up (along the Y axis)
raises the pitch. The mouse location has been mapped to the grid by
subtracting the grid's left and top coordinates from the mouse's X and Y
coordinates, respectively. (The upper left-hand corner of the screen is

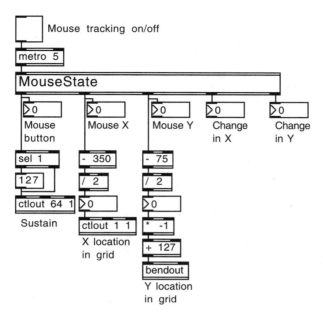

Figure 5.13
Using the mouse: MouseState

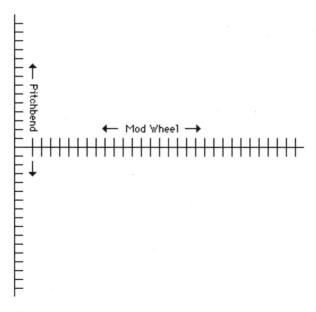

Figure 5.14
Grid (graphic) showing mouse control

located at coordinates (0, 0).) The upper left-hand corner of the grid is located at (350, 75). Since the grid is 256 by 256 pixels, and the control values are only 0–127, the modified mouse location is also divided by two and then limited to a maximum of 127 by the **number box** *info*. Thus, in figure 5.14, the mouse's X location affects the modulation wheel, its Y location changes pitchbend, and the mouse button triggers the sustain pedal. For multimedia projects, Max can also report X, Y coordinates of mouse locations within a playing video image (imported as a QuickTime movie; see chapter 10).

Key and **keyup** are objects that translate keystrokes from the computer typing keyboard into numbers. **Key** sends a number when a key is struck; **keyup** sends a number when a key is released. Both objects send ASCII code, the standard numbers that represent keyboard characters. **Key** also sends Apple computer keyboard code, a different set of numbers, out the right outlet. You can see the difference by pressing 8 on both the keypad and the keyboard. The ASCII output will stay the same, and the keyboard code will change. **Keyup** is similar to **key** in that it will report the last key pressed. However, **keyup** waits until the key has been released to send out a number. **Keyup** only reports ASCII numbers.

In figure 5.15, keyboard strokes are used to play percussion instruments in a General MIDI drum set, which demonstrates the potential for building musical instruments using the keyboard and mouse. **Sel** identifies alphanumeric keys and maps them to a corresponding drum sound. Various other maps could be stored in a **table** or **coll**, with the entering values used as indexes.

Interface and Encapsulation: A Programming Example

This chapter ends with six figures that show the step-by-step process of creating usable software by commenting, formatting, encapsulating, and making a user interface. The program has two main components. The custom object called **Scale** takes incoming notes and moves them to the nearest note in a predetermined scale. In the final version, the selectable scale can be chromatic, pentatonic, major, or minor. The second component, **MakeRandomMelody**, is a random pitch generator that creates notes to be processed by **Scale**. The tempo and range can be set for **MakeRandomMelody**. **Scale** and other composition objects will be discussed more fully in the next chapter.

This patch implements a keyboard-driven
drum set. Keys from the computer
keyboard will be mapped to MIDI notes sent
to a General MIDI drumset (set on channel
10). The keys are mapped as follows:

Space = Kick
b = Snare
j, k, and l = Hi-hat
a, s, d, and f = Toms
Return = Crash
u = Ride

This patch provides high
speed kick drum (key =
tab) and hi-hat (key = ~)
action by playing them on
keyup as well as
keydown.

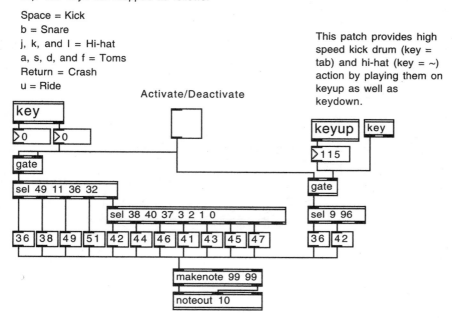

Figure 5.15
key and **keyup**

One useful technique for a large collection of patches is to create
a "peel-off" interface that is entirely detached from the non-interface
objects (see disk examples). A peel-off interface could look much like
the final version in figure 5.21, with all connections made remotely.
One benefit of this method is that each interface object can send to
multiple locations without dealing with complex and confusing physical connections. It is especially useful for sending parameter information to deeply imbedded objects (objects within objects). Also, as a
large interface takes shape, it will be easier to reposition the essential
on-screen controls as purely graphical elements than to maintain readability with numerous attached objects. Keep in mind, however, that
remote messages require message lookup and therefore are less efficient
than most direct connections. Finally, a **preset** object can be added at
any stage to store and recall multiple interface configurations. (See
chapter five disk examples for advanced tutorials on designing custom
objects and interface automation.)

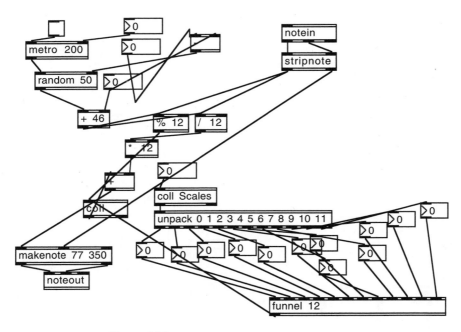

Figure 5.16
Screen graphics 1: a very messy patch

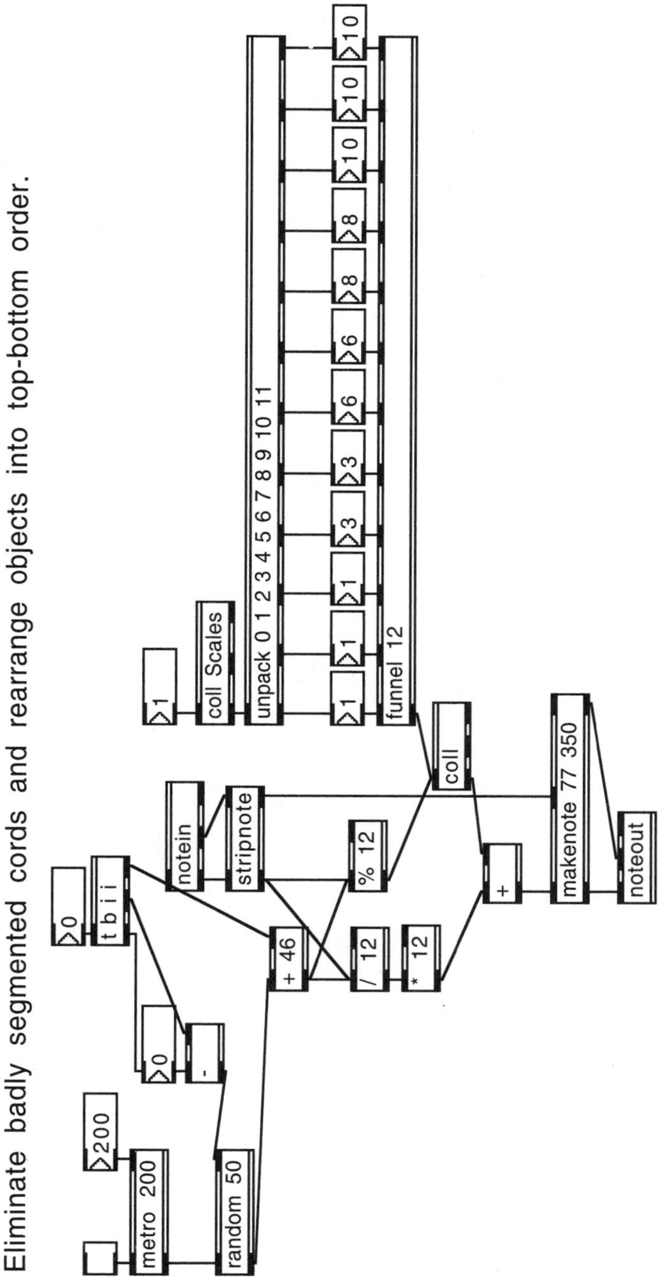

Eliminate badly segmented cords and rearrange objects into top-bottom order.

Figure 5.17

Screen graphics 2: reposition objects and segment chords

Begin encapsulation with small single-purpose algorithms

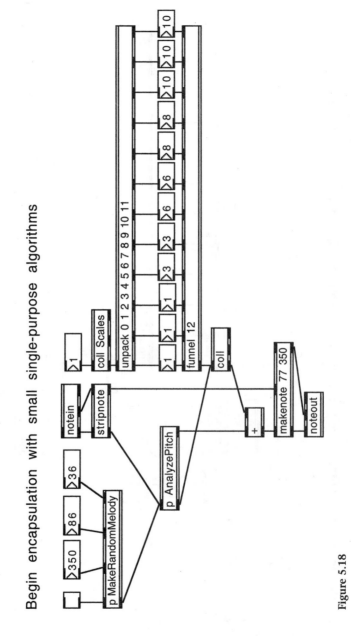

Figure 5.18
Screen graphics 3: encapsulate algorithms

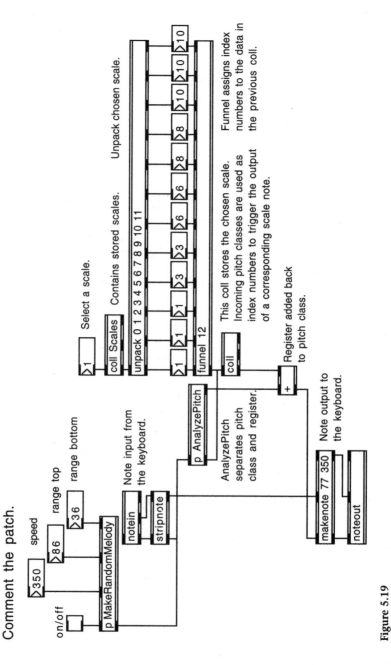

Figure 5.19

Screen graphics 4: comment the patch

Encapsulate the main algorithm and add instructions.

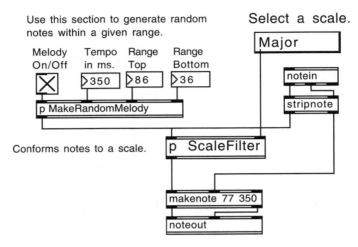

Figure 5.20
Screen graphics 5: encapsulate the main algorithm

Expand the interface, make the non-essential objects invisible.

Figure 5.21
Screen graphics 6: build the performance interface

III   Core Components

6 The Computer as Listener: Analyzing and Storing Performance Data

At the heart of interactive composition lies software capable of recognizing and analyzing the features of a musical performance. What does this software need to know? To help answer this question, we will begin by examining the human processes involved in making and perceiving music, and attempt to apply these to the computer.

A sound is physically produced by striking, blowing, bowing, or plucking an instrument to create sound waves. Sound is perceived when these sound waves enter the ears. Listening begins by focusing attention on the sound and noticing sonic components such as melody, timbre, and register. Each listener's understanding of music is based on the past memories and associations triggered by the music, and by his or her concepts of music in general. While the emotional complexity associated with experiencing music is lost on the computer, it can understand music by comparing an on-going performance to "memories" of basic musical materials, past musical events, and stored musical concepts. Pitches and dynamics are some of the basic materials immediately recognizable by the computer. Past musical events are stored musical patterns that can later be matched by the computer. Musical concepts are abstract ideas about music or musical processes, such as the notion of keys, chord types, or transposition. All these elements may work together in both humans and computers to give a comprehensive view of a work at different levels of detail. The process of understanding a performance begins with two interrelated activities: listening to music and understanding music.

Listening to Music

Listening and hearing are different. Hearing is the passive perception of sound. Listening implies active involvement and focus. We hear the radio turn on, but listen to the news. We hear the telephone ring, but we listen to a telephone conversation.

The computer "hears" the stream of MIDI numbers as they enter, but requires software like Max to "listen" to a performance by focusing on specific aspects of the MIDI data. MIDI makes interactive composition possible by providing accurate performance information about two primary musical parameters: **pitch** (MIDI note number) and **loudness** (MIDI velocity number). The essential parameter of **time** is provided in Max by objects built for timing incoming MIDI data. These three basic parameters are the building blocks for "listener objects," which use analysis techniques to identify complex events immediately or to track events as they change over time. Unfortunately, a fourth important musical parameter, **timbre**, is not provided by MIDI, except for information that can be gleaned from synthesizer voices linking velocity to timbre, or from continuous controllers assigned to control the parameters that affect the sound. (See chapter 8 for more on timbre.)

Analysis: What Can Be Understood?

Musical understanding, in both humans and computers, occurs when an event or series of events can be matched in memory with a similar event or with a concept of the event. This could be the recognition of simple data, such as middle C; the matching of musical patterns, such as a melodic or rhythmic motive; the concept of an intervallic relationship, such as a "major chord"; or a description of a process, such as "delay." Musical memories are referenced to provide insight into the listening situation of the moment (Laske 1980).

Since MIDI input provides Max with the knowledge of basic musical elements, simple algorithms immediately identify a wide variety of common musical features. More elaborate memory schemes can be used to store larger musical patterns to be used at a later time. In this way, the musical present can be understood and shaped based on information gleaned from the musical past.

This chapter contains many examples of listener objects that may be used either as is, or modified to fit a composer's needs. These examples do not, by any means, cover the extensive research done in this area. (In fact, several volumes could be written just describing recent efforts in performance analysis.) Careful consideration of the musical context will yield the most appropriate listener objects, and an exhaustive list will definitely not ensure a successful piece. Often the effective use of just a few analysis tools will produce excellent results. What are the salient qualities of a particular performance that will inform compositional decisions? What interactive techniques are appropriate for a specific work? The deft use of a few simple techniques might carry an entire piece, while some of the most complex examples might be appropriate for only brief improvisational sections. Identifying the necessary performance information is the first step in fashioning compelling links with computer-generated music.

Musicians best loved for their passionate performances exhibit their personal style in the control of minute variations in timing, articulation, and dynamics. These are the aspects of performance that best impart human interpretive skills to the computer. How can these variable characteristics be isolated and understood?

Time

Music is a temporal art, an art that rests upon the organization of musical elements in time. Musical elements and structures create coherence in a time flow, their meaning dependent on their order and duration. An entire musical work can be viewed from its largest time structures, which differentiate sections that define the overall shape of a piece, to ever-increasing smaller levels, which consist of the smaller subsections that make up larger sections, phrases contained within the subsections, short rhythmic motives within each phrase, and finally, the placement in time and the duration of a single pitch. (Even pitch is a function of time, with frequency determined by the number of cycles per second.)

Max Timing Objects

Correct analysis of timing is essential to interactive composition because it enables the computer to recognize the tempo and rhythm of the music being played and respond accordingly. Flexible timing between computers and performers is crucial for simulating musical interaction. Max comes with several objects designed to control tempo and measure time. **Metro** and **tempo** are both used to output *bangs* at a specified rate, usually to control tempo (figs. 6.1 and 6.2). **Metro** works in milliseconds, while **tempo** takes more familiar arguments in beats per second (corresponding to the metronome markings found in a score). **Metro** is more efficient if all that is needed is a *bang* every x number of milliseconds.

Tempo, which is ideal for following the changing meters and metronome markings found in many contemporary music scores, takes three optional arguments (fig. 6.2). The first sets the initial tempo, in beats per minute, representing the speed of a quarter note. The second is a beat multiplier, which scales the tempo; a multiplier of 2, for example, would cause **tempo** to output every two quarter notes (or every half note). The third value sets the pulse to be sent out; a 4 will send out quarter-note pulses, an 8 will send out eighth-note pulses, and a 16 will send out sixteenth-note pulses.

Timer and **clocker** both count milliseconds (fig. 6.3). **Timer** behaves like a stopwatch. A *bang* in the left inlet starts the **timer** counting from 0; a *bang* in the right reports the elapsed time in milliseconds. A second *bang* to the right inlet will update the elapsed time, while a second

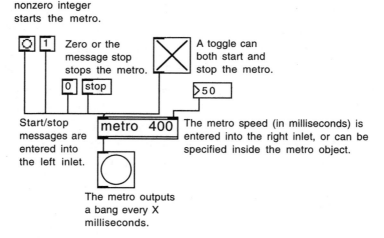

Figure 6.1
metro

Tempo is a metronome-like object that counts out locations in a measure. Unlike similar Max objects, its speed is set in beats per minute rather than milliseconds. Tempo also includes an inlet for setting the divisions of a whole note, so that any beat value can be counted (whole note, quarter note, septuplet), and a beat multiplier.

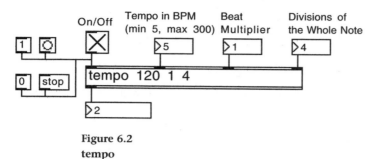

Figure 6.2
tempo

The timer object gives the length of time (in milliseconds) between two bangs. The left inlet starts the timer running, and the right outputs the elapsed time.

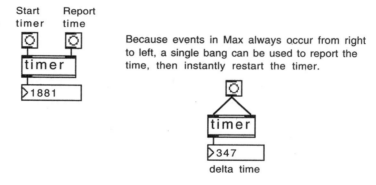

Figure 6.3
timer

bang to the left will restart the clock at 0. A single *bang* to the right and left inlet will report the time and immediately restart the clock (right to left order). Use **timer** to get the time between events.

Clocker is similar to **metro**, but instead of sending a *bang* per beat, it automatically reports elapsed time at a specified rate. As with **metro**, **clocker** takes an optional argument representing milliseconds to specify how often it outputs its running time (fig. 6.4). Since **clocker** is continuously updated, it can keep track of time after a specific musical event has begun, and may be used to automate a single change or several periodic changes to the program.

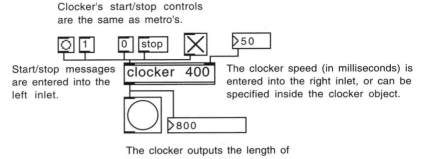

Figure 6.4
clocker

Timing Analysis

You can choose to control or display tempo in either millisecond format or, in a format more familiar to musicians, beats per minute (bpm).
Figure 6.5 shows a formula for converting timing in milliseconds to
the number of beats per minute, and bpm back to milliseconds. Notice
that the two objects on the left may be expressed as a single **expr** statement. The floating point version on the right will produce more accurate results.

"Delta time," which enables tempo-following and other interactive
timing functions, is the term for the time between events, that is, the
time from the beginning of one note to the beginning of the next. An
analysis of delta time can yield data on speed, density, and beats,
among other things. Max timing objects, such as **metro**, take arguments to specify a delta time. "Note duration" is the length of an individual note (as opposed to the time between two notes). A long delta
time coupled with short note durations will produce slow staccato
notes. In general, the closer the note duration gets to the delta time,
the more legato the passage will be. (The perception of legato, staccato,
and other articulations is also dependent upon the envelopes of the
computer sounds.)

"Duration" is the length that a note sounds. As far as Max is concerned, duration on a keyboard it is determined by measuring the time
between the striking of a key, and the release of that key (even though
a sound may last well beyond the key release). Figure 6.6 shows a

Milliseconds to BPM

converts from milliseconds to Beats Per Minute (BPM)

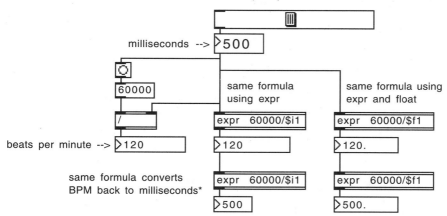

* The int millisecond time and the float millisecond time may differ because of rounding errors caused by using an int instead of a float (int truncates any fractional part of the number). Being off by one millesecond will probably not be significant for tempo, but for calculations requiring more accuracy, use floats.

Figure 6.5
Converting milliseconds to beats per minute (BPM)

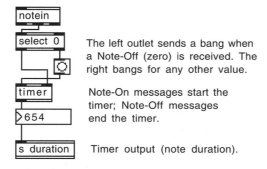

The left outlet sends a bang when a Note-Off (zero) is received. The right bangs for any other value.

Note-On messages start the timer; Note-Off messages end the timer.

Timer output (note duration).

Figure 6.6
Note duration

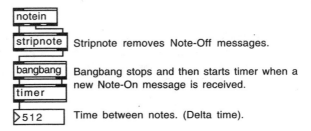

Figure 6.7
Delta time

simple patch for reporting the current duration using a timer to count the time between *Note-On* and *Note-Off* messages. Using velocity data, **select** 0 sends a *bang* out the left outlet when a *Note-Off* message is received and triggers a *bang* each time a nonzero value is passed out the right outlet. These two *bang* messages are used to start and stop a **timer.**

A similar technique measures delta time by timing each successive *Note-On* message (fig. 6.7). When a *Note-On* message is received, it sends out two *bang* messages, outputting the previous time (right inlet), and then restarting the clock (left inlet). Duration and delta time will be identical if there are no pauses or overlap between notes (virtually impossible for a live performance). Delta time partly determines rhythm. It also reflects the overall speed of a performance, and therefore may be used to determine tempo. When the rhythm played is one note per beat, then delta time and tempo are the same. One thing to take into consideration is the fact that the performed delta time will always be one unit ahead of the computer-analyzed delta time, since delta time can only be determined after a second note is played.

Since most music involves a variety of rhythmic values, one strategy in analyzing rhythm is to use a performer to input the beat by tapping a foot pedal. Since many musicians are used to keeping time by tapping a foot anyway, this is a natural solution that utilizes their existing performance habits (Dannenberg 1987). In figure 6.8, a patcher called **FootTempo** uses the sustain pedal, continuous controller 64, to get tempo information. The sustain pedal outputs 127 in the down position, and 0 in the up position. Each time **select** receives 127, it outputs the new time since the previous beat. While the foot keeps the beat for the computer, the performer is free to play anything on the keyboard without altering the tempo of the computer music.

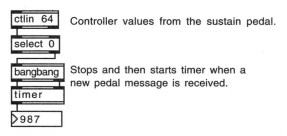

Figure 6.8
Foot tempo

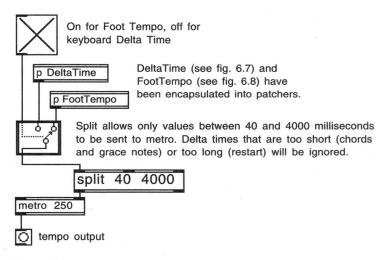

Figure 6.9
Get tempo

In figure 6.9, the two previous examples are encapsulated into sub-patches, and the toggle switch chooses between the tempo controlled by a keyboard and by a foot pedal. The **split** object defines valid tempo values as between 40 and 4000 milliseconds, which represents metro-nome values of beats per minute between 15 and 1500. It is used after determining delta time as a simple error-detector, rejecting any tempo values that are below 40 or above 4000 milliseconds. Delta times below 40 are undesirable in this example for a number of reasons. First, such short delta times may be a result of a performance error (such as acci-dentally hitting two keys with one finger). Second, playing chords or grace notes will generate very short values not intended to represent the tempo. Filtering out these values will enable performers to control the tempo by playing single lines or chords. (This is a somewhat arbitrary range, 40 to 4000 milliseconds, which may be shifted up or down depending on the musical context. In many instances, a higher minimum value will prove more dependable.)

If someone stops playing, the **timer** will keep going until it receives the next message. So rather than accept a tempo of 120000 after a coffee break, **split** will ignore that value and wait for the next valid one (assuming that delta times over four seconds are pauses in a performance or rehearsal). Valid tempo values can be tailored to fit a particular musical situation. As demonstrated here, **split** is a very useful object for selecting a range of values, or filtering out unwanted values. (See fig. 6.19 for a more accurate error filter.) The interface range object, **rslider**, can be used in conjunction with **split** to select and display a range of values graphically.

Max contains several objects designed to analyze and capture listener data. The most useful single object is **Borax**, a "Swiss Army Knife" for music analysis (fig. 6.10). It takes pitch and velocity information from a **notein** object, and sends out nine different parameters associated

Borax is a standard Max object that, among other things, outputs the duration and delta time of notes entering it. Unlike previous examples, Borax also corrects for beginning a second note before the first is finished.

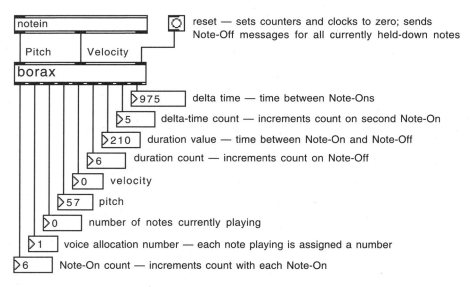

Figure 6.10
Timing analysis with **Borax**

with the performance. While each one of these functions could be simply written many by smaller objects, having all these features in one object is very convenient. In the time domain, **Borax** reports duration values (time between *Note-Ons* and *Note-Offs*) and delta time (time between *Note-Ons*). It is also a simple counter, sending out separate event numbers for MIDI *Note-On,* duration, and delta time. This could be useful because the MIDI *Note-On* is counted as soon as a key is pressed, the duration is reported only after the key is released, and the delta time is reported only after the next note is played, so that it is always one less than the count for MIDI *Note-On.* **Borax** also sends out a report of how many notes are simultaneously held down. If several of these parameters are used in a patch, **Borax** is a very handy object. However, any single action would be handled more clearly and efficiently with a single object, such as a **counter.**

Tempo Follower2 integrates several timing methods to control a **metro** object that randomly selects notes from a predefined scale (fig. 6.11). The computer music tempo can be continually adjusted in real time by either the keyboard or the sustain pedal. In keyboard mode, playing the upper register of the keyboard will produce a bass line in tempo. In foot pedal mode, tapping the sustain pedal will produce a bass line, along with a higher computer-produced melody. Since tempo is based on delta time, two notes (or foot taps) must be played to determine a single tempo; the new tempo is calculated as soon as the second note is played. Changes in the tempo are detected only after the change has already taken place, so the performer's tempo will always be one beat ahead of the computer's tempo.

The keyboard and the sustain pedal options produce different musical results. In keyboard mode playing rhythmic values other than the beat may determine the tempo. A **menu** selects options for playing divisions of the beat, using **BeatConfig**, which simply multiplies the delta time by the rhythmic value (fig. 6.12). Quarter, eighth, triplet, or sixteenth notes are selected from a menu to inform the computer what division of the beat will be played. When the chosen rhythmic value is played on the keyboard, the computer will respond by generating a bass line at the tempo of the quarter note. Assuming that a quarter note gets one beat, the time value of a single eighth note will be half the time value for one beat. So if eighth notes are being played, multiplying the delta time by two will give the correct quarter-note tempo.

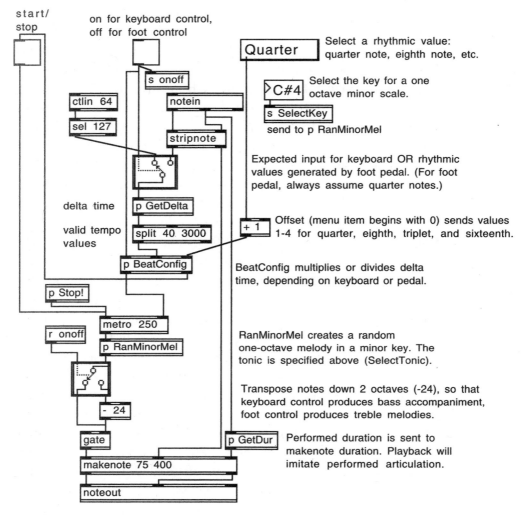

Figure 6.11
Tempo follower 2

If sixteenth notes are played, then multiplying the delta time by four will give the quarter-note tempo.

In foot tempo mode, the sustain pedal always keeps the quarter-note beat and creates a bass line, while a melody is created in the chosen rhythmic value by dividing the beat to get shorter delta times. So if the foot is tapping every 1000 milliseconds (a quarter note equals sixty bpm) and sixteenth notes are selected from the menu, the computer will play an upper melody of sixteenth notes by dividing 1000 by 4, reversing the process in the previous example (where the computer

BeatConfig multiplies or divides delta time by a modifier, depending on the tempo source.

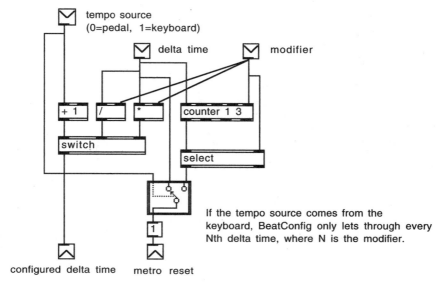

Figure 6.12
BeatConfig: determining rhythmic values (subpatch of fig. 6.11)

kept the beat while the performer played other rhythmic values). Melody and bass lines are created with the patcher **RanMinorMel**, which generates a random melody in a minor key that is selectable from the interface (fig. 6.13).

Another method accepts multiple rhythmic durations using windowing techniques to allow the tempo to change only by a small specified amount. **TempoWindow** checks each new delta time to see if it falls within a given range based on the previous delta time (fig. 6.14). The range of values is specified by a **slider** that determines the maximum and minimum window values based on a percentage of the current tempo. The object accepts a new delta time as the new tempo only if it fits within the prescribed range. The old tempo remains current until a valid tempo is received.

This kind of window, which specifies a range of values defined by a variable upper and lower limit, was previously seen in the **split** object. Figure 6.15 uses the lengthy **if** statement: [*if(i1) >= $i2 − ($i2 ∗ $f3)) && ($i1 <= $i2 + ($i2 ∗ $f3)) then $i1*].

Variable $i1 (variable 1, type integer) represents the new delta time; $i2 (variable 2, type integer) represents the old tempo; and $f3 (variable

RanMinorMel generates random notes in a one-octave minor scale.

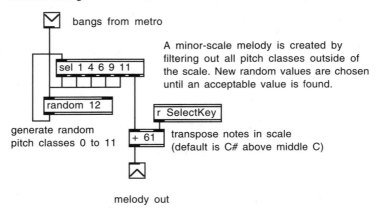

Figure 6.13
RanMinorMel: algorithm to produce a minor melody (subpatch of fig. 6.11)

TempoWindow allows only a certain percentage change in tempo; large jumps are ignored.

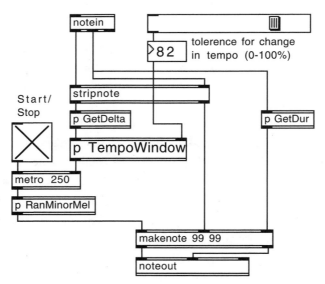

Figure 6.14
Restricting tempo changes

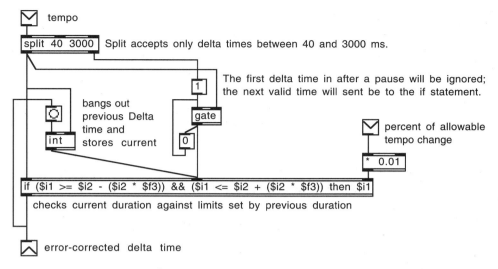

Figure 6.15
TempoWindow (subpatch of fig. 6.14)

3, type float) represents the maximum percentage of change allowed for a new delta time to be accepted as a new tempo. (A decimal number is multiplied to get percentages—times .10 for 10%; times .50 for 50%.)

The statement reads: **if** (the new delta time *is greater than or equal to* the old tempo *minus* (a percentage of the old tempo)) *AND* (the new delta time *is less than or equal to* the old tempo *plus* (a percentage of the old tempo)) **then** it is a *valid* new tempo and send the value out the left outlet to change the **metro** speed. If these conditions are not met (**else**) then *nothing* is sent out the left outlet.

This method has a number of advantages over the previous examples. Primarily, since it doesn't use a foot pedal, it allows the performer to play many different rhythmic values, such as triplets or sixteenth notes, without changing the tempo. It is designed so that gradual changes in successive quarter notes will be registered and they will, in turn, become the new center point for any tempo changes. Although this restricts tempo changes to quarter-note values, this is the kind of technical challenge whose limitations may push a composer into an unknown direction to produce interesting musical results.

· The **slider** value in figure 6.14 specifies how much quarter-note values can fluctuate and still count as valid tempo changes. A value of 100% will accept most delta times as the new tempo, while a value of 15% will allow for only very gradual changes in the tempo. For example, if the current tempo is 1000 and the window percentage is set at 20%, only delta times between 800 (1000 − 20%) to 1200 (1000 + 20%) will change the tempo. Sixteenth notes (delta time 250), triplets (delta time 333), and eighth notes (delta time 500) can all be played without affecting the computer's tempo. These values need to be chosen for a specific musical context; in this case the computer will never respond to a sudden change in tempo that is faster than 20% of the previous delta time. A simple reset feature (perhaps controlled by a foot pedal) can be programmed to get around this problem by allowing a new tempo to be set immediately, regardless of the previous tempo. TempoWindow has the built-in benefit of rejecting tempos that will be very long (because of pauses) or very short (because of playing chords, or hitting the cracks, or other errors).

Some tempo-following strategies rely on score-following techniques in which the computer contains a predefined score and gets tempo information as notes are matched in the score, even remembering and anticipating tempo changes from previous performances. Other techniques involve mixing a percentage of the old delta time with a percentage of the new, thus providing a smoothing algorithm to reduce abrupt changes in the tempo. A simple example using a stored score is included on disk, called "Conductor Model." It uses the foot pedal as a conductor, providing beats that index a score (of a Chopin Prelude) stored in a **coll.** (More score-following techniques and references for beat-tracking will be presented in chap. 9.)

Rhythm Analysis

Rhythm may also be analyzed and stored separately from other musical parameters. Figure 6.16 presents a method of recording rhythms from incoming MIDI data. Using **RhythmAnalysis**, you can analyze the rhythm of a performance by first determining the beat from a foot pedal or by tapping the space bar, and then comparing the delta times of incoming notes with the beat time to get the rhythmic values. This simplified model analyzes only sixteenth-note divisions of the beat.

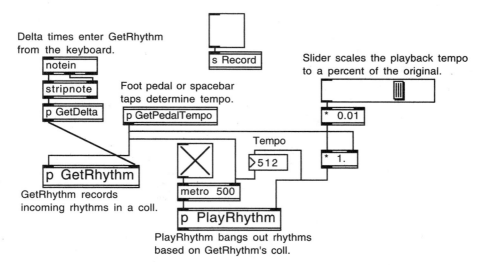

Figure 6.16
Simple rhythm analysis

Even so, it provides a more abstract analysis than simple delta times which may be used to generate complex rhythmic variations.

The patch works by first turning on the record switch. Hitting the space bar or the sustain pedal four times will set the tempo of the recording. When a phrase is played on the keyboard, **GetRhythm** will analyze the performance and record the rhythm in the **coll, CM-Rhythm.coll** (fig. 6.17). **PlayRhythm** uses a copy of the **coll**, with the identical name, to access the rhythmic values for playback (fig. 6.18). The record switch toggles to stop the recording. (Note that the last note played will be ignored, since two notes are always needed to create one delta time.) The **slider** adjusts the tempo of the playback, and the switch above the **metro** turns playback on and off.

Improving Listener Data

To err is human, but computers are unforgiving. Simple Max patches can reject common human performance errors and errors specific to various MIDI controllers. Double triggers are common errors for both performers and pitch-to-MIDI converters. A typical double-trigger error may occur when a keyboardist accidentally hits two adjacent keys with the same finger, or a wind player executes an awkward fingering, acci-

Delta times of incoming notes will be turned into rhythmic
values and stored in the coll object below, CMRhythm.c.

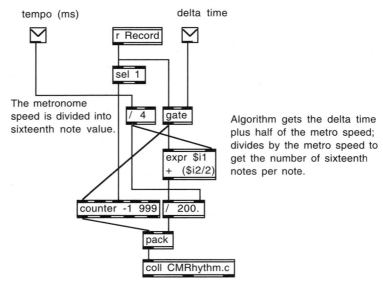

Figure 6.17
GetRhythm (subpatch of fig. 6.16)

dentally playing two notes instead of one. Pitch-to-MIDI converters are
sometimes confused by unstable pitches, timbres with strong upper
harmonics, wide vibrato, or notes played out of tune. Human listeners
take this all in stride, realizing the limitations of the instruments and
accepting these anomalies as normal within the tradition of performance. But imagine what would happen in a slow piece if the computer assumed a double trigger was the current tempo, and instead of
playing music at MM 60, it suddenly jumped to MM 600? By defining
a single musical event as anything occurring within a given time limit,
the computer manages to avoid many common errors occurring within
the first few milliseconds of the note attack. While this doesn't insure
complete note accuracy, it does reduce tempo errors and permits grace
notes and chords to be played without the computer analyzing the
very short values for tempo information. It also overcomes similar errors that occur when pitch-to-MIDI converters are confused by wide
vibrato, strong overtones, or pitches lying between the notes of the
tempered scale.

In figure 6.19, **ErrorFilter** accepts the first note in and ignores other
pitches that arrive too close together. It may be placed directly after

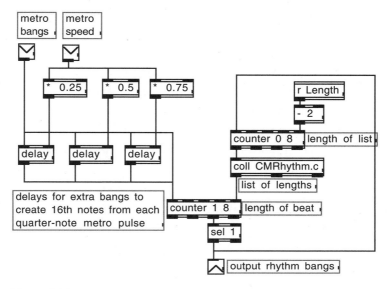

Figure 6.18
PlayRhythm (subpatch of fig. 6.16)

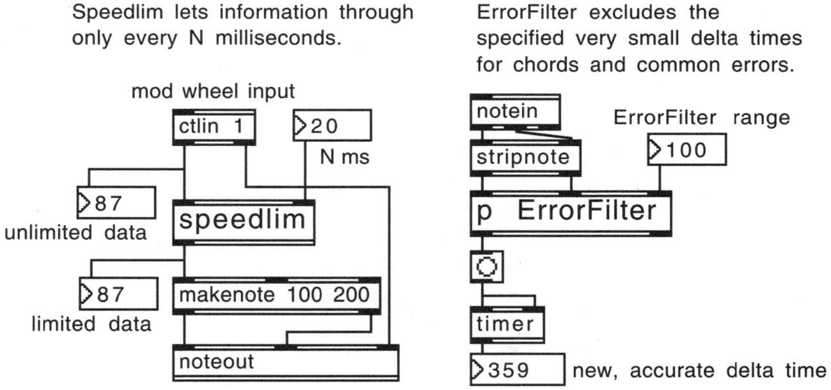

Speedlim lets information through only every N milliseconds.

mod wheel input

ErrorFilter excludes the specified very small delta times for chords and common errors.

Figure 6.19
Improving listener data

notein and **splitnote** to prevent erroneous data from entering the system. It stores incoming velocity and pitch information, outputting a note only if the timing was greater than *n* number of milliseconds. The minimum delta time allowed for a note to get through is specified in the right inlet.

ErrorFilter (fig. 6.20) can be used to calculate a more accurate delta time than we found in the previous delta time example (fig. 6.7). It contains two **ints** for velocity and pitch, only letting them into the system when a valid delta time has been received. These represent the starting point of "valid" musical events. Timing these events will produce a more accurate measurement of a performer's tempo. **ErrorFilter** produces a *bang* whenever it receives an acceptable time between events. Next, it sends out the pitch and velocity information associated with the last valid events. Getting delta time from these velocity values will yield the starting point of each valid event entering the system (such as the starting point of one chord to the starting point of the next). In the previous delta time example, a chord rolled slightly would produce an error by measuring delta time starting from the end of the roll rather than the beginning. If each note of a five-note chord was played 25 milliseconds apart, this would produce an error in rhythm of 100 milliseconds.

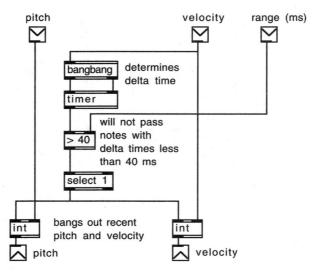

Figure 6.20
ErrorFilter (subpatch of fig. 6.19)

If the tempo of a musical passage is more or less predetermined, then **ErrorFilter** could be set slightly less than the fastest expected beat, and any subdivision of the beat would be ignored by the computer as a tempo change (with results similar to TempoWindow in figure 6.14).

Max's standard object, **speedlim**, lets one event pass through every *n* milliseconds, as specified by the right inlet. **Speedlim** is especially good for thinning out continuous data, such as continuous control messages, so that the program does not receive more information than it needs.

Space

Musical space can be viewed as a two-dimensional graph of pitch over time. Although time remains the essential medium of music, the vast majority of theories of music have concerned themselves with musical space. How pitches move through time and how they combine simultaneously are the basic starting points for music theories that describe melody, counterpoint, and harmony. From an accurate reading of pitch by incoming MIDI note numbers, many aspects of music related to musical space can be described.

Figure 6.21 shows three simple ways of analyzing pitch information based on pitch class, interval, and register. This example also shows the numerical representation of each pitch along with the note name. (The note-name feature is available by using GET INFO on a **number box** and choosing NOTE NAMES in the display option.)

Pitch Analysis

Pitch class looks at the note names only of incoming MIDI data, ignoring the register. The % object (modulo operator) divides two numbers and outputs the remainder. Using [% 12] (mod 12) on any MIDI note will reduce it to the lowest octave, giving numbers between 0 and 11 corresponding to the 12 notes in each octave: 0 for C, 1 for C#, 2 for D, 3 for D#, 4 for E, and so on. For instance, 7 would represent all G's, not just a particular note. Pitch-class information can be used as abstracted "themes" to generate melodies and chords based on the notes played.

This patch uses the pitch of an incoming note to determine its pitch class (the pitch of a note regardless of its octave), interval from the previous note, and register (the octave in which the note resides).

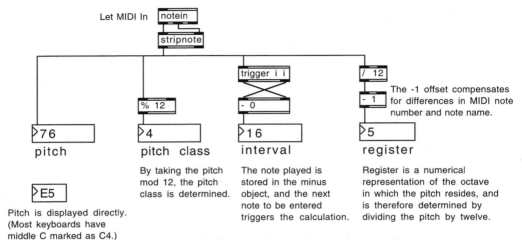

Figure 6.21
Pitch analysis

Intervals are determined by calculating the difference between one MIDI note number and the next. Subtracting the first pitch from the second pitch will give information about the interval and its direction; ascending intervals are positive numbers, and descending intervals are negative numbers. For example, if middle C (60) is played followed by the G above (67), the difference (67 − 60) will be 7 semitones, or a perfect fifth. Playing the upper note G first, followed by middle C (60 − 67), will result in −7, a descending perfect fifth. The **abs** object (absolute value) can be used to look only at the interval content regardless of direction by insuring that the value will always be a positive integer. This might be useful in storing interval information for the computer to generate harmony. Since two notes are required to create one interval, the results of playing the initial note should be ignored.

Register may be determined by dividing the note numbers by 12. Since middle C (60) is called C4 on most MIDI synthesizers, and 60/12 = 5, an offset of 1 is subtracted from the resulting numbers to adjust it to the proper register. Register is an effective device for interactive composition, because it can reveal basic concepts of high and low and track larger melodic direction over time.

Melodic Analysis

These simple analysis objects may be used to detect melodic shape and direction. For instance, register may be mapped to alter timbre or adjust the duration of a computer sequence. Pitch class sets can be captured and manipulated in real time to produce variations. Intervals can be captured and stored from a performer's melodic line and then used by the computer to create chords. More sophisticated objects that can be used to track melodic changes and capture phrasing information will be discussed at the end of this chapter.

Harmonic Analysis

The computer may be programmed to recognize chords by looking for two or more MIDI notes received within a short specified time and analyzing the intervals of pairs of notes. Since humans will never play all members of a chord at exactly the same time and MIDI data is transmitted serially, several notes sound as a chord when played within 0 − 60 milliseconds of each other (depending on the musical context and the number of notes in a chord). As the time between notes gets longer, they will separate into a series of individual notes, creating arpeggios or melodies.

Figure 6.22 demonstrates a patch that defines near-simultaneous notes as chords. It reports the number of notes in each chord, and shows the intervals in each chord for up to seven-note chords, in high-to-low order. The algorithm involves several steps:

1. **Thresh** creates a list out of notes received within 60 milliseconds of each other.

2. **Sort** places the notes in low to high order. (Note: This is not a standard Max object.)

3. **Iter** sends out elements in the list, one at a time, and **counter** counts the number of notes in the chord.

4. To determine the intervals, **unpack** sends out the sorted list to a series of **expr** statements that subtract the lower pitch from the upper pitch for each adjacent pair. The result shows the interval makeup of the chord, from low to high. Mod 12 may be used on these numbers to reduce all intervals to within a one-octave range.

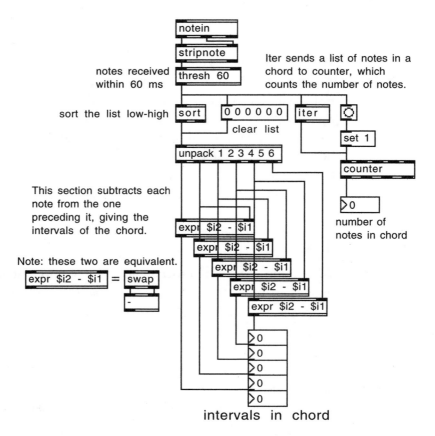

Figure 6.22
Chord analysis: intervals and order

The results of these chords could easily be indexed to "match lists" or algorithms to determine interval content and chord type. As an example, figure 6.23 shows a method for analyzing major and minor triads played in closed position (within one octave). It reports the type of chord, inversion, bass note, and root. Here is the technique:

1. Triads are sent to **sort**, and the two intervals are placed from high to low order. The lowest note is the bass.

2. The next step identifies inversion with a series of **if** statements in the subpatch, **TriadAnalysis** (fig. 6.24). Since root position chords are the only inversion not to include a fourth, the first statement reads: **If** the lower interval is not 5 (a perfect fourth) *and* the upper interval is not 5, then the chord is in root position. If this is not the case, then

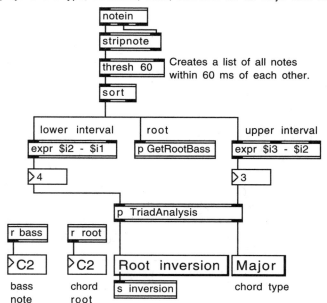

Figure 6.23
Chord analysis: chord type, root, inversion

the next statement looks for a fourth in the lower interval. If there is a fourth, then the chord is in second position. Anything else must be a first inversion chord.

3. To determine the root, root position chords have their root on the bottom, first inversion chords have their root on the top, and second inversion chords have their root in the middle (fig. 6.25).

TriadAnalysis sends out two numbers as indexes to **menus** to display inversion and chord type. Although this example is rather limited in the types of chords it recognizes, similar approaches could be generalized to include the identification of a larger variety of harmonic changes.

A brute-force method would attempt to match each chord to a list of possible interval combinations. This method could recognize chords made up of fourths and fifths, for example, as well as thirds. It could also be used to recognize chords with more than three notes. By assuming that any chord is possible, it might attempt to match whatever chord information is needed. For example, the formula for identifying

TriadAnalysis determines if a triad is major or minor and in what inversion.

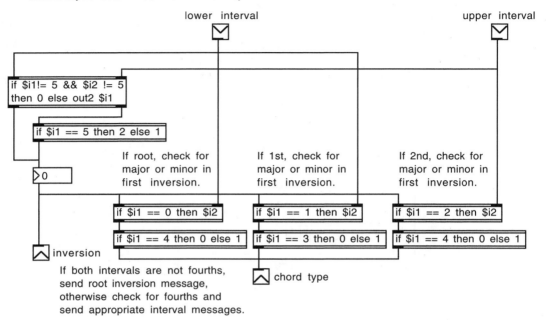

lower interval

upper interval

if $i1!= 5 && $i2 != 5
then 0 else out2 $i1

if $i1 == 5 then 2 else 1

> 0

If root, check for major or minor in first inversion.

If 1st, check for major or minor in first inversion.

If 2nd, check for major or minor in first inversion.

if $i1 == 0 then $i2

if $i1 == 1 then $i2

if $i1 == 2 then $i2

if $i1 == 4 then 0 else 1

if $i1 == 3 then 0 else 1

if $i1 == 4 then 0 else 1

inversion

chord type

If both intervals are not fourths, send root inversion message, otherwise check for fourths and send appropriate interval messages.

Figure 6.24
TriadAnalysis (subpatch of fig. 6.23)

GetRootBass gets the root and bass of a triad.

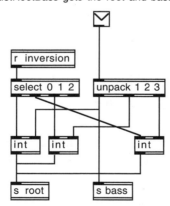

r inversion

select 0 1 2   unpack 1 2 3

int   int   int

s root   s bass

Figure 6.25
GetRootBass (subpatch of fig. 6.23)

a dominant seventh chord in root position would read: **If** the number of notes in a chord is 4 *and* the lowest interval is a 4 (major third) *and* the next interval is a 3 *and* the next interval is a 3, **then** the chord is a dominant seventh chord in root position and output a 0, **else** (if there is no match) out 2 (send the number out the second outlet to the next statement to be checked). The next statement might look for inversions, chords made up of fourths, any five-note chord with a minor second as the first interval, or any harmonic information that will be used in a piece.

Identifying Musical Features and Tracking Their Changes Over Time

Max provides many useful standard objects designed to analyze performances. **Borax** has already been mentioned as an all-in-one analysis object. **Select** and **match** both "look" for specific numbers, sending out a *bang* when a match is found. Both are very useful in triggering a computer's response based on pitch information. **Select** looks only for single values, sending a *bang* out the corresponding outlet when a number in the argument list is received. Figure 6.26 uses **select** to identify and then harmonize each note belonging to a D harmonic minor scale. It separates pitch class and register so that any notes in the scale will be harmonized.

Because **match** looks for lists of numbers in a specified order, it can be useful for identifying melodic passages in a score or for triggering events based on the specific harmonic content of an improvised melody. Values in a match list (arguments) must arrive consecutively. Figure 6.27 shows an example that will trigger a chord whenever the interval of a major third is followed immediately by an interval of a minor third.

Max includes analysis objects for understanding changing data. **Past** sends a *bang* each time a number or list of numbers rises above (or equals) a threshold setting (fig. 6.28). After sending a *bang,* the object waits to receive a number below the threshold point before it will rest and begin to look again for another number above the threshold point; if values begin higher than the limit and descend, **past** will remain inactive.

Peak finds the largest value in a stream of numbers (fig. 6.29). It outputs the highest number out the left outlet and reports if the current value is or is not a new peak. An arbitrary high point can be set at

Select is set to pick out the pitch values of a D harmonic minor scale (D E F G A Bb C#) and add the correct notes to form a diatonic chord. Each time an incoming value matches a number in select, it will send a bang out the corresponding outlet, creating a chord which is then transposed back to the original register.

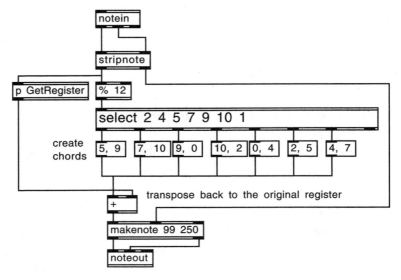

Figure 6.26
select

Match checks whether a list of entering numbers matches its arguments. This differs from select in that the list entering match must arrive in the correct order to trigger an output. Match sends out the list by default, but can send a bang using the bang button, as seen below.

Play a major 3rd followed by a minor 3rd (e.g., C E G)

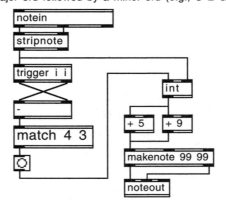

Figure 6.27
match

Past sends out a bang when a series of numbers exceeds a preset limit.

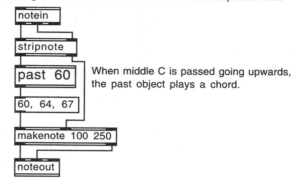

When middle C is passed going upwards, the past object plays a chord.

Figure 6.28
past

When numbers are sent through Peak, it will pick out the largest one entered so far and remember it.

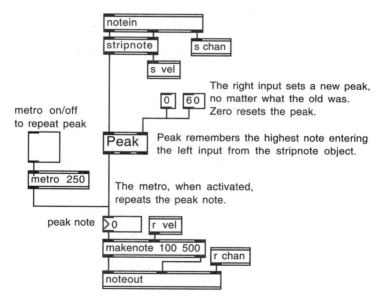

The right input sets a new peak, no matter what the old was. Zero resets the peak.

Peak remembers the highest note entering the left input from the stripnote object.

metro on/off to repeat peak

The metro, when activated, repeats the peak note.

peak note

Figure 6.29
peak

any time through the right inlet. **Peak** can be used to monitor a on-going performance, whether it is to view the loudest note played, or to track the high points of melodic contours. Various tracks of sound, for instance, could be added each time a new melodic high point is reached. The opposite of **Peak** is **Trough**, which finds and stores minimum values.

A useful performance-analysis technique involves keeping a running count, or histogram, of performance data. **Histo** counts how many times it receives each number between 0 and a specified limit (fig. 6.30). The numbers received by **Histo** represent an address (index), and the running count for each number (data) is stored there. Each time a number goes into **Histo,** the quantity (the count) at that address is increased by 1 and sent out the right outlet, while the entering number (the index) is sent out the left outlet. A number sent to the right inlet will query **Histo** and send the current total of that number out the right outlet. Since **Histo** keeps track of changing variables, it plays an important role in building listener objects, and can be used to analyze such things as the predominance of certain notes, the number of chords played in a section, or general changes in register.

Histo is a simple array. It counts the number of occurrences of any given number. When you enter a number into the other input, it will tell you how many occurrences of the number it contains in memory.

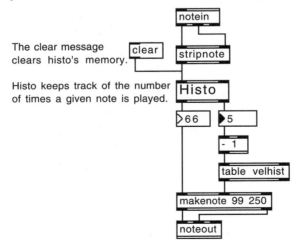

Figure 6.30
histo

In figure 6.30, the number of occurrences of a given note is used to determine its velocity—the more times a note is played, the quieter it becomes. After ten times it becomes silent (velocity 0). Each time a note is sent to **Histo**, the count is sent out the right and used as an index to the **table** *velhist,* which contains ten velocity numbers stored in descending values. The velocity values correspond to index numbers 0 through 9.

Much of the interest in listening to music lies in how musical ideas and various elements change over time. Several custom patches that may be used to track parameters as they change over time are described below.

RunAve (Running Average) looks at changing variables and determines if they are increasing, decreasing, or staying the same (fig. 6.31). It averages the values of a specified number of items. For example, if ten is the number of items to average, the program will produce an average of the first ten items, then the next ten items, and so on. (A smoother ongoing image of changing states would continuously average the last ten values every time a new value is received, rather than once every ten values.)

Compare2 is a subpatch within **RunAve** that compares the average of the new group to that of the old group to determine changing states (fig. 6.32). A report is sent out the right outlet based on a comparison of every two groups of averages, with 0 for decreasing averages, 1 for increasing averages, and 2 for little or no change. The right inlet determines the amount considered a significant change by defining the upper and lower values of a window. If the new average falls within the range of this window, then it reports a 2, meaning little or no change. If the new average is above or below this window, then it will report a change, either a 1 or a 0. This object has been generalized for many types of musical data, since the average and window values can be changed to work in a number of situations. The left inlet takes any changing data. The middle inlet determines the number of items to average. The left outlet sends out the current average.

An object that attempts to report the current state of crescendo and diminuendo continuously can be created by sending velocity to **Run-Ave**. This example averages the velocity of every ten notes, and if the average value is ten greater or less than the previous average, it will report a 1 for crescendo, a 0 for decrescendo, or a 2 if the new average was within 10 above or below the old value.

RunAve takes in any kind of real-time data and puts out a running average. It compares the current average with the previous average and reports any changes. Here it identifies change in dynamics (crescendo and diminuendo).

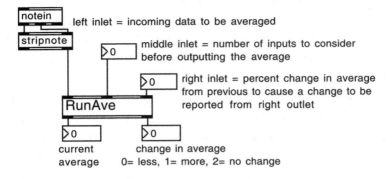

notein   left inlet = incoming data to be averaged

stripnote

▷ 0   middle inlet = number of inputs to consider
        before outputting the average

        ▷ 0   right inlet = percent change in average
                from previous to cause a change to be
                reported from right outlet

RunAve

▷ 0   ▷ 0
current   change in average
average   0= less, 1= more, 2= no change

RunAve

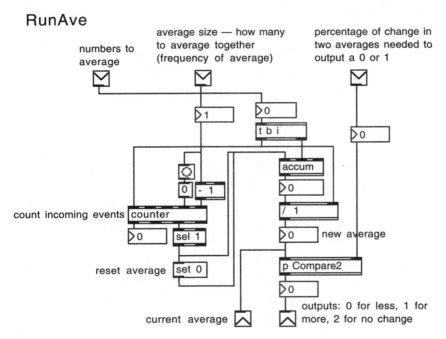

numbers to average

average size — how many to average together (frequency of average)

percentage of change in two averages needed to output a 0 or 1

count incoming events   counter

reset average   set 0

new average

current average

outputs: 0 for less, 1 for more, 2 for no change

Figure 6.31
RunAve (Running Average)

Compare2 compares the old average to the new average. In the if statement, $f1 is the new average, $f2 is the old average, and $f3 is the percentage to count as a change.

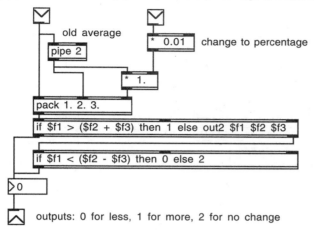

Figure 6.32
Compare2 (subpatch of fig. 6.31)

Simply changing velocity data to delta time would create an instant analysis tool for tempo changes, allowing **RunAve** to keep track of fluctuations in tempi, reporting a 1 for accelerando, 0 for ritardando, and a 2 if there is no change to the tempo above or below the specified amount to be considered a change.

RunAve could also be used to track overall direction changes in a melodic line; the music might change, for example, if a performer is playing ascending lines or descending lines. Similar techniques could be used to view how dynamics, register, or chord density change over larger sections of a piece. Besides reporting immediate changes, information from **RunAve** could be stored in a histogram to compare larger overall changes in the music.

Figure 6.33 shows another example that demonstrates the continuous tracking of parameters over time. **VelHist** (velocity history) uses **table** to display a graphic representation of a histogram (using **histo**), keeping a running count of five different dynamic levels, from pp to ff. Velocity messages are sent to a series of cascading if-then-else statements. The first **if** statement checks to see if the velocity value is greater than 85. If it is greater than 85 (*f-ff*), it sends a 1 out the left outlet and waits for the next note. If not, then it sends the number (*$i1*) out the left outlet (*out2 $1*) to the next statement, which checks to see if

VelHist divides the incoming velocity of notes played into five categories. The number of notes played in each category is then stored in a table that can be viewed graphically.

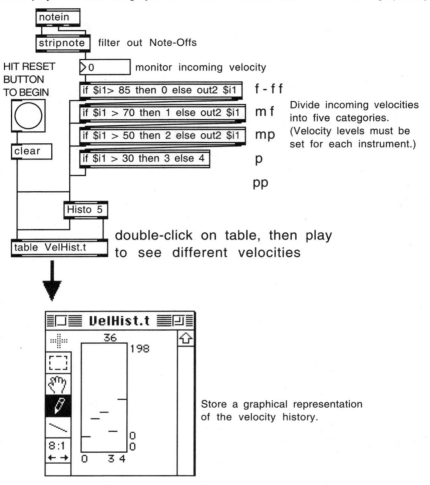

double-click on table, then play
to see different velocities

Store a graphical representation
of the velocity history.

Figure 6.33
Velocity **histo**

the number is greater than 70 (*mf*). If it is greater then 70 it sends out a 2; if not it passes the number on to the next statement. Since the process begins with the highest category and is always checking for a condition greater than that number, all velocity values will be checked and the process will continue until a category match is found. Playing a variety of dynamic levels while viewing the **table** in the analysis example will animate the **table** values as they are continuously updated. The number in each column will increase when the corresponding dynamic level is played.

A more elaborate histogram, **DurHist** (duration history), keeps a continuous count of 4 types of articulation: legato, tenuto, detached, and staccato (fig. 6.34). These are determined as ratios between duration and delta time. For example, legato is defined as "smooth" playing, with little or no break between notes. Thus, **DurHist** counts a legato note when the duration time and the delta time are almost the same (within 90 percent of each other). The series of if-then-else statements checks for the various articulations. The numbers to be analyzed are sent into the left inlet. Each time a conditional statement is matched, a number representing four types of articulation is sent out the left outlet. If a statement is false, then the two numbers for delta time and duration get sent out the right outlet and are passed on to the next level to be checked.

The first two **if** statements identify staccato notes for slow and fast delta times. Staccato poses a special problem since the perception of short notes changes depending on the speed of the notes. A 1 will be added to the third column each time a staccato note is played. After that, if the duration time is 90% or more of the delta time, the passage is considered legato: no breaks exist between notes. **DurHist** will add a 1 to column 0 for each legato note. If the duration is between 60 to 90 percent of the delta time, **DurHist** will count it as tenuto, and so on.

Articulation data could be used in numerous musical situations, such as programming the envelope shapes on a synthesizer to move with the changing articulations of a live performer, or subtly altering timbre or reverberation to reflect broad changes in articulation. Many other types of articulation can be analyzed by viewing dynamics along with duration and delta time. For example, a sforzando, or heavily accented note, would have a high velocity number with a relatively short duration. Besides these traditional notions of articulation, changing

DurHist keeps track of 4 different articulations by comparing duration with delta times.

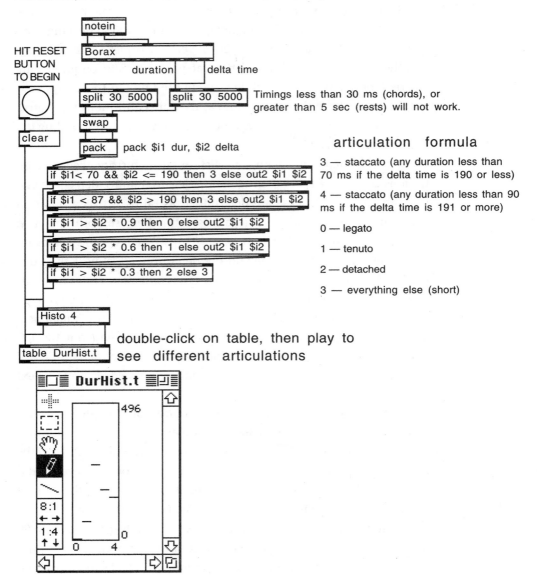

notein

HIT RESET
BUTTON
TO BEGIN

Borax

duration   delta time

split 30 5000   split 30 5000

Timings less than 30 ms (chords), or
greater than 5 sec (rests) will not work.

clear

swap

pack   pack $i1 dur, $i2 delta

if $i1< 70 && $i2 <= 190 then 3 else out2 $i1 $i2

if $i1 < 87 && $i2 > 190 then 3 else out2 $i1 $i2

if $i1 > $i2 * 0.9 then 0 else out2 $i1 $i2

if $i1 > $i2 * 0.6 then 1 else out2 $i1 $i2

if $i1 > $i2 * 0.3 then 2 else 3

articulation   formula

3 — staccato (any duration less than
70 ms if the delta time is 190 or less)

4 — staccato (any duration less than 90
ms if the delta time is 191 or more)

0 — legato

1 — tenuto

2 — detached

3 — everything else (short)

Histo 4

table DurHist.t

**double-click on table, then play to
see different articulations**

DurHist.t

496

8:1

1:4

0

0   4

Figure 6.34
Duration **histo**

amplitude shapes (envelopes) of individual notes could be discerned during a performance through continuous controller information, such as aftertouch or breath control. Pitch-to-MIDI converters also send out continuous amplitude information in the form of a continuous-controller message. This continuous information representing human actions could be captured with a **seq** or other data storage object and later applied to shape computer-generated music.

Timing Maps are created by storing delta times. This information can then be used by the computer to perform music with a human touch. Timing Maps can be scaled to play back at different speeds, or processed to control other parameters. Capturing dynamic information along with a Timing Map gives a phrase level analysis of musical performance. Since timing and dynamics are the parameters associated with "expressive" playing, this is valuable information that may directly impart human performance characteristics to machine-generated music. Chapter 7 will discuss **CaptureGesture**, an object designed to store and play back duration, dynamics, and timing information (fig. 7.39). In this way, a phrase from a performer can be captured, and that musical gesture applied to a new melody created by the computer, or interpreted to add a human element to other computer processes.

Efficient Use of Listener Objects

Listener objects should look at the minimal amount of information necessary to achieve desired musical results. By limiting the focus, reducing the data stream, and storing in memory only what will be needed at a later time, objects will use less memory and have more accurate results. For maximum efficiency, try to get the most use out of a few flexible listener objects that can be used in many situations rather than using many narrowly defined objects. Before creating a complex listener object, consider what specific aspects of a performance will best suit a musical idea, which data will be useful in producing musical material by influencing musical processes. For example, if the software needs to track the direction of a melody over a large span of time, a simple routine that detects octave changes might work better than an elaborate procedure for analyzing the melodic direction of every note.

There really isn't any mystery in creating listener objects; they should simply represent musical information as accurately as possible. With the basic parameters of pitch, velocity, and time provided by MIDI, researchers continue to create much more elaborate analysis algorithms than the ones presented here. However, even the simplest methods provide a composer with plenty of material with which to begin the real work of composition. How is computer music shaped by this information? It is up to the composer to invent the imaginative ways that this raw material can now be turned into music.

7   *Composer Objects*

Composer objects represent musical processes, known in computer music as compositional algorithms. Algorithms are plans (methods) for performing actions, operations, or procedures on musical material or other data. Programmers break down procedures into sequences of simple operations, with each step clearly defined. For hundreds of years composers have used processes to create musical material and musical structures. A canon (round) is a very old compositional algorithm; the plan is for one person to begin singing a melody, and after a set amount of time (or beats), a second person comes in singing the same melody while the first one continues. The method for action is to *delay* the second voice. The material (data) to be processed is the original *melody*. Transposition is another example of a simple algorithm. Transposition modifies notes by adding or subtracting a specified number of semitones. The plan is to *add*. The data are the *notes*.

Many musical processes, especially those used in twentieth century acoustic music, lend themselves well to computer implementation. Perhaps even more interesting are the complex and sometimes unique processes that would be difficult or impossible to create without the use of a computer. Many composers have, in fact, used the computer as a tool to generate algorithmic music that is then scored for traditional ensembles. Pioneering work, such as Lejaren Hiller's *Illiac Suite for String Quartet,* began to appear in the late 1950s with the birth of computer music (Hiller 1959). In general, compositional algorithms are the methods computers use to create music.

Composer objects serve a double role in creating interactive works; not only are they the response mechanism to a performer's actions, but they also serve as a computer-aided sketchpad for the composer to create a new work. Composer objects provide an intuitive platform for real-time exploration of musical processes, with selected variables controlled by the composer from the computer keyboard or by a performer. This immediacy in generating and manipulating musical materials provides the composer with an interactive laboratory where musical ideas and time-varying compositional algorithms are quickly realized and refined. The benefits of receiving immediate aural feedback from this kind of experimentation cannot be overemphasized. Complex processes, which at first seem confusing, can be mastered and understood with practice and rehearsal. Compositional algorithms, coupled with a well-designed user interface, allow composers to generate scores for acoustic works, improvise with other musicians, perform solo pieces from the computer, or shape interactive pieces on-the-spot during rehearsals or performances.

Other music programs, running concurrently with Max, create a powerful working environment for composers. Music generated with Max can be recorded with **seq** or routed directly to many sequencer or notation programs through Opcode's Inter-Application Communication Bus (IAC). From there, the music can be viewed and edited. This is helpful in understanding the musical capabilities inherent in each process. It also makes it possible to produce a score for musicians using Max, perhaps based on similar music that would be played by the computer during a performance.

The study of compositional algorithms is so large that existing literature comprises hundreds of volumes. These are rich resources for composers wishing to expand their musical technique using the computer. This chapter discusses some general concepts about algorithms and describes various types of composer objects common to interactive composition.

Creative Response to Listener Date

Composer objects create music directly or indirectly by responding to performance data. Composer objects are algorithms that embody the thought processes, taste, and skill of a composer. They represent a program's entire range and potential for musical production. Possibilities for composer objects are endless; it is in their design that the composer can be most imaginative.

Listener objects, on the other hand, only need to be factual to provide accurate and dependable data about a performance. They answer a limited number of questions, such as what note, how loud, how fast, and how parameters change over time. Listener objects, in and of themselves, may not be artistically interesting; they simply need to work. The real work for composers begins by interpreting listener data so that it can influence musical production, showing a mutual cause and effect relationship between performers and computers. The basic principles of object and program design are applicable to compositional algorithms. They should be consistent in how they work, have a clear function, be generalized for expanded use, and be foolproof to prevent unwanted side effects. Compositional ideas need to be represented as a step-by-step process, with each step having exact limits and a precise purpose essential to the outcome.

The logic involved in creating an algorithm does not imply that a composer's talents, which involve craft, imagination, and refined artistic judgment, are secondary. Such strict "rules" are the limitations that shape form and create musical style. Music history is full of examples of music predicated on a strict adherence to rules (that are at times intentionally but tastefully broken). Taste, artistic values, and even "breaking the rules" are all aspects of composition that can be programmed into an interactive piece. The beauty of interactive composition is that a thoroughly logical and even uninteresting algorithmic process can be made to sound quite expressive when a performer "messes it up" by manipulating variables according to his or her own interpretation.

Which variables should the performer alter? The ability to alter or change a variable in real time is precisely what makes an algorithm interactive. With the potential to have numerous composer objects simultaneously producing music, it is important to make a few significant variables available for manipulation.

Composer Object Design

Performers may affect computer output in one of two ways. The computer may look for a specific note, a condition, or other listener data to trigger a prerecorded sequence or to begin a compositional process. When a specified conditional is met, playback or processing will commence. Performers may also have continuous control over specific parameters of a process, such as controlling the dynamic level or the tempo, which continually shapes the musical outcome. The composer determines the range, scale and time frame for a performer to influence a musical process. Performer actions may not always be so obvious as a one-to-one correspondence with composer objects; performer actions may be stored, delayed, accumulated, or interpreted in other ways that produce compelling musical results. Triggers may even cause a chain reaction of automated actions.

Data Sources

Composer objects may receive data from a variety of sources. Listener objects provide *real-time data* via MIDI, or from the computer keyboard and mouse. They also provide *captured data,* useful musical material and analysis information that has been stored during a performance via one of Max's data storage objects. Storage objects may also hold *predetermined data,* musical material or potential material that is loaded into a program prior to a performance. Predetermined data could be anything from a complete musical score, waiting for playback, to raw material, such as a few intervals used to create new melodies or chords. **Seq, table, coll,** and **detonate** are used in most cases for this purpose, since they can retrieve large amounts of information in real time, and in an organized fashion. *Generated data* is produced by algorithms that create data from a small subset of stored or real-time data. The computer may use a mathematical formula or statement to internally generate numbers used for musical input, without needing outside input or stored data. Such an example has already been shown using the **random** object to generate melodies using random numbers within a given range. Other, more complex formulas have been used by composers to generate pitches and timbres based on fractals, the golden-mean ratio, and other such phenomena. Finally, *processed data* results when data from any source is modified by an algorithm. Several composer objects may be linked so that processed data is passed out one object and into another object for further processing.

RandomMelody provides a straightforward interface for a random-melody generator (fig. 7.1). The simple algorithm within **Random-PitchRange** is used throughout this text to create random notes within a given range (fig. 7.2). The **random** object generates values from 0 to the maximum, which are offset to reside within a reasonable range for

RandomPitchRange uses metro to start/stop and set
the tempo. The range size is set with the second inlet,
and the range minimum is set with the third inlet.

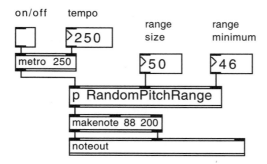

Figure 7.1
Random melody

Generates a range of random notes. The lowest note is set by the + object;
the range size is set by the random object.

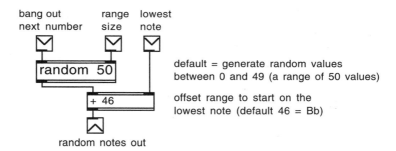

Figure 7.2
RandomPitchRange (subpatch of fig. 7.1)

MIDI melodies. Other types of random-number generators in Max will
produce different melodic results, such as **urn**, which outputs random
numbers without duplicates, and **drunk**, which outputs numbers
within a moving range, a "random walk" with a specified step size.

Types of Composition Algorithms

In *Interactive Music Systems,* Robert Rowe defines three basic methods
by which composer objects respond to data input: generative, sequenced, and transformative. Generative algorithms use elementary or

fragmentary source material, such as a set of intervals for producing chords and melodies. The music may be generated from musical fragments captured from a live performance, from fragments stored before a performance begins, or from equations or formulae that generate numbers, such as a random-number generator. Rowe (1993) writes:

Generative methods use sets of rules to produce complete musical output from the stored fundamental material.

Sequenced techniques use prerecorded music fragments in response to some real-time input. Some aspects of these fragments may be varied in performance, such as tempo playback, dynamic shape, slight rhythmic variations, etc.

Transformative methods take some existing musical material and apply transformation to it to produce variants. According to the technique, these variants may or may not be recognizably related to the original. For transformative algorithms, the source material is complete musical input.

Transforming Musical Material

Source material may come from one of several sources: a live performance, a stored sequence, or a generative algorithm. Transformative methods may be used to alter musical material from any source. They are represented as musical processors, taking existing material as input, and shaping it to produce new versions based on some aspect of the original. Thus, they are the primary means for creating variations. The transformation may alter a single parameter, such as pitch transposition, or may alter several parameters so drastically as to produce results that are unrecognizable, yet formally related, to the original. Processors are analogous to MIDI effects boxes (signal processors): the input signal is warped, distorted, colored, or otherwise altered according to the selected algorithm. In fact, previous examples have shown that it is possible to create Max objects that mimic some functions of a signal processor, such as delay, pitch shift, arpeggios, and panning. A few basic categories of processor types are discussed below.

Filtering

Filters take in a performance or sequence, and alter the data by reducing, distorting, or eliminating some aspect of the performance. Simple filters can throw out certain pitches or registers, thin data, or set up restrictive conditions for data to be able to pass through. **Select** and **split** are Max objects useful for setting up simple filters by selecting data to accept or reject. A **counter** or **timer**, coupled with a **gate**, may also be used as a filter by allowing one out of every *x* number of events to pass through, for instance, playing every third note, or allowing events to pass during specific time frames (also known as "windowing").

Limiting

Limiters are types of filters that modify or eliminate values outside of a specified range. The **split** object is the most obvious limiter, specifying allowable high and low values. **Split** may be used to reject velocity values that are too loud, ignore tempo changes that are too slow, or accept only short duration values. A limiter may be used in conjunction with a formula to alter the rejected values. In figure 7.3, **Range-Loop**

This example uses RandomPitchRange to create pitches that are then further limited by split. The allowable range of values is set with the low and high split inlets. When the GSwitch is sending to the left outlet, it chooses new random notes until it gets one within that range. When the GSwitch is sending to the right outlet, notes outside the range will not sound.

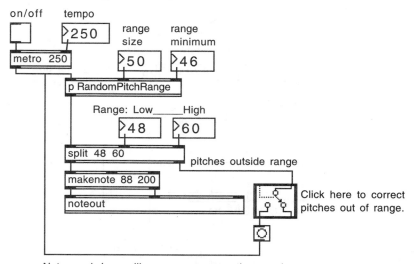

Note: each loop will use up processor time on the computer; use this method with caution!

Figure 7.3
Range loop

plays notes only within a predefined range using a single **split** object. Each *bang* from **metro** produces a random value from **RandomPitchRange**, with pitches out of **split** being ignored. This makes the object fairly limited, but it does create interesting rhythms because values outside of the **split** range will produce rests (they do not go to **makenote**). Fine tuning the range of random values from **RandomPitchRange** and the range of notes to play from **split** will produce continuous rhythmic variations that are somewhat predictable, since the values are highly constrained. Many algorithms that improvise and produce constant variations use constrained random values. In this example, a simple correction algorithm may be added by clicking on the **GSwitch**, which creates a feedback loop by sending a *bang* back to **RandomPitchRange** for each out-of-range value. Such feedback loops should be used with caution, since indeterminately endless looping can use up processor time on the computer. However, this should not be a problem if an appropriate value is generated within a short time.

Figure 7.4 shows the output of an arpeggio-generating algorithm, **AddArpeggio**, being processed by a more generalized algorithm, **RangeMod**, to place values within a predefined range. **RangeMod** takes in melodies (or any other data) in the first inlet and alters pitches that fall outside the selectable minimum and maximum range using

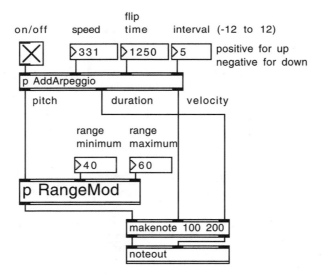

Figure 7.4
Constrained arpeggio

the % object (the modulo operator), which divides two numbers and outputs the remainder. The size of the range is determined by subtracting the maximum from the minimum. (1 is added to include the specified end points.) The number received in the right inlet of % (the divisor) determines the maximum value of the range; the middle inlet determines the minimum value (fig. 7.5). Values sent to % will result in numbers between 0 and the range size. A previous example showed the use of [% 12] (mod 12) to analyze incoming notes as pitch classes, reducing all values to fall within a range of 0 to 11 (fig. 6.14).

RangeMod first checks to see if values are in range using **split**; if they are, the values are sent out without further processing (fig. 7.5). The **expr** object calculates the size of the range. To be fail-safe, an **abs** object (absolute value) is used to convert any possible negative numbers to positive. Next, the **modulo** operator creates new values within the specified range, starting at 0. To get the new values in the proper register, the minimum value (*Range Minimum*) is added to offset the results. (See figures 7.30 and 7.31 for a third range method.)

Each **notein** to **AddArpeggio** begins a new arpeggio from the last note played (fig. 7.6). *Speed* controls the arpeggio speed and is sent out to the duration inlet of **makenote** to assure that the duration and the

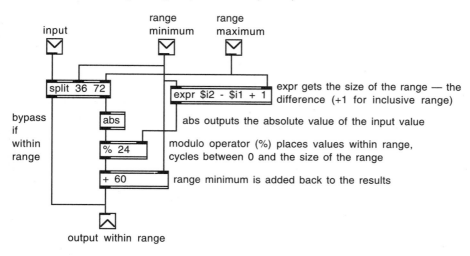

RangeMod will take any value and place it within a predescribed range using % (the modulo operator).

Figure 7.5
RangeMod (subpatch of fig. 7.4)

AddArpeggio takes a note played on the keyboard as a starting point and adds or subtracts a specified interval repeatedly, creating an arpeggio. The addition/subtraction will restart each time a note is played on the keyboard. In regular time intervals (flip time), the arpeggio direction will be reversed by multiplying the original interval by -1.

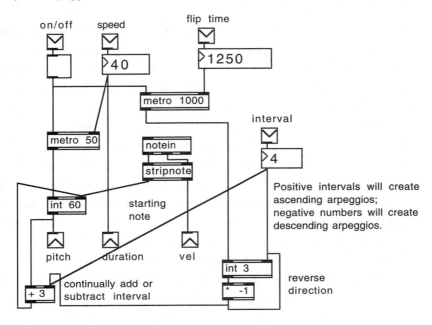

Figure 7.6
AddArepeggio (subpatch of figure 7.4)

speed are equal (legato). Arpeggios in this example are created by continuously adding or subtracting a single interval, as specified in the right inlet, producing ascending and descending lines. An **int** is used to hold the starting keyboard pitch, which gets replaced each time an interval is added or subtracted. *Flip time,* in milliseconds, determines how often the direction of the arpeggio will change using a second **metro.** With each *bang* from the **metro,** the direction of the arpeggio is reversed by multiplying the arpeggio interval by −1.

Scaling

Another approach to **Range** would be to use a compression algorithm to scale data outside of the range. Such a process would generate a larger scalar factor for numbers farthest away, pulling them within the range, with smaller corrections made to numbers just outside the range. Scaling can be used to increase or decrease a range of values, usually by multiplying or dividing the values, sometimes with an added offset. (See Scaling Parameters in fig. 8.22.)

To build and operate many composer objects, it is essential to know the allowable input value range and to be able to scale data to accommodate that range. Scaling is an important technique for interpreting listener data and processed data for composer objects because incoming MIDI data is often scaled or offset before it is used. 0 to 127 is a perfect range for MIDI velocity values, but what happens if those values are intended to control another parameter, such as the speed of a **metro?** With time in milliseconds, 0 to 127 would make for a truly exhilarating experience! With a loud note, the slowest tempo would be around mm = 480, and playing quietly could result in the computer playing at impossibly fast speeds (with the increased risk of crashing the computer). By adding an offset (plus 10), and scaling the velocity (multiplying by 10), the numbers are transformed from 0 to 127 to usable metronome speeds between 100 and 1370 (fig. 7.7). In this way, the range of incoming performance data can grow or shrink to accommodate each situation.

On the other hand, linking velocity numbers to pitch may result in too many extreme highs and (mostly inaudible) lows, so the scale factor would be needed to condense the range. Adding 60 to the velocity number and multiplying by 0.5 would yield more usable pitches in a range between 30 and 93.

Selecting

The **select** object is a very useful tool for matching and obtaining a *bang* for desirable numbers specified as arguments. However, it can also

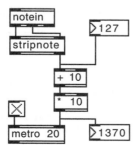

Figure 7.7
Scaling

be used in reverse, to remove numbers from a data stream, since all nonmatching values are output through the right outlet. Figure 7.8 shows a self-operating version of the **RanMinorMel** subpatch from figure 6.13. **Random 24** creates values representing a two-octave range. All pitches entering the **select** object will pass out the right outlet except for the note numbers *outside* the C minor scale: 1, 4, 6, 9, 11, 13, 16, 18, 21, 23. The results are then transposed to place them in a chosen tonic and register. Any type of scale, even one that changes in each octave, could be produced in this way.

The **gate** below **select** causes pitches outside C minor to output a new note, until a note in the scale is found. The feedback loop ensures that all beats will be played. Like the previous **RangeLoop** example, unhooking the feedback loop produces more interesting rhythms.

Timing Processes

Objects dealing with timing processes use techniques such as thinning, speed change, delaying, gating, and switching to create variations in rhythm, texture, and speed. Thinning, gating, and switching are related, cutting out part of a signal for a specified amount of time. In

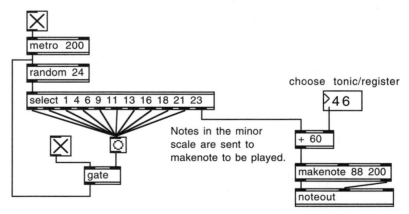

If the gate is open, notes outside the minor scale "re-bang" the random number generator until an acceptable value is found. When the gate is closed, notes outside the minor scale will not sound, creating "rests."

Note: care should be taken when using this method since the computer could spend much of its time looping if a desired value is not found.

Figure 7.8
Select scale

thinning, this is usually done at regular intervals; gating and switching let data pass through at variable times. Delay techniques create canons, echoes, and other structures with delay lines.

Thinning

Speedlim (chap. 6) is the data-thinner of choice for many composition functions, especially when a continuous controller from the keyboard is used to control compositional processes, since the rate of data change sent from controllers is faster than many algorithms require. **Speedlim** keeps data streams to a minimum, which improves efficiency for the overall program. **Speedlim** allows only one value output every X milliseconds. For example, if the modulation wheel is used to determine the register of a melody, looking at its position once every 40 milliseconds might be just as effective as looking at it every millisecond, with forty times less information to process. In figure 7.9, **Mod-WheelMelody** scales modulation-wheel values to fall between 60 and 85, and sends them to **select** to create a melody. (The tonic is not variable in this example; **select** will reject any notes outside a C minor scale.) The right inlet is a variable that controls the maximum speed of the melody by thinning the data-transfer rate with **speedlim**. **Sliders** can generate a thinned data stream by using an offset and a multiplier in GET INFO. Here the **slider** values go from 50 to 1000 (millisecond speed for melody), in increments of 10. This makes the

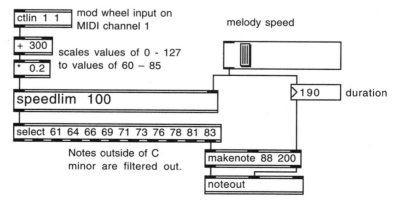

Figure 7.9
Modulation wheel melody

slider smoother to operate since the data stream has been reduced. In this case, speed changes of less than 10 milliseconds offer more detail than is needed.

Gating

In figure 7.10, the subpatch **Rest** is an elaborate switching filter that takes in steady metronome beats and creates varied rhythm and phrasing (fig. 7.10). Two variables control the operation of **Rest.** Both numbers represent constrained random values between 1 and the specified maximum number (i.e., a value of six means random values between one and six). The middle inlet represents the rest phrase length, the maximum number of notes that will be played continuously before a rest. The right inlet determines the rest size, the maximum duration of a rest. As soon a phrase is completed, a new rest size number is issued, and the melody waits that number of **metro** beats. Then, the algorithm gets a new number for the phrase length and plays that number of beats, and so on. A **GSwitch** alternately switches back and forth between the two (fig. 7.11). When it switches to phrases, *bangs* are output, when it switches to rests, the signal is blocked. (A similar effect could be achieved using a **gate** to open for X number of beats for the phrase, and close for Y number of beats for the rest.) For example, long

Rest generates rhythm in a melody or other
functions involving a steady metronome.

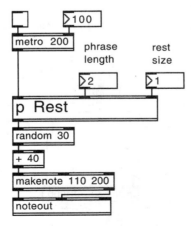

Figure 7.10
Rest example

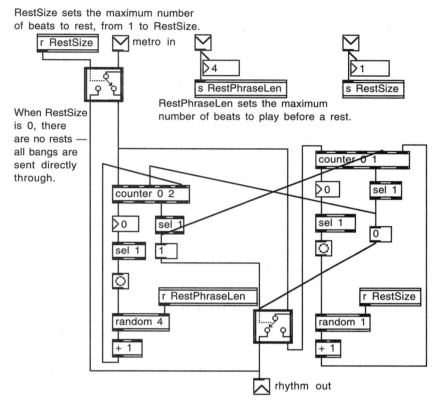

Rest takes metro bangs in and outputs a variable subset of them.

RestSize sets the maximum number
of beats to rest, from 1 to RestSize.

metro in

r RestSize

s RestPhraseLen

s RestSize

RestPhraseLen sets the maximum
number of beats to play before a rest.

When RestSize
is 0, there
are no rests —
all bangs are
sent directly
through.

counter 0 2

counter 0 1

sel 1

sel 1

sel 1

sel 1

r RestPhraseLen

r RestSize

random 4

random 1

+ 1

+ 1

rhythm out

Figure 7.11
Rest (subpatch of fig. 7.10)

phrases with infrequent rests of one or two beats would result from
choosing 25 for the phrase length and 2 for the rest size, whereas
choppy, pointillistic rhythms would result from a phrase length of 4
and a rest size of 8. When the rest size is 0, the beat is continuous and
bangs from **metro** will bypass the entire algorithm to prevent unnecessary computer calculations. (Note: Remote sends in fig. 7.11 are used
to improve the readability of the example.)

Automated and Delayed Functions

Delay may be used to postpone a reaction to performance data or to
automate actions. Chaining delay lines together, or using one delay
line with a variable delay time, can set up a time frame for specific

actions. The **line** object can also be used to automate the increase or decrease of variable values in a composer object, and to create "ramp" values that interpolate between two end points.

Line takes four variables: a starting value, an ending value, the time it takes to get from the starting value to the ending value, and the time "grain," the number of milliseconds it takes to output an updated value (a thinning value). A single number to the left inlet is the starting value; a pair of numbers to the left inlet [*0 500*] represents the starting value (0) and the time (500). The middle inlet is the destination value, and the right inlet is the time grain. Perhaps the easiest way to use **line** is to send a message of three variables in the form of [*0, 200 5000*], where 0 is the starting point, 200 is the destination value, and 5000 is the time in milliseconds to output values between 0 and 200. Optionally, **line** takes two typed-in arguments that represent the starting value and the time grain.

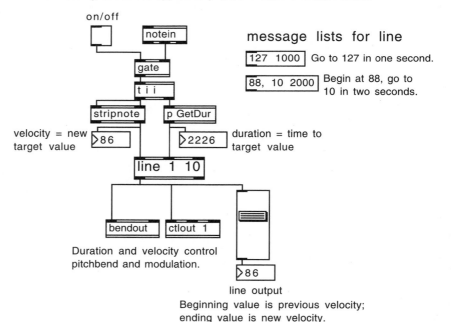

Line creates a continuously changing function using velocity and duration. The resulting values are applied to pitchbend and modulation wheel.

Figure 7.12
Interpolator

An example called **Interpolator** uses **line** to map discrete velocity values as continuous changes over time (fig. 7.12). The velocity values act as points connected in time to create a function. The time between points is dependent on the duration. The patch creates a continuous function that is a mapping of dynamic level and duration (articulation). Staccato notes will cause **Interpolator** to jump rapidly to the next velocity value. Legato playing will cause **Interpolator** to move smoothly between two velocity values. The output is a function (a contour), with values between 0 and 127. In this example, the **line** object alters pitchbend and modulation, while its changing values are "animated" by a **slider** for display. Using message lists in series is another way to create ramped functions using **line**. Functions with multiple break-point values can be edited and viewed graphically using the **env** (envelope) object.

An excellent use of **delay** as a compositional technique can be seen in Robert Gibson's Canon program, which uses delay lines and ramped delays to create canons (fig. 7.13). The object reads a single standard MIDI file into two **seq** objects and delays the playback of the second by a user-specified amount. The following is a short description of its features and operation, which can be seen in the carefully designed user interface.

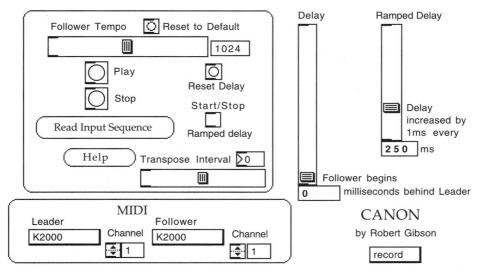

Figure 7.13
Canon by Robert Gibson

The *Follower Tempo* **slider** sets the tempo of the "follower" voice. The default is 1024—the same tempo as the "leader" (the original tempo of the **sequence**). Values higher than 1024 create canons in diminution (e.g., 2048 plays the follower at twice the speed of the leader); values less than 1024 produce canons in augmentation. The *Delay* **slider** sets the number of milliseconds between the start of the leader and the start of the follower. The *Ramped Delay* **slider** sets the rate of an optionally increasing time interval between the leader and the follower, triggered by clicking on the *start/stop* **toggle** for *Ramped Delay.* This can create phasing effects, as the two versions slowly drift out of synch. The pitch interval of the follower can be set by selecting a number (in half steps above or below the leader) with the *Transpose Interval* **slider.** The **slider** has a four-octave range (−24 to +24). The default is 0 (unison). The device (or port) and channel of the leader and follower can be set in the MIDI menu. The final result can be recorded.

Using this program, Gibson has successfully created new computer pieces as well as renditions of several acoustic pieces, including Georg Philip Teleman's *Allegro (III)* from *Six Canonic Sonatas* and Steve Reich's *Piano Phase.*

Mapping

Mapping is one of the most effective and commonly used techniques in interactive music. Mapping is typically used as a transformative method to link performer actions to composer object parameters. In this broad definition, parameter mapping usually associates one prominent musical feature with another. For example, mapping velocity to delay time so that louder notes will have a longer delay time, and shorter notes will have a shorter delay time.

More specific data mapping techniques use mapping in the mathematical sense; to take an element in one set and match it with another element in the same set or a different set. Data mapping may take place within the same parameter, such as mapping all pitch input to play a specific scale, or harmonizing a melody by using pitch numbers as the index to a **coll** to output stored chords. A **table** is also a useful data structure for mapping, since pitch or dynamic information may be used as the index to output other values. Output from one **table** may, in turn, be used as the index to another **table**. **Select** and **match** are often used to define an initial set of data.

After choosing the variable that will alter a process, the composer must select the performance feature(s) that will control the variable. A clear example of performance feature to variable mapping can be seen in the user interface of Robert Rowe's Cypher program (fig. 7.14). Note that the clearly marked performance features above (listener objects) can be connected to influence any of the music-producing parameters below (composer objects). The user simply draws a line between them to map (connect) any listener feature to a composition method. In this example, the first two rows of connected ovals will cause the following to occur (from left to right): a slower performance tempo will increase the tempo of the computer (accelerando), a soft dynamic level will

Cypher by Robert Rowe

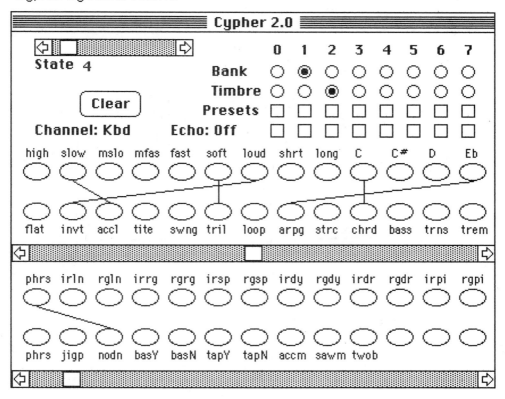

Figure 7.14
Cypher by Robert Rowe

produce a trill, playing loudly will invert the melody, playing any C will produce a chord, and playing any E♭ will produce an arpeggio. The bottom two rows of connections handle responses based on larger changes over time, such as phrasing features or detecting regular or irregular skips in register. (Note: Cypher is not a Max program).

Allen Strange's MIDI reMap demonstrates a Max program with a similar approach to mapping parameters (fig. 7.15). In this clearly designed interface, a **menu** selects a MIDI performance control, such as velocity, aftertouch, or mod wheel, and maps this controller onto specified composition parameters, such as panning or duration. In the description provided with the program, Strange writes:

This instrument allows the player to remap various MIDI controls to selected parameters of a free running instrument. Each data stream can be "inverted" with the **toggle** to give reciprocal values [i.e. duration can be the inversion of velocity]. Each parameter can also be determined by a free running **random** object or controlled by a screen **slider.**

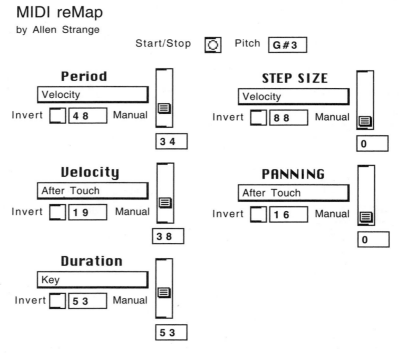

Figure 7.15
MIDI reMap by Allen Strange

The pitches are determined by a "Brown Noise" generator [the Max **drunk** object] accessing a **table** consisting of various pitches in related modes. The possible deviation from the last sounded pitch to the next is controlled by the STEP SIZE parameter. Any key pressed on the MIDI keyboard instantly resets the "seed" for the selection of the next pitch.

In figure 7.15, period (tempo) is controlled by velocity, while panning is controlled by aftertouch. Panning location, left and right, would be reversed if invert mode was selected. On-screen controls of all the parameters makes this a very usable "instrument" for performance from the computer keyboard.

Constrained Pitch Output: Comparative Programming Examples

Sometimes algorithmic output needs to be shaped with a filter to achieve the desired musical results, such as altering incoming notes to conform to a scale. Three different objects for mapping pitch information to a "correct" scale or pitch will show the diverse structures available in Max.

Tonicize is the simplest and most limited example (figs. 7.16 and 7.17). **Tonicize** takes incoming notes and forces notes near a chosen tonic to become the tonic note. This creates a "black hole" effect: the Tonic Strength setting specifies a range of semitones, centered around the tonic, that will be "sucked" into the tonic. The larger the range

Tonicize takes the notes immediately surrounding a selected tonic, and moves those notes to the tonic.

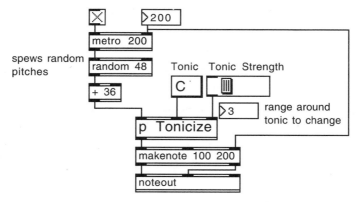

Figure 7.16
Tonicize tutorial

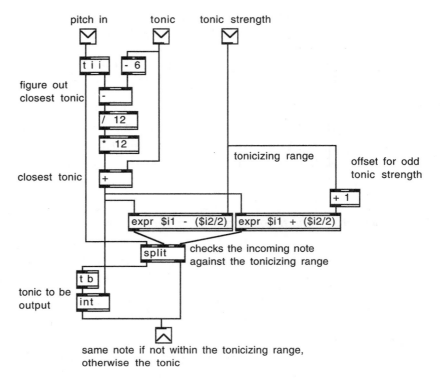

Figure 7.17
Tonicize (subpatch of fig. 7.16)

setting, the stronger the force of the tonic note. For example, a range of six will map to the tonic any pitch that is three semitones above or below the tonic so that a selected C♯ tonic will cause any A♯, B, C, D, D♯, or E to be changed to a C♯. This creates a variable situation where the prominence or weight of a single note can be controlled in terms of the frequency of occurrence and its isolation from surrounding pitches.

Quantization is a technique that takes a large set of continuous values and changes them to a smaller set of discrete values. This may be done using a rounding function, a formula, or mapping techniques. **PitchQuant** (pitch quantization) is a custom object that maps incoming pitches to a predetermined scale (fig. 7.18). It may be used in the typical sense of quantizing a scale, for example changing chromatic scale input to major scale output, but is flexible enough to allow for quite unusual mapping. The interface asks for the input note, the new note to map it to, and the percentage of time that the mapping will occur (quantization strength). The store button updates a **coll** that con-

PitchQuant maps incoming pitches to a predetermined scale. The percentage chance that a pitch
will be mapped is specified by the user. The Note menu selects which pitch class should be
changed. The New Note menu selects the new value of that pitch class. Chance of quantization
specifies the percentage chance of the original pitch class being changed when played.

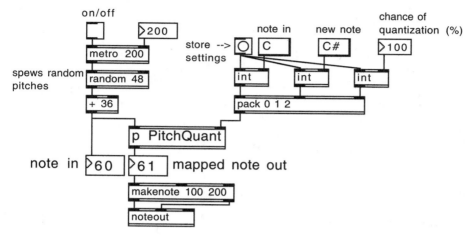

Figure 7.18
PitchQuant tutorial

tains all the mapping information. Each line of the **coll** contains pitch
class $(0 - 11)$ as the address, followed by the new note, followed by
the percentage chance that the original has to change. Thus, (4, 5, 50)
in the **coll** would mean to change all Es to Fs fifty percent of the time.
A user monitor gives feedback about which pitch is entering **Pitch-
Quant** and which pitch is being output.

When a note enters **PitchQuant**, an analysis object separates pitch
class from register, a technique that allows similar processing of notes
for all octaves (fig. 7.19). Register is later added back to the final pitch
class. Pitch class goes into the **coll**, acting as the address to trigger the
new note and percentage change. The new note and the old note are
stored in **ints**. The percentage algorithm chooses how often to output
an altered note. Each note input generates a random value between 1
and 100. A less-than ($<$) operation sets the percentage range: All values
below the percentage change will trigger the new note; all values above
will trigger the old note. The $<$ object works by sending a 1 if the
condition is true, or a 0 if the condition is false.

How could **PitchQuant** be improved? Although **PitchQuant** is set
up to work on all octaves the same way, it could be easily expanded so

PitchQuant maps incoming pitches to a predetermined scale.

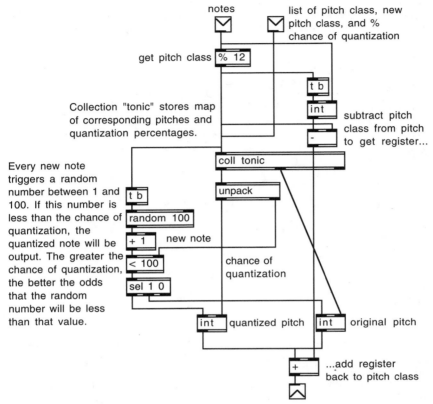

notes

list of pitch class, new
pitch class, and %
chance of quantization

get pitch class % 12

t b

int

subtract pitch
class from pitch
to get register...

−

Collection "tonic" stores map
of corresponding pitches and
quantization percentages.

coll tonic

unpack

Every new note
triggers a random
number between 1 and
100. If this number is
less than the chance of
quantization, the
quantized note will be
output. The greater the
chance of quantization,
the better the odds
that the random
number will be less
than that value.

t b

random 100

+ 1   new note

< 100

sel 1 0

chance of
quantization

int quantized pitch   int original pitch

+   ...add register
back to pitch class

Figure 7.19
PitchQuant (subpatch of fig. 7.18)

that various octaves could have different mappings. More important is
the lack of a data structure to create and store multiple mappings. A
nice added feature would allow many different scales to be stored and
recalled with a **menu** or **preset** object.

The next example, **Scale**, simplifies the previous idea, providing a
menu of available scales in the interface (fig. 7.20). It is easier to use
than **PitchQuant**, but less flexible, since it does not have the percentage feature or an interface for creating custom mappings. Instead, **Scale**
always maps every note input to a predefined scale, available in a
menu. Variables to **Scale** are scale selection and pitch input. Any note
received outside the selected scale will get mapped to the nearest
scale note.

All notes passing through the Scale object will conform to a pre-defined scale type, selectable from a menu. Scale uses a different algorithm than PitchQuant to map incoming notes.

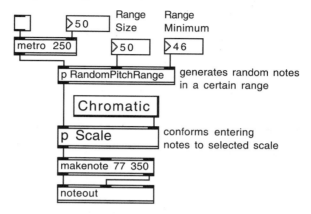

Figure 7.20
Scale tutorial

The user interface contains a list of scale names in a **menu.** Selecting Get Info on the **menu** reveals the contents: [Chromatic, Pentatonic, C major, C minor].

When selected, each item is output as an index to a previously stored **coll.** Inside the **coll**, the list following the address represents the mapping of each pitch class, in order (fig. 7.21). Adding more scale types would entail adding a name to the **menu**, then specifying the mapping to **coll.** The definition of the scales are typed in directly and stored with the program. The inside of the **coll** looks like figure 7.21.

Although not very user-friendly, the **coll** mappings are quite flexible. For example adding Wild Scale to the menu (item 4) and adding a new line to the **coll**: [*Wild Scale, 24 11 10 9 8 7 6 5 4 3 2 1*] would cause all Cs to play two octaves higher, and would invert each octave of the keyboard for the other pitches, so that D♭ = B, D = B♭, E♭ = A, and so forth.

The first **coll** is convenient for storing and retrieving multiple scales, but it is not in a form usable for mapping. To make it usable, the contents of each scale is sent out and reformatted into a second **coll**, where the index number is an incoming pitch class, and the data is the mapped pitch class. Figure 7.22 shows the mapping of a chromatic scale to a major scale. In figure 7.23, **unpack** separates the list of items

Chromatic, 0 1 2 3 4 5 6 7 8 9 10 11;
Pentatonic, 1 1 1 3 3 6 6 8 8 10 10 10;
C_major, 0 0 2 4 4 5 5 7 7 9 9 11;
C_minor, 0 0 2 3 3 5 5 7 7 8 8 10;

Figure 7.21
Scales stored in first **coll**, raw storage

0, 0;
1, 0;
2, 2;
3, 4;
4, 4;
5, 5;
6, 5;
7, 7;
8, 7;
9, 9;
10, 9;
11, 11;

Figure 7.22
Scales stored in second **coll**, usable for mapping

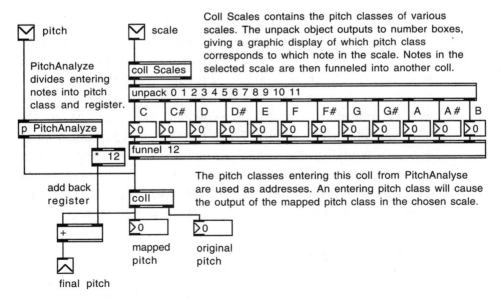

pitch
scale
Coll Scales contains the pitch classes of various scales. The unpack object outputs to number boxes, giving a graphic display of which pitch class corresponds to which note in the scale. Notes in the selected scale are then funneled into another coll.
PitchAnalyze divides entering notes into pitch class and register.
coll Scales
unpack 0 1 2 3 4 5 6 7 8 9 10 11
C
C#
D
D#
E
F
F#
G
G#
A
A#
B
p PitchAnalyze
* 12
funnel 12
The pitch classes entering this coll from PitchAnalyse are used as addresses. An entering pitch class will cause the output of the mapped pitch class in the chosen scale.
add back register
coll
+
mapped pitch
original pitch
final pitch

Figure 7.23
Scale (subpatch of fig. 7.20)

in the first **coll**, giving a graphic display to the user who can check the mapping for each pitch class and easily experiment with different scales. **Funnel** takes single values in and creates ordered pairs, supplying the address numbers for the next **coll**. As in the previous example, this **coll** uses the pitch class as the index to output the mapped note, adding back the register at the end. **PitchAnalyze** is simply an encapsulated version of an algorithm that separates pitch class from register. The second **coll** below is reformatted, as in figure 7.22.

Scale is straightforward and easy to use. It could easily be expanded to include the features found in the previous two examples. However, beware of "feature creep." Feature creep refers to commercial software companies' constant addition of new features to old software, even though the old software is perfect for the job. The new features may add confusion or be rarely used. Composer objects may have so many capabilities that they lose their single purpose, or offer so many options that their operation becomes confusing.

MelodicContour: A Progressive Study in Generative Methods

Generative algorithms create complete musical statements from "scratch" using basic musical elements or mathematical formulas. A random-number generator, for instance, is a generative algorithm that is the mainstay of most computer-music systems. Other formulas or numbers, such as those derived from fractal geometry, chaos theory, or even a phone number, may be used to generate pitch, velocity, duration, and rhythm.

Generative algorithms can be thought of in a traditional compositional sense as creating larger musical structures from basic musical motives or cells. This could be a short melodic fragment, a rhythmic idea, or even a small set of intervals. Many traditional techniques for motivic development can be coded as algorithms to produce complex structures and variations based on a single musical idea. Computer music, in general, lends itself well to this type of organic thinking, where a single cell spawns and mutates to grow into a larger form.

Generative algorithms may be mapped to a performer's incoming pitches or other triggers to cause augmentation and elaboration of musical material. For example, specific pitches may produce trills, grace notes, or arpeggios, using a portion of the current input.

A **table** is a useful structure for storing such raw material, since it stores single items and can be viewed graphically. **Tables** can be used to store aspects of a performance and then to play them back in a different order, or to use portions to create ostinatos or other variations. **Coll** also is an obvious choice for holding raw material that will be used to generate variations for a piece.

Several versions of a patch, **MelodicContour,** will show how a generative algorithm can be further developed with additional transformative processes.

MelodicContour: the Easy Version is a small program that generates melodies based on a set of three intervals (fig. 7.24). The intervals are analyzed from a keyboard performance; the last three intervals played will be the raw material used to create a melody. A pause of one second or more will cause the interval recorder to reset and wait to count the next three intervals. The performer controls the interval content, dynamic level, and starting note (register) of the melody.

Takes notes played from the keyboard and generates a melody based on the intervals played.

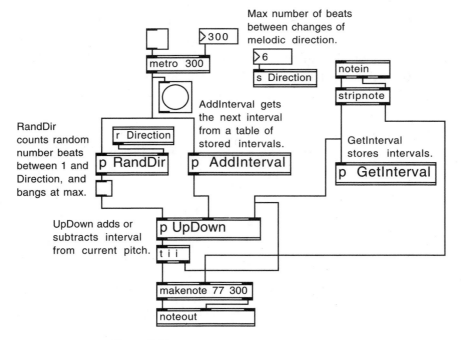

Figure 7.24
Melodic contour: the easy version

The four subpatches operate as follows: **GetInterval** records intervals, **AddInterval** plays back those intervals, **RandDir** (Random Direction) determines how often the direction of the melody will change, and **UpDown** adds or subtracts intervals from the last pitch to create a melody.

GetInterval is the analysis and recording object (fig. 7.25). It simply stores the last three intervals played into a **table** called "intervals." After a pause of approximately one second, the **counter** is reset so that the next four notes will store three intervals in the first three addresses of the **table.** In this way, harmony can be changed "on the fly" either by playing continuously or by pausing to record a complete set of new intervals. **AddInterval** plays back those intervals using a copy of the same **table** (fig. 7.26). Each *bang* from **metro** goes to a **counter** that continuously cycles through the **table.** The starting note to create the melody is always the last note played, which could be from the performer or the computer. In other words, while a performer is playing, the computer creates a response in the same register as the performer. Once a performer pauses, the computer continues to play, taking its last note as a starting point. To generate the melody, a number is sent by the user, **s Direction,** to the object **RandDir** (random direction), which determines the maximum number of intervals that can go consecutively in any one direction (fig. 7.27). The direction value represents the maximum of a randomly generated number. With each *bang,* the

Gets intervals from incoming pitches, and stores them in table intervals.

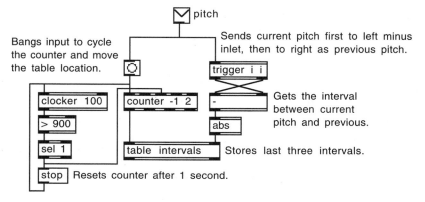

Figure 7.25
GetInterval (subpatch of fig. 7.24)

Outputs intervals in table when banged.

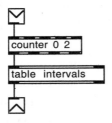

Figure 7.26
AddInterval (subpatch of fig. 7.24)

Counts a random number between 1 and Direction (maximum range);
bangs highest number reached and chooses new number.

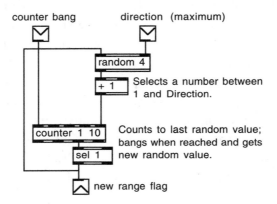

Figure 7.27
RandDir (subpatch of fig. 7.24)

melody ascends or descends a certain number of times, by adding or
subtracting the intervals in the **table** beginning with the starting pitch.
After the end of each ascent or descent, a new number is issued by
RandDir that represents the number of intervals to go in the opposite
direction, and the **toggle** changes a **GSwitch** inside **UpDown** so that
it adds or subtracts (fig. 7.28). This process continues over and over
again, with **RandDir** sending new random numbers, and **UpDown** alternately adding and subtracting the numbers. Eventually, numbers
generated outside the MIDI notenumber range will cause playback
problems.

Interval is added to or subtracted from old pitch.

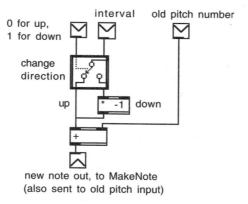

Figure 7.28
UpDown (subpatch of fig. 7.24)

In **MelodicContour: the medium version** (fig. 7.29), notes out of range are corrected with **RangeFlip**, which alters pitches to fit within a user-definable range. **RangeFlip** uses an approach different from the previously mentioned **RangeLoop** and **RangeMod** (figs. 7.2 to 7.5). User controls to set **RangeFlip** are provided to the right of the screen; they set minimum and maximum values for the range, and specify exact intervals (in semitones) to add or subtract to numbers falling outside the range to make the correction. In this way, a pitch outside a range can be transposed up or down by an exact interval.

RangeFlip is particularly useful for processes sensitive to pitch (fig. 7.30). For example, a value of 24 or 36 to *RangeLowAdd* or *RangeHighSub* would transpose out of range pitches by two or three octaves, preserving the original pitch class. Parameter *RangeMin* sets the minimum value and *RangeMax* sets the maximum value. *RangeLowAdd* specifies the number to add to values below *RangeMin*. *RangeHighSub* specifies the number to subtract from values above *RangeMax*. If one addition or subtraction does not "correct" the value, **RangeFlip** will continue to add or subtract numbers until it is within range. With *LowAdd* and *HiSub* set to 12, the object would always transpose melodies up or down by one or more octaves until they fit inside the specified range.

In figure 7.29, melodies will go up or down between one and five notes before changing direction. Larger direction values would create broader, more sweeping melodic contours, whereas smaller values

Takes notes played from the keyboard and generates a melody based on the intervals played. The melody is kept within a user-specified range.

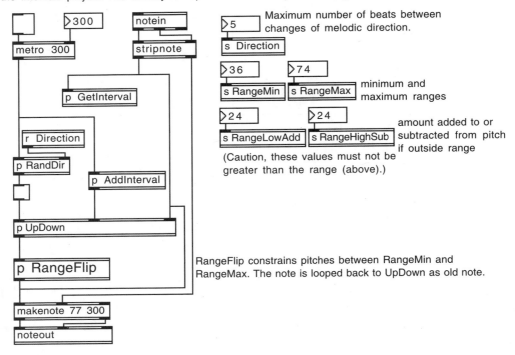

Maximum number of beats between changes of melodic direction.

minimum and maximum ranges

amount added to or subtracted from pitch if outside range (Caution, these values must not be greater than the range (above).)

RangeFlip constrains pitches between RangeMin and RangeMax. The note is looped back to UpDown as old note.

Figure 7.29
Melodic contour: the medium version

Places pitches within a specified range by adding to a low number or subtracting from a high number.

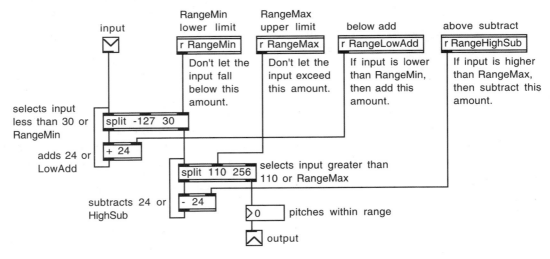

Figure 7.30
RangeFlip (subpatch of fig. 7.29)

would create "creeping" melodies that constantly change direction. The range is set between 36 and 74, excluding the highest and lowest notes on a keyboard. All values outside the range will be "corrected" by adding or subtracting 24 (two octaves). If the number 70 is sent, it will pass through unchanged. If the number 30 is sent it will be changed to 54 (30 + 24). If the number 300 is sent, 24 will be subtracted ten times until the number is within range (300 − (24 ∗ 10) = 60). Sending the object data that is closer to the desired range will improve efficiency. Also, this object is a bit dangerous to use, since if the values to add or subtract are not smaller than the entire range, a note could be flipped back and forth, continuously falling outside the chosen range.

In the "tricky" version of **MelodicContour,** (fig. 7.31) a simple object, **VoiceNum,** adds a tremendous amount of variety to the previous

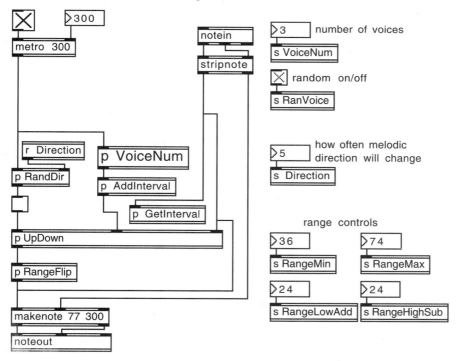

Figure 7.31
Melodic contour: the tricky version

number of voices per beat, either by VoiceNum or randomly.

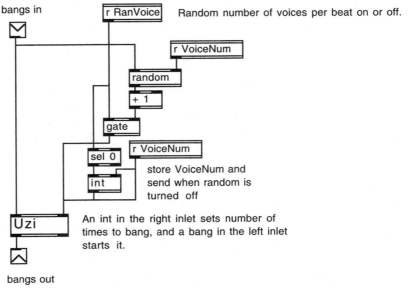

Figure 7.32
VoiceNum (subpatch of fig. 7.31)

version. **VoiceNum** sends out one or more *bangs* for each one received using **Uzi** (fig. 7.32). A single number to the left inlet of **Uzi** sends out that many *bangs* immediately. A *bang* to the left inlet will continue to send out multiple *bangs*. The number may also be set by the right inlet (as in this example) or as an argument. In this way, it is possible to make chords of two, three, four, or more notes with each **metro** *bang*, all based on the same interval set. Another option, [s **RanVoice**], uses constrained random numbers to create a mixture of single notes and chords, with the maximum number of notes per chord specified by [s **VoiceNum**]. Thus, setting [s **VoiceNum**] to *3* and [s **RanVoice**] to *on* will generate music with a mixture of single notes, dyads (two-note chords), and triads (three-note chords).

ParamColl: Parameter Analysis and Playback

ParamColl (parameter collection) is a complex program that shows an integration of listener and composer objects (fig. 7.33). **ParamColl** has two main components: a recording section and a playback section. It

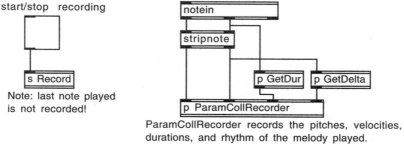

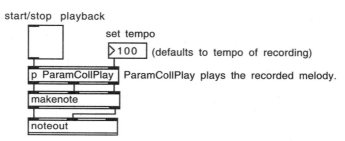

Figure 7.33
ParamColl example

takes in a live performance, analyzing a single melody for four performance features: pitch, velocity, duration, and rhythm (using algorithms from chapter 5). It stores each parameter in a separate **coll.**

In example 7.33, all four **colls** play back together, using the same **counter** to recreate the original performance. However, since all the parameters are stored separately, a number of processes may be used to generate variations. For example, by giving each **coll** a separate **counter** with a different length, the various parameters could be constantly cycled through, generating a kaleidoscopic mixture of the four parameters. The **counters** could be set to cycle through the first ten pitches, the first nine velocities, the first eight durations, and the first seven rhythms. Irregular cycling of pitch and rhythmic values can reproduce isorhythmic techniques similar to those common in fourteenth-century music. Further variations could be generated using the features found in **counter. Counters** could be set up to play portions of the **coll** beginning at a given spot, loop up and down, or always play in reverse. Messages sent directly to **coll** can also manipulate the stored data, such as *goto, delete, sort,* or *insert.* Finally, one or more parameters could be replaced with a different source. Rhythm, for

ParamCollRecorder uses four colls to store pitch, velocity, duration, and rhythm. All
subpatches use counters to pack the current event number (used as the index) with the data.

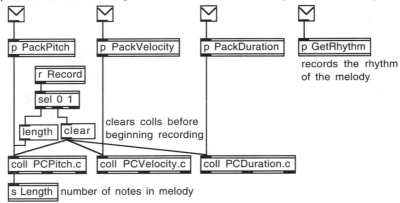

Figure 7.34
ParamCollRecorder (subpatch of fig. 7.33)

example, could be supplied by another algorithm or a human performer, with the remaining recorded parameters playing back in response.

ParamColl Recorder uses listener objects to analyze pitch, velocity,
duration, and rhythm (fig. 7.34). Before recording, a tempo is set by
tapping the beat with the foot pedal or the spacebar of the keyboard.
Rhythms are limited in this example to sixteenth-note values. A further
variation could store delta times in a **coll**, rather than sixteenth-note
rhythms, and use the delta times to play back the other parameters
with the original rhythm or a scaled version of the original. In this
way, the rhythm would not be limited to sixteenth notes.

The algorithm for playing the **colls** is very simple. In **ParamCollPlay**
(fig. 7.35), three **colls** share a **counter** that can be set to any length by
sending a remote message to [**r Length**] (which defaults to the number
of notes originally recorded). Any *bang* into the **counter** will output
the next item in each **coll**. (Again, separate **counters** for each **coll**
would offer further possibilities for variation.) **PlayRhythm** can output
all the original rhythmic values, or, since it has its own **counter**, could
be set to cycle through portions of the collection. (See figures 6.16 to
6.18 for rhythmic analysis.) If the **metro** *bangs* bypassed **PlayRhythm**,
it would send constant beats to the other three **colls** below. With a few
modifications, a performer could control the whole timing mechanism
for playback, using the rhythm or tempo of a new melody to trigger
the parameters based on previously played material.

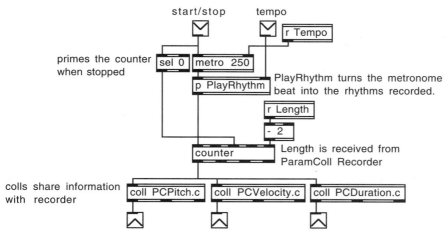

Figure 7.35
ParamCollPlayer (subpatch of fig. 7.33)

Sequencer Methods

The previous example showed how whole sequences or performances can be broken down to create raw material for generating new melodies. Sequencer fragments or large sections can be recorded live, prerecorded, or imported as a standard MIDI file from another MIDI application. Although **coll** may be used to record entire performances, **seq** and **detonate** are specifically designed for that purpose. **Seq** files record and play back the entire MIDI stream. Since their primary function is playback via a trigger, they have limited possibilities for variation. What they do well is to provide quick and easy playback of numerous files, from short melodic fragments to long multichannel arrangements. The primary variable control is playback speed. Short **seq** files may be mapped to **notein** input to create ornamentation and decoration around chosen notes. Longer files may be started to provide a tape-style accompaniment for a section of a performance. (See fig. 9.6 for more information.)

Seq is ideal for playing music that a composer has carefully crafted with a commercial sequencer, and will be played back the same way each time. It is also useful for capturing generated material or a live performance for playback. Virtually any performance condition or feature is capable of triggering a **seq**. **Seq** may also be used to feed listener objects, replacing a live performer. In fact, an interesting working method for a live interactive piece is for the composer to record the performer's part using a **seq**, and then work with that file as a virtual performer to do much of the programming and rehearsing without the performer being there physically. That way, any problems that arise within the program or the music can be discovered and ironed out without wasting the performer's time. Analysis can be done on **seq** using **midiparse** to separate the various parameters, but this is a job more easily handled by **detonate**.

While **ParamColl** is a good study of how several analysis objects can be coordinated with **colls** to generate musical variations, it is not a very practical example since the **detonate** object already exists to record, edit, and playback most of the same information. In addition, **detonate** records on multiple tracks, reads and writes MIDI files, and displays all the data in a full-featured graphical editing window. In fact, **detonate** uses delta time in the way suggested above for **ParamColl**. Since it does not have an automatic timing mechanism, as does **seq**, it usually gets its timing data from an analysis of the performed delta times, stored in its left inlet. Other inlets are used to record pitch, velocity, track number, MIDI channel, and there are two extra unspecified inlets for any type of data (which could store the sixteenth-note rhythmic values, for instance, or data from a modulation wheel or foot pedal). All these parameters can then be viewed and edited in a graphic score, or altered for playback with a variety of messages. Upon playback, **detonate** sends analysis data out separate outlets representing delta time, velocity, pitch, duration, MIDI channel, track number, and the two unspecified data tracks. **Detonate** is also very useful for understanding how complex and unpredictable composer objects work, by capturing and displaying the musical output that shows the variations that result from parameter changes.

Humanizing Algorithms: The Computer as Performer

Composition variables can be used with absolute values or constrained random values to determine how much variation will occur from performance to performance. Constrained random values define a range of possible outcomes. These techniques allow a computer to "improvise," producing music that is constantly changing and unpredictable yet within a given style.

Similar techniques can be used to simulate interesting and expressive performance qualities in computer-generated music. Humans cannot possibly play with the accuracy of a computer, yet many musicians strive in vain for such perfection in their technique. Ironically, it turns out that listeners often find composer algorithms *too* perfect; the lack of constant small imperfections creates music that is missing some of the richness and complexity produced by real musicians. With many algorithms, adding slight errors and the "jitter" associated with human performance creates a more musically satisfying result. Jitter is the continuous, small fluctuating movement in many parameters that characterizes all human performances and adds life to computer-music performances. Pitch in wind instruments, for instance, is never steady, but continuously fluctuates around the idealized target pitch. Some algorithms add subtle and constant variation to pitch, velocity, duration, or tempo, which gives a more human-sounding performance. Controlling a parameter like tempo with constrained random values, for example, gives a wide continuum, from subtle fluctuations to wild, irregularly spaced rhythms. Other humanizing algorithms attempt to impart expressive phrasing and timing information to computer music.

Using Constrained Random Numbers

The custom object, **Randomize**, is an example of a very useful all-purpose object that adds random fluctuations to selected parameters. In figure 7.36, the user selects the range of random fluctuations for velocity using the **Randomize** object. The right inlet is the original value to randomize, the middle inlet is the maximum percentage of change allowed above or below that value, and a *bang* to the left inlet sends out the new, randomized value. With each **metro** pulse, **Randomize** takes the last played velocity value and changes it by adding or subtracting a random percentage between 0 and *n*. Small random values almost always improve the performance of dynamics; it is virtually impossible for any performer to maintain a constant dynamic level. The same object could also be used to randomize tempo, duration, or any type of musical data. Randomizing the tempo by 4%, for example, would make the pulse more human by adding slight unsteadiness to the beat. Randomizing the tempo at 50% would produce

Randomize changes a given number by up to a certain percent around it. In this example, the velocity of the melody is being randomized.

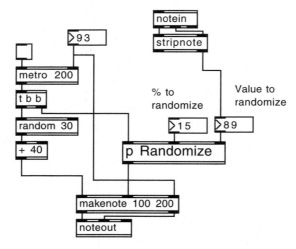

Figure 7.36
Randomize example

melodies with the disjunct rhythms associated with certain styles of twentieth century music, but with the overall speed still tied to the **metro.** Randomizing duration adds variety to the articulation of music. Small changes add subtle interest to all these parameters, while larger fluctuations seem to make the computer's performance more passionate (or even wildly out of control).

In figure 7.37, a percentage of the current value is determined by multiplying the percentage number (percentage number ∗ .01) times the current value. The percentage number is sent to **random,** representing a range of new numbers, and thus, how wide the possible fluctuation will be from the original. Rather than simply add this number to the original, the entire range of random values is shifted downward by half so that half of the values are positive and half are negative, and therefore the randomization will take place above and below the original value.

In the final version of **MelodicContour: the hard version,** several humanizing and improvising features have been added that use constrained random values (fig. 7.38). **Randomize** has been inserted to process duration, dynamics, and tempo. Also, two variable controls work together to alter **UpDown** by influencing the longer term me-

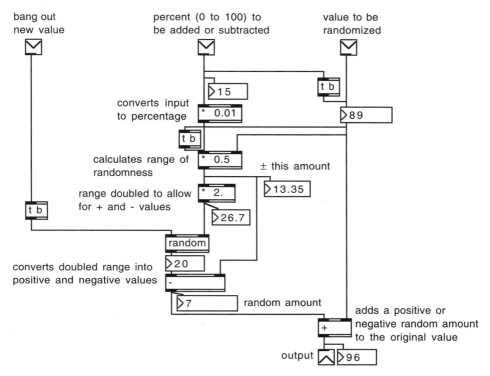

Figure 7.37
Randomize (subpatch of fig. 7.36)

lodic drift. *UpOrDown* is a variable that determines if the melody will generally drift higher or lower over time. **UpDown,** by itself, drifts randomly; it has no preference for direction. *DirectionPull* determines how quickly the melody will reach the end points of the range. A zero may be sent to bypass its effect. The strongest *DirectionPull* value is 1, creating arpeggios that go only in a single direction; the weakest value is 20. Over a large span of time, the melody will tend to go higher or lower. In between there is more or less influence on the overall melodic direction.

This series of examples show how subpatches are added to the processing chain to generate complex variations and explore musical material. Additional performance controls would create further interaction, such as using a performer's Delta time to control tempo or using continuous controllers to alter one or more of these compositional parameters.

Takes notes played from the keyboard and generates melodies based on the intervals played. These melodies are kept within a user-specified range and may tend toward one end or the other of that range.

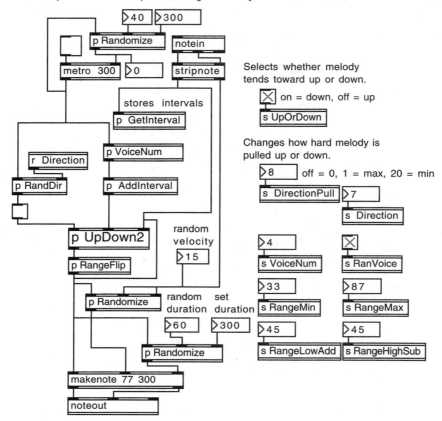

Figure 7.38
Melodic contour: the hard version

CaptureGesture: Applying Human Phrasing to Computer Processes

Rather than simply simulate the irregularities of a human performer, actual phrasing, timing, and dynamic information can be captured from a performer and applied as input to compositional algorithms. **CaptureGesture** is an example of a complex object that captures and plays back gestural information regarding a performance (fig. 7.39). **CaptureGesture** records and plays back musical gestures representing the "expressive" information of a live performance: tempo, rhythm, articulation, and dynamics. The playback module, **PlayGesture**, has been separated from the recording module to facilitate ease of pro-

These patches capture and play back musical gestures —
the rhythm, articulation, and dynamics of a musical phrase.
CaptureGesture uses both a seq and a coll to store the data it needs —
the coll is for durations, and the seq is for rhythm and velocity.

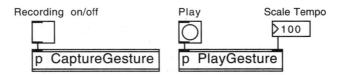

Figure 7.39
CaptureGesture example

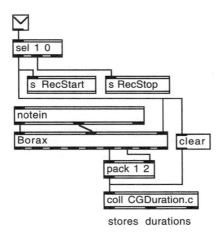

stores durations

Figure 7.40
CaptureGesture (subpatch of fig. 7.39)

gramming. **CaptureGesture** uses both a **seq** and a **coll** to store the data it needs; the **coll** stores durations and the **seq** stores rhythm and velocity (fig. 7.40). **CaptureGesture** can use a **seq** to record a portion of a performance or a prerecorded **seq.** On playback, it is parsed for delta time, velocity, and duration (fig. 7.41). In this way, it stores a tempo map in a very compact form. It can then use this timing and dynamic information, based on phrasing and other expressive playing techniques, to impart those qualities to composer algorithms. In figure 7.41, the *bang* outputs are used to drive a random pitch-generating algorithm, accompanied by the original "feel" of the performance. In this way, a phrase from a performer can be captured, and that musical gesture applied to a different computer melody or other parameters.

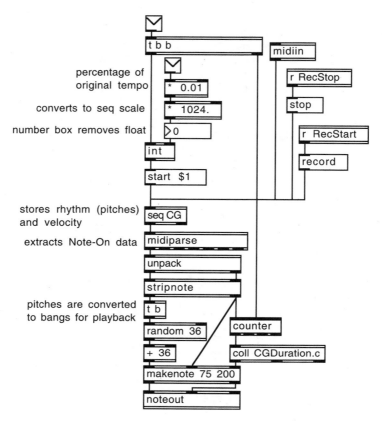

Figure 7.41
PlayGesture (subpatch of fig. 7.39)

The phrase can be played back slower or faster using *tempo scale*. This is an interesting abstraction of a performance, since timing and dynamic information do not have a life of their own separated from sound (Desain and Honing 1991). Composers will then find inventive ways to apply these uniquely human properties to influence computer music output.

CaptureGesture can also generate time-varying functions in conjunction with **Interpolator,** which uses the **line** object to continuously represent dynamic changes over time (fig. 7.12). These functions can be used to control any parameters over time anywhere in the program, imparting a live performance quality to the variable changes. These continuous changes are especially effective for the continuous control of timbre, vibrato, and signal-processing parameters.

These composer objects have shown just some of the diverse approaches to creating computer music using performer input based on transformative, generative, and sequenced methods. These algorithms, which represent a composer's tools and techniques, produce the materials and musical processes for a composition. In some cases, a few simple algorithms may be very effective in producing short works. How larger collections of objects are connected and how their events are synchronized will be the focus of chapter 9. Resources for further study are numerous, and additional examples are provided on the accompanying CD-Rom. Of special note are several Internet sites where Max programs are available for downloading.

IV   *Advanced Techniques and Concepts*

8 *Sound Design*

The ability to create unique sounds and fashion them within a musical context has always been a primary attraction of computer music. A large amount of computer music research has focused on the quest for new timbres, new ways to produce them, new ways to organize them, and new ways to control them. Synthesis methods, sampling techniques, and signal-processing algorithms may have variable parameters that can be shaped by a performer's input, imparting expressive control to the creation of timbre. A performer may also participate in interactive orchestration by using the computer to select timbres and mix multiple channels of sound.

The selection of timbre is of great importance as it creates the "sound world" that characterizes a work. A performer might play with a virtual band, use an acoustic instrument to trigger sampled sounds from everyday life, or use the computer keyboard and mouse to create abstract "soundscapes" fashioned from gestural input. Sound design reflects the basic concept of a piece, whether it will be based on traditional models, combinations of pitched and nonpitched sounds, or the exploration of a particular sound as the subject of a composition, avoiding traditional notions of pitch, instrument, and orchestration.

Top down and bottom up approaches both serve their purpose in sound design. Strong musical content or clear preconceived ideas may provide the impetus to discovering and creating specific sounds for a compositional goal. Starting from the top, an overall structure, written score, or diagram can help pinpoint specific timbral and orchestrational needs. On the other hand, composers may begin by discovering a captivating sound that is the imaginative spark that suggests an entire composition. Sound processing and manipulation is the primary area of focus of a vast number of computer-music compositions. Sounds lend themselves well to musical development, spawning larger, related structures of greater complexity. With the ability to sample, process, and synthesize an enormous variety of sounds, these compositions suggest new methods for expression and structure that depart from the traditional focus in music on pitch and rhythm. Continuous control of timbral parameters gives sound the flexibility it needs to transform into an endless variety of permutations. Timbral ideas may also develop by choosing from a large library of related sounds, either synthesized or sampled.

Unfortunately, MIDI reinforces traditional biases by relying upon code to represent the dominant parameters of written musical scores, namely pitch (MIDI note number) and dynamics (velocity) over time (duration). It is impossible for MIDI to describe even the basic parameters of a sound, such as brightness, attack characteristics, or vibrato (except as synthesizer-specific continuous controller values). In acoustic music, these parameters fall in the general category of interpretation, a source of endless debate and speculation, yet always residing within well-defined limits determined by traditional performance practice. With just a few decades of history and no performance practice to speak of, computer music must describe all aspects of a sound and the manner in which a sound is played.

Many synthesizers offer sophisticated user-programmability and real-time control over powerful synthesis and sample-processing algorithms, which encourage composers to go beyond the traditional note/ rhythm paradigm. The extra time devoted to exploring the timbral capabilities of any particular MIDI synthesizer is well worth the effort, and Max provides the means to construct an intuitive user interface for viewing and controlling a large number of parameters for sound synthesis and sample processing, parameters that might normally be hidden or buried somewhere inside a tiny two-line synthesizer display window. Unfortunately, MIDI synthesizers are too often sold strictly on the basis of the 127 most popular presets, and as a result, the large majority of users never learn to program original sounds.

MIDI Limitations for Listener Objects

The opportunities for sound production and control are rich for composer objects, yet the limitations of MIDI create few possibilities for timbral analysis via listener objects. MIDI was designed to be an affordable and practical standard that could be used to transmit and receive gestural information using any MIDI device. It is important to understand that MIDI works as well as it does because it is a simplified code that greatly reduces the data stream by allowing limited types of data to be transmitted at a fixed rate. MIDI transmits data serially, that is, one bit at a time at the rate of 31,250 bits per second. This is slow compared to other data transmission protocols, and too slow to digitally transfer audio information representing the sound or wave form. (A single digital audio sample is usually represented by sixteen bits, with 44,100 samples played per second to recreate a mono audio signal.) In fact, the slow speed of MIDI can even produce a delay when transferring the basic performance information that it is optimized to represent. Since it takes a little less than 1 millisecond to transmit one **Note-On** message (320 microseconds for each MIDI word), a twelve-note chord will introduce approximately a 10-millisecond delay. (Rothstein 1994) Add more notes, pitchbend, and a few streams of continuous controller data and the delay time would become discernable, creating synchronizing problems for performers, and adding unwanted delays to large composer algorithms.

Of the four basic parameters of music—pitch, amplitude, time, and timbre—only timbre cannot be represented simply as MIDI. Velocity, divided into 127 levels, seems to offer a large spectrum of dynamic levels, and computers are fast enough to calculate accurate timing information based on incoming data. Pitch poses additional problems, since MIDI note messages are modelled after a piano keyboard, and the limitation of twelve notes per octave excludes a description of the multitude of microtones and the variety of tuning systems available in many systems (although, in some cases, pitchbend may be effectively used). Timbre is the most structurally complex and varied, requiring multiple parameters to be described simultaneously in fine detail to be effective.

One possible solution to the problem of describing sounds would be to extend the basic MIDI parameters to include concepts of spectrum, noise, envelopes, microtones, and other features of sound that would produce similar results regardless of the hardware platform. Another approach is to represent the audio signal itself, along with instructions for specific processes. MIDI cannot accept audio signal input directly from a microphone or other audio source, such as an electric guitar or tape recorder. Both of these methods would require a much higher "bandwidth" than is currently feasible via MIDI (i.e., more data travelling at faster rates). Unfortunately, this means that direct timbral analysis information and software synthesis is currently unavailable to Max (although several non-Opcode versions of Max do have this capability). However, based on studies of acoustics and orchestration, some general assumptions can be made about how a particular instrument's timbre will change with velocity (attack level), continuous dynamic level (sustain level), and duration. These parameters are available to MIDI.

The General MIDI standard is a part of the MIDI specification that tries to address this problem by adopting a standardized set of 128 sounds and corresponding program numbers that can be consistent from one machine to another. Although this assures game manufacturers and other software developers that a sound will be similar across synthesizer platforms, the whole idea of standardizing sounds goes against a main attraction of composing music with computers, which is to explore new, nonstandard timbres that only computers can create. Therefore, a small standardized set of sounds holds little interest to composers interested in developing original sounds for their compositions.

The original MIDI specification was created fifteen years ago and designed to be very efficient so that it could run on slow processors. Currently available communication chips allow maximum speeds more than six hundred times that of MIDI. Although several solutions have been proposed to address the shortcomings of the current MIDI specification, there has been no agreement on a protocol to specify characteristics of timbre that would allow the transmission to the computer of vital information in real time during a performance, and would insure similar results for various machines from different manufacturers. (For more information, see the proposal for the ZIPI protocol in McMillen, Wessel, and Wright 1994.)

Participation by Musicians Playing Nondigital Instruments

Although digital instruments have proliferated in the last ten years, the most highly esteemed musicians perform primarily on nondigital acoustic or electric instruments. Finding ways to include these master musicians in the creation of digital music is the purpose behind much of the research in interactive composition. MIDI versions of acoustic instruments and pitch-to-MIDI convertors help to solve the problem by transferring some gestural information to the computer. MIDI instruments translate into digital signals a performer's physical motion and position, such as hand and finger position on a MIDI guitar, breath pressure on a wind controller, or drum pad hits on a MIDI drum set. Pitch-to-MIDI convertors translate the musical gestures that are a result of a performer's physical gestures on an acoustic instrument. Although these devices can provide a somewhat accurate analysis of pitch and dynamic information in the form of MIDI data, they are incapable of translating information regarding timbre. Real-time spectral analysis (timbre analysis) of the audio signal has been demonstrated in several specialized systems (discussed at the end of this chapter), and the current generation of home computers shows promise as it approaches the speed and memory requirements needed to handle this computationally demanding task.

For now, it is unfortunate that listener objects are unaware of timbral information from acoustic musicians, because sound quality often represents a high point of their achievement, and using aspects of their sound would impart richness and refinement to computer-synthesized tones. The constant fluctuations in timbre naturally produced by non-digital instruments are integral parts of expressive performance and interpretation, inextricably tied to register, tempo, phrasing, dynamics, and articulation. Examples would include the subtleties of color and pitchbend in a jazz saxophone performance, the range of sounds and textures available from a string quartet, or the screaming distorted sound of an electric guitar solo. In fact, musicians work for years on controlling the subtle changes of color occurring within each note and within each phrase. Indeed, high praise from one musician to another is a mention of their wonderful "sound." One currently feasible method for incorporating the sound of an instrument into a computer-music composition is through the use of MIDI controllable digital signal processors (effects boxes); devices that allow an audio signal to be sampled, altered and changed under computer control. (Interactive signal processing will be covered later in this chapter.)

Composer Objects for Timbre Selection, Creation, and Manipulation

While input analysis of timbre is still not available via Max on Macintosh computers, output options for creating and altering timbre are numerous. Objects may be specifically tailored for timbre selection, synthesis design, modulation control, mixing, sample playback, and signal processing via external MIDI effects boxes. All these techniques depend on a specific brand and model of MIDI device for the final creation of the sound. Each device will have different parameters and sound capabilities that can be controlled by MIDI, usually programmable by the user. Recent designs in MIDI devices show manufacturers adding more and more MIDI-controllable parameters to alter the sound, with many parameters easily assignable to a specified continuous-controller number.

A simple and very effective way to alter timbre is via program changes. Data from listener objects may be linked to select one of several synthesizer sounds. For example, parallel links could use dynamic levels to switch the computer output to different string patches, with low velocity values triggering quiet, legato, muted strings, and high velocity values triggering loud and aggressive marcato passages. In fact, any number of performance features could be programmed to crossfade seamlessly between a group of samples. Similarly, a performer's articulation, in the form of duration, could be mapped to trigger legato or pizzicato string sounds. More imaginative techniques could use conditional statements to link timbre changes to tempo, note density, or harmony.

Timbral changes may be used in improvisational situations to surprise and motivate a performer. Since most timbre changes are immediately perceived, they provide a salient feature to provoke a performer's response. In improvisational settings, the sounds themselves will inspire different reactions and playing styles. Constrained random values may be used to select from a set of related timbres, with the sounds narrowed to function for the musical context, and the variation offering freshness from one performance to the next. More broadly randomized timbre parameters can yield a consistent sound world with unexpected results.

Timbre selection may also be achieved by switching the data output to a different MIDI channel that is set to play a different timbre (by sending an **int** to the right inlet of **noteout**). When switching MIDI channels it is essential to remember that each MIDI *Note-On* message needs a matching *Note-Off* message. If a *Note-On* message is sent on one channel, and the corresponding *Note-Off* message is sent on another channel, the note will get "stuck," playing the sound indefinitely. The **flush** object is specially designed to avoid stuck notes. (As described in chapter 4, **flush** keeps track of every *Note-On* message on every MIDI channel, and supplies an appropriate *Note-Off* message when it receives a *bang*.) Inserting **flush** between **makenote** and **noteout** and sending a *bang* to **flush** just before channels are changed will insure that all notes receive a timely *Note-Off* command. For monophonic performances, this is a solution that works well. However, for keyboard performances, all overlapping notes and held chords will be cut off whenever a **flush** receives a *bang*. **Borax** has features that may be useful in this situation. First, a *bang* to the right inlet resets all values to zero and supplies all held notes with a *Note-Off* message. Since **Borax** "tags" each event as it is received with a number, it is possible to use it in conjunction with a **coll** to supply *Note-Off* messages to the proper channel, using methods like those described below.

An elegant solution to the problem of changing MIDI channels can be seen in Richard Zvonar's **Hocketizer** patch (fig. 8.1). **Hocketizer** takes its name from a compositional technique developed in the 13th century in which a single melody is distributed between two or more singers or instruments, so that successive pitches are played, in order, by different musicians. In this example, successive notes create a hocketing effect by cycling between two to sixteen different MIDI channels. Timbre is assigned to each channel via program changes from sixteen **number boxes**, and these settings may be saved in a **preset** object. As each new note enters the program it gets routed or "channelized" to play on a specified MIDI channel according to one of three methods (using the menu labelled Hocket Type): Random, Cycle, or Table. All three types are continuously calculated with the results going to a **switch** object; the **menu** selects one of the three types to pass through the **switch**. **Random** simply outputs a new random channel number with each incoming note. The size of **random** determines how many channels will be used. Each new note also cycles through numbers from a **counter**, the **counter** maximum determining the maximum number of output channels. The **counter's** output is also available as an index to a **table**, so that a specified pattern of MIDI channels may be cycled through.

On the disk provided with the software, Zvonar describes his useful solution to the problem of assigning *Note-Off* information when changing channels:

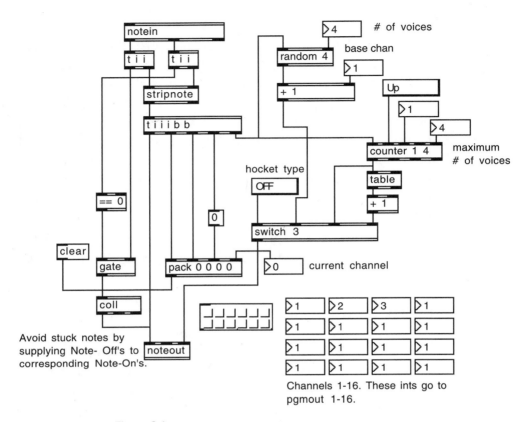

Figure 8.1
Hocketizer

In order to avoid stuck notes, we must insure that each note's **Note-Off** is assigned to the same channel as the **Note-On,** and we do this as follows: Each channelized **Note-On** message, such as C4, is passed through to a **noteout** object, and a corresponding **Note-Off** message, complete with the proper channel information, is formatted and stored in a **coll.** When a C4 **Note-Off** message enters the patch, it triggers recall of the stored channelized **Note-Off** for C4, thereby shutting off the channelized note.

The formatting of the **Note-Off**s is done with a **pack** object, which creates a list: [*note note 0*]. This list is sent into the **coll,** where it stores the list [*note 0 chan*] at the index "note." When a **Note-Off** message arrives, the presence of zero velocity causes a **gate** to open and the note value is passed as an index to the **coll,** triggering the proper **Note-Off.** When a **Note-On** arrives, the presence of non-zero velocity causes the **gate** to close again, so that a **Note-Off** is not sent.

Sample Playback via Max

Sample playback via Max expands the sound resources beyond the limited synthesis algorithms found on some MIDI synthesizers. Samples may be played from a MIDI sampler, from sound files stored on disk, or from an audio CD. Besides samples that are captured via microphone or CD, sample playback opens up the possibilities of including interesting sounds created with sophisticated signal-processing, filtering, and synthesis techniques found in many non real-time computer-music programs (such as CSOUND). These well-developed programs create original and compelling sounds by using transformative algorithms to process digital sound files or by generating sound files "from scratch" using a large array of powerful synthesis algorithms. Max can incorporated these unique sounds in a live situation; the immediate response and feedback in sample playback allows composers and performers to play with the material in a way that is impossible outside a real-time environment.

MIDI samplers usually have features that allow real-time shaping of various aspects of the sound via continuous controller data, such as envelope shape, loop point, filtering, and other processes. Max has several objects for accessing samples from internal sources, playing them out the Macintosh speaker, the computer's audio output jack, or an installed digital audio card. The **snd** object plays back standard Macintosh sound files that are stored on disk using the Apple Sound Manager. The **cd** object plays specified cues from audio CDs via an Apple CD-ROM drive. **AiffPlayer** is an unsupported object written by Eric Singer that plays back standard Macintosh AIFF sound files from disk. A final option, using sound only from QuickTime movies, will be discussed in the final chapter on multimedia extensions.

The snd Object

Snd plays samples stored on disk as standard Apple Sound Manager "snd" resources (fig. 8.2). Sample quality can be selected, including 44.1K/16-bit stereo sound files, the specification for CD-quality sound. Max is capable of playing up to 32 voices simultaneously (depending on the speed of the hardware, among other things). A *1* or *bang* sent to the left inlet will play back the original sample. A 0 will stop the sound. Values 2 to 127, representing pitch, will transpose the sample up or down so that melodies can be produced using the samples stored on disk. 60 (middle C) is the default transposition, representing the original pitch. In figure 8.2 the pitch may be controlled by the **graphic keyboard,** or by using a **number box.** The remaining three inlets specify duration, voice number, and volume.

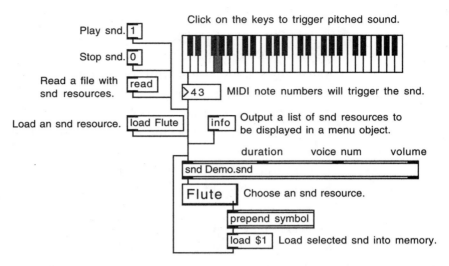

Figure 8.2
snd

A **snd** file may contain a single sound, or many sounds stored as separate resources. Several applications, such as Sound Edit (Macromedia) and SoundApp (freeware) can create files with multiple **snd** resources. **Snd** takes two arguments that represent a file name and a resource within the file. Messages to **snd** include *load,* to load another resource, and *read,* to read in a file off a disk.

Max will always default to the first sound resource when it loads a sound file. One way to select different **snd** resources from the same sound file is to use a **menu** object. Clicking on the *info* message will automatically set a **menu** object with the names of the **snd** resources currently available. A new resource is then easily chosen from the **menu.**

The cd Object

Audio CDs offer vast resources for sound material and musical clips. (For professional work, copyright rules may apply to the use of commercial recordings.) Composers can create a custom library of their own samples and digital audio files using a CD-ROM writer to press a disk. This is a practical and affordable way to access up to 720 MB of sound files designed for a specific composition. The **cd** object receives messages to start and stop playback from anywhere on an audio CD, played from the Apple CD-ROM drive (fig. 8.3). A single number begins

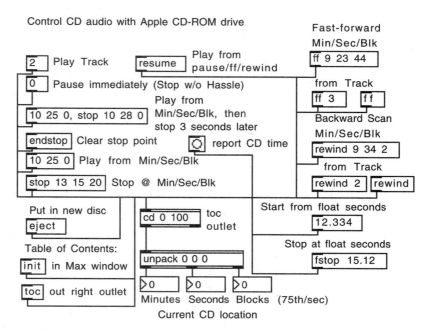

Figure 8.3
cd

playback at the beginning of a track. Within the track, location is speci-fied by a three-number message that represents minutes, seconds, and blocks (75th sec). Sending *stop* followed by three numbers specifies the stop location [*stop 1 3 0*]. The stop point remains until the message *endstop* is sent. Sending the message, *init,* places the CD's entire table of contents in a Max window. Playback is not instantaneous, unfortu-nately, as there is a very slight delay while the file's location on the disk is found. For many applications, the delay will not pose a problem. However, it can be minimized by positioning and then pausing the CD before it is required to play. Another solution to quicker response is to measure the delay time and try to compensate for it by beginning play-back slightly early during a performance according to a trigger note that precedes the CD playback. Because of the lag time, the **cd** object may not be a good substitute for a sampler or a sound file played from disk when a performer expects an immediate response from a physical gesture. For time-critical playback, audio applications such as Sound Hack and Sound Edit can store clips from a CD onto disk. The **cd** object is a valuable addition to Max's sound capabilities, an inexpensive way to trigger long or short segments of prerecorded material. Multiple CD-ROM drives can be used simultaneously.

Cd takes two optional arguments. The first is the drive's SCSI ID. This needs to be specified only if multiple CD-ROM drives are used. The second argument is how often (in milliseconds) the CD's current time will be reported. A *bang* to **cd** will also report the time (location of the CD).

AIFFPlayer

Eric Singer's **AiffPlayer** is an external object (written in C) designed to play back soundfiles directly from a hard disk in the standard Macintosh AIFF file format (fig. 8.4). It uses Apple's Sound Manager to play soundfiles out the computer audio jacks or through Digidesign hardware, such as an AudioMedia sound card. It uses a playback buffer so that large files can be played back without loading them entirely into memory.

AiffPlayer can play back multiple files simultaneously; the default is 4. The maximum number depends on a several factors, including the speed of the computer, the speed of the hard drive, the resolution of the soundfiles, and how much other processing is going on. Files must

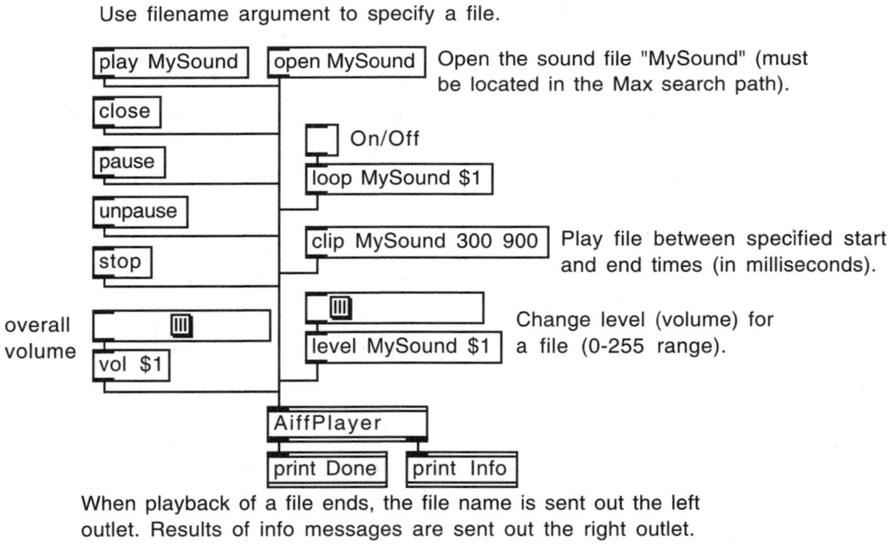

Use filename argument to specify a file.

| play MySound | | open MySound | | Open the sound file "MySound" (must be located in the Max search path).

| close |

| | On/Off
| pause |
| loop MySound $1 |

| unpause |

| | clip MySound 300 900 | Play file between specified start
| stop | and end times (in milliseconds).

overall | ▥ | | ▥ | Change level (volume) for
volume | vol $1 | | level MySound $1 | a file (0-255 range).

| AiffPlayer |

| print Done | | print Info |

When playback of a file ends, the file name is sent out the left outlet. Results of info messages are sent out the right outlet.

Figure 8.4
AiffPlayer

first be opened and their names automatically stored in an internal file list. Then the *play* message, followed by the name of an opened file, will play the sound. Arguments to **AiffPlayer** are (from left to right): filename, number of voices (default 4), audio channel outputs (default stereo), playback buffer size, and maximum number of files that can be opened (default 32). The optional *clip* message can specify start and end times for playback, and files can be looped. Other messages to control playback include *stop, pause, unpause, level* (for a single file), and *volume* (overall volume) (Singer 1996).

Synthesis Design and Assigning Control Parameters

Since each synthesizer and sampler has device-specific methods to produce its sound, it is difficult to discuss particular parameters. At one time, a sampler was primarily a device that recorded and played back sounds, while a synthesizer was a device that used a synthesis algorithm to create music "from scratch," with stored waveforms, modulation techniques, additive synthesis, or other synthesis algorithms. Today the distinction between synthesizers and samplers is often blurred, with sample-based synthesizers, and samplers with powerful synthesis and processing capabilities. However, many of these devices have some basic categories of sound design in common. These include the ability to mix several layers of sound, alter the attack characteristics and overall amplitude envelope of a sound, control the depth and speed of modulating oscillators, and change filter settings. Most recent synthesizers offer users the ability to assign continuous controller numbers to specific synthesis and processing parameters, creating a powerful real-time synthesis engine where numerous parameters can change continuously under computer control. Parameters not assignable to continuous controllers can usually be altered via system-exclusive data, a MIDI protocol which allows the control of parameters specific to a particular make and model of synthesizer.

Thus, numerous aspects of a sound can be altered according to a score, an algorithm, or in direct response to a performance. Listener-object data may be routed directly or indirectly to influence these parameters. As with other MIDI continuous controller data, Max may need to to scale the output range between 0 and 127 or within a narrower range to achieve subtler effects. Scaling algorithms, described in previous chapters, are often needed to prepare data for synthesis control.

In addition to synthesis methods, many synthesizers come equipped with an internal signal processor for generating effects, such as reverb, echo, and chorusing. Many of these parameters can also be assigned controller numbers. The Kurzweil K2500, for instance, incorporates a fully functional signal processor inside each synth, complete with variable performance controls that can assign any signal-processing parameter a continuous-controller number. It also has a separate DSP architecture, incorporating highly sophisticated and programmable synthesis processes, such as nonlinear distortion and modulation functions, whose parameters are also assignable to particular continuous controllers or to automated functions. The techniques presented here that use continuous controllers to create and alter timbres during a performance are applicable to both synthesis and signal-processing algorithms.

In figure 8.5, **ContinuousControlMapper** can be used to experiment with various synthesis control structures. It takes any controller input and maps it to the controller number and MIDI channel specified by the fourth and fifth inlet. Any controller, such as a foot pedal, modulation wheel, or data slider, can be used as input. These controllers can be made to effect only the parameter assigned to the output of the mapper by making sure that no assignments are made inside the synthesizer, or by turning local control off. The second inlet allows the range of values to be offset higher or lower. The range can also be offset with the third inlet to provide a more useful set of data for a specific synthesis parameter.

System Exclusive Messages

The **sysexformat** object can prepare messages for model-specific synthesis parameters sent via **midiout**. The *system exclusive* (*sys ex*) protocol was created to accommodate the differences in synthesis techniques and other synthesizer operations, such as bulk storage of programs (bulk dump) that are outside of the standard MIDI messages. Since *sys ex* messages contain code that describes the manufacturer and the model of the synthesizer along with the parameter data, they are much less efficient and more complex than similar continuous controller messages. On certain synthesizer models (especially older mod-

Takes any incoming continuous controller and maps it to a use- specified controller number and MIDI channel. Scale factor adds or subtracts the number before output. Speedlim 10 thins data stream to make Max run more efficiently.

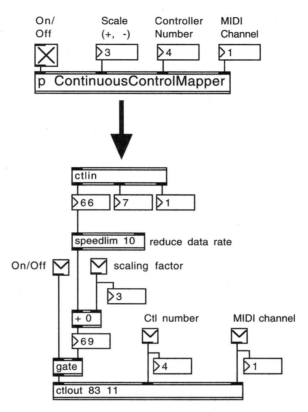

Figure 8.5
ContinuousControlMapper

els) *sys ex* messages are the only way to control many parameters. On newer models, however, many synthesis parameters are assignable to continuous-controller numbers. A *sys ex* message always begins with the number 240 and ends with 247 (hexidecimal numbers FOH and F7H), and the manufacturer's identification number is in between, followed by any number of data bytes required by the manufacturer's specification.

Sysexin, like **notein** and **ctlin,** receives *sys ex* data directly from the serial port. **Capture** or **print** will display an incoming *sys ex* message represented by a list of numbers. Between each number, 240 and 247, is a complete *sys ex* message. Usually there will be only one or two values that change in the long *sys ex* message. These changing values represent a changeable synthesis parameter. All the other data bytes are constants—they never change. To create a message for output back to the synthesizer, variables are represented by the strings *is $1*\\ and *is $2*\\ in the **sysexformat** object. Like **midiformat** (see chap. 2), the **sysexformat** object prepares a complete MIDI message before sending it via **midiout.**

Figure 8.6 shows the process of identifying and using the *sys ex* format. This data represents one of the amplitude envelopes for a sound on the Yamaha SY77 synthesizer. A full message would read [*sxformat 240 67 16 52 8 32 0 16 0 100 247*]. Obviously, this format is considerably longer than a three-byte continuous-controller message.

Automated Mixing and Multitrack Parameter Control

Several commercially available mixers offer MIDI control of various functions, such as level control, panning, and equalization. Most of them treat mixer faders as individual continuous controllers, recording and playing back fader movement either internally or via MIDI to a software sequencer. Some offer the ability to take "screen snapshots" that can reconfigure an entire mixing board instantaneously with a punch of a button or be triggered via program change messages. Ideal mixing, panning, and signal-processing levels can be set by the composer or engineer for each performance, or they can be altered inter-

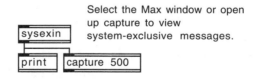

Select the Max window or open up capture to view system-exclusive messages.

Yamaha SY77 Example:

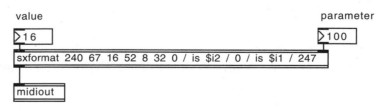

Figure 8.6
sysexin and **sxformat**

actively by a performer sending continuous-control messages. Other mixer functions, such as auxiliary sends and returns and main mix level, may also be controlled via MIDI. A MIDI mixer is essential when interactive level control and automation of several audio signals is desired, such as controlling the levels and effecting the sends of an acoustic ensemble. Figure 8.7 shows the front panel of a software editor created by Charles Maynes for the Yamaha DMP11 MIDI mixer and signal processor. The intuitive interface design makes editing functions on the DMP11 simple to understand and easy to use, enabling the rapid configuration of a complex system.

The programming complexities are hidden from the user's view using a graphic template (overlay), **sliders, pcontrol,** and **ubuttons.** (All the continuous control outputs and editing mechanisms are hidden.) Editing functions for the DMP11 are sent from Max as continuous-controller numbers. Among other things, the DMP11 has eight level faders, eight pan position controls, muting for each channel, and eq settings. The DMP11 also contains two signal processors, fx1 and fx2, with separate sends for each channel. All effects are editable via subpatches that contain all parameters. The full example, included on disk, is worth studying as a model for creating editors for other signal

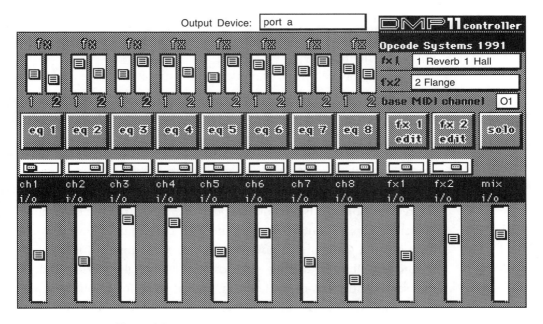

Figure 8.7
DMP11 Controller by Charles Maynes

processors and synthesizers that can be programmed rapidly and used in performance situations. Imagine a performer controlling parameters that can pan, mix, filter, process, and output up to eight separate audio inputs from an ensemble, band, or orchestra.

MIDI controlled mixers can be simulated in software without the need for additional hardware using Max. The MIDI protocol specifies continuous-controller number seven as the volume control for each MIDI channel. MIDI volume control is different from velocity. Velocity values, representing the amount of force used to play a particular note, are often tied to loudness and timbre, since the timbre of most acoustic instruments changes when played at different dynamic levels. A piano string, for example, will produce many more upper harmonics and more "noise" from the hammer mechanism when played loudly (velocity). MIDI volume, unlike velocity, is designed simply to increase or decrease the gain without altering the envelope or spectrum of a sound. Controller number seven works like the volume-control slider on a synthesizer, with a different level possible on each MIDI channel. Max can act as a "virtual" mixer using MIDI volume by sending continuous-controller messages on each MIDI channel. Figure 8.8 shows an example of an eight-track MIDI mixer. Each level has a remote-control receive object (r Lev1, r Lev2, etc.) so that values for automated mixes can be generated and sent from other sources in the program. Each **ctlout** sends **slider** data for controller seven to a different MIDI channel.

Although the following examples demonstrate automated mixing, even more important, they demonstrate ways to receive, transmit, interpret, automate, and scale continuous-controller data. The controller-number assignments, specified by the middle inlet or as arguments, could easily be changed to address parameters on devices that alter panning position, synthesis parameters, or signal-processing functions.

While this arrangement offers complex automated mixing through the **receive** object, it is not an ideal performance instrument since only one slider can be controlled at a time with the mouse. However, this simple patch turns into a powerful real-time instrument for shaping timbre as well as for mixing when coupled with eight physical faders that send continuous-controller data, such as those found on the Kurzweil K2500 synthesizer, most MIDI mixers, or a MIDI fader unit. The JR Cooper FaderMaster is a set of eight high-quality faders that translates fader movement into MIDI messages. This stand-alone controller

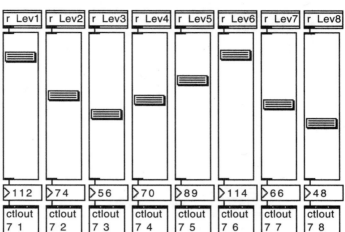

Figure 8.8
Virtual mixing

is highly programmable and has patch changes that can immediately reconfigure the range, controller number, and MIDI channel output for each fader.

KeyCtl attempts to solve the problem of the one-point mouse source with software, by turning the computer keyboard into a mixing board, simulating continuous controllers with various keys (fig. 8.9). **KeyCtl** produces continuous values between 0 and 127, using one key to raise the value and another key to lower the value. The "u" key (select 117) raises the value; the "j" key (select 106) lowers the value. The keys start a **metro** object, and each **metro** *bang* adds or subtracts 1 from the previous value, thus determining how fast a fader will move. The **number box** limits values between 0 and 127. **Keyup** stops the **metro** and halts the value changes.

Multiple **KeyCtl** objects can be used to control several faders or other continuous processes, in effect mimicking a set of hardware faders (although much less responsively). Figure 8.10 shows four volume **sliders** controlled in this way. The right hand moves each fader up and down at the selected speed. Keys [u, i, o, p] raise the levels of **sliders** 1, 2, 3 and 4. Keys [j, k, l, ;] lower the level of **sliders** 1, 2, 3, and 4. The **slider** speed parameter sets the speed of a **metro** object.

Line and **delay** are effective in automating many functions. In this example, the initial *bang* causes **line** to raise **slider** 4 from 0 to 127

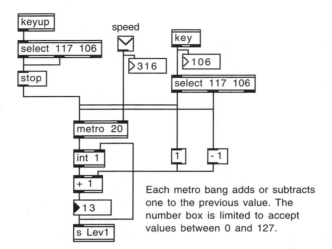

Figure 8.9
KeyCtl

Automated sliders using the computer keyboard.

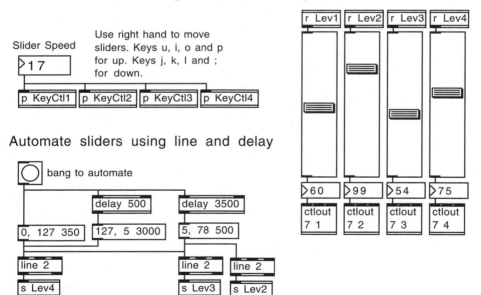

Figure 8.10
Automated sliders

over 350 milliseconds. Then, after a 500 millisecond pause, **slider** 4 is lowered to a level of 5 over 3 seconds. After **slider** 4 reaches 5, **sliders** 2, 3, and 4 begin to rise, reaching 78 in 500 milliseconds.

The **mtr** object is a special data storage object designed to record any type of Max message, numbers, lists, or symbols, using a multitrack tape recorder as a model (fig. 8.11). It is ideally suited for recording and playing back automated mixes. An argument specifies the number of tracks, from one to thirty-two. The left inlet is the master control; messages sent to the left inlet affect all the tracks. Messages include *stop, record, play, rewind, next, mute, unmute, delay [0], first [0], read,* and *write.* A message sent to any individual tracks will affect that track only. Individual tracks can be separately recorded, played back, stopped, delayed, and muted. Max can read and write **mtr** files from disk.

Layering and Crossfading

Many synthesizers and samplers can combine two or more basic sounds into a single "instrument," playable on the same note and MIDI

Multitrack recorder for any kind of message.

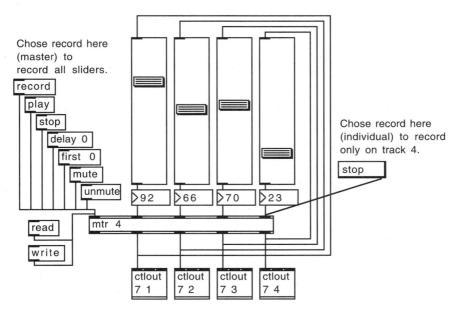

Figure 8.11
mtr

channel. Typically, several samples are accessed in response to velocity, so that a sample of the instrument played quietly is heard at low velocity levels, and a different sample of the instrument played loudly is heard at high velocity levels. Usually the layers are crossfaded, providing a smooth transition between one and the next, with one sound fading out as the other becomes more prominent. Velocity Switching selects only one sound at a time, abruptly changing to a new sound at specified velocity levels. The balance of the various layers can also be assigned to controller sources, offering continuously varying control by a performer or the computer. Long sustained sounds consisting of multiple layers create effective situations for interactive shaping and control of timbre.

Envelopes

Amplitude control on the envelope level allows the user to create and alter attack, sustain, and decay portions of the sound. Envelopes are usually composed of multiple segments defined by their beginning and ending levels and their overall time. A typical envelope consists of an initial attack segment, a decay segment, a sustain segment, and a release segment, called an "ADSR envelope" (fig. 8.12). Many synthesizers provide more segments to describe more interesting shapes. Segments can be altered according to velocity, register, or controller values. A typical example is to program a piano or harp sound so that the decay time shortens as the pitch goes up, which models their acoustical counterparts. Interactive control of the attack portion of the amplitude envelope creates the most dramatic changes in the sound, going from sharp percussive attacks to smoother "bowed" sounds. Larger controller values normally increase the rate of the initial attack.

Envelopes can serve as functions to control other parameters besides amplitude. Pitch envelopes, for instance, can be used to create fine-tuned pitchbending effects to model acoustical instruments, such as congas, tablas, or guitars. Filter settings, synthesis parameters, crossfading, and sound location can all be shaped using envelopes, and the envelopes, in turn, can be made responsive to computer control. The **env** object can create and output envelope functions in response to automated messages or performance features.

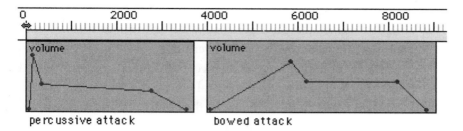

Figure 8.12
Envelope control

Panning

Perceived spatial location is determined primarily by panning position, available on the final output on most synthesizers, as well as on each individual sound. Continuous controller #10 is the MIDI standard for panning. Controllers assigned to panning position create movement and action in the stereo field. Under computer control, panning, like mixing, becomes interesting and complex, with strong possibilities for using spatial location and movement as central concepts in a composition. With multiple sound sources, or a single synthesizer with multiple outputs, the computer can describe how sound can be "flown" around a space using four or more speakers.

Interactive Signal Processing

MIDI-controlled signal processors have proliferated in the last few years, offering sophisticated programmable algorithms that transform a sound in real time. Any audio signal may be processed, including acoustic, electronic, or prerecorded sounds. These devices allow composers the opportunity to digitally transform instruments and sounds so that they may be fully incorporated into the texture of a computer-music composition. Although these effects boxes use limited types of processes, their portability, price, and programmability make them attractive tools for use in concert performance. Increased flexibility is gained by using computers to send continuous-controller messages to alter various parameters, which allows for subtle, dynamic control over all the aspects of the processed sound. As the control of these processes becomes more flexible, their use becomes more musical by responding to a skilled musician whose performance gestures and musical cues control how the parameters change over time.

Typically, a musician may influence both signal processing and computer-music algorithms by simultaneously sending audio data to the signal processor and MIDI data to the computer. The audio signal may come from any sound source that is digitized (sampled) as it enters the processor. From there, various algorithms transform the sampled sounds in real time. Composer objects may respond to performance data by sending ***continuous-controller*** messages out to control signal-processing parameters, giving performers immediate feedback and the ability to alter their sounds. Signal processors can then respond to a particular performer or performance, empowering the musician with an extension of his or her sound, which is sensitive to their musical nuance.

Some synthesizers, such as the Kurzweil K2500, come equipped with built-in signal-processing capabilities, with the ability to process both synthesized sounds and audio signals available through external inputs. Like their stand-alone counterparts, these "internal" effects boxes alter signal-processing parameters in response to continuous-controller data. The control data could come directly from a physical controller on the synthesizer, such as a foot pedal or data slider, or from messages sent by the computer. In this way, musicians may use performance gestures to specify exactly how the processing will take place.

Many composers are especially interested in using signal-processing techniques to transform the sounds of acoustic instruments and voices during live performance. These techniques invite musicians to participate in performing computer music that is controlled, in part, by their performance, and created with their own sound. When used as integral parts of music compositions, they provide a common sound world where synthesized sounds and acoustic instruments can blend, while expanding the coloristic and expressive range of the instruments. Besides providing pitch information, most pitch to MIDI convertors, such as the IVL PitchRider 4000, send out continuous-controller messages that correspond to continuous changes in the dynamic level. These dynamic changes are well-suited to control signal-processing variables.

Basic Categories of Signal Processing

Although the available effects differ from one signal processor to another, there are several basic categories of processing common to most units. Each processing technique has one or more parameters that may be controlled directly from a MIDI device, or from the computer. These processes may be applicable to synthesis methods as well, such as modulation techniques using low-frequency oscillators (LFO) and filtering. Also, Max may be used to simulate many of these audio processes in MIDI, modeling time delay and pitch-shifting effects. Described here are a few types of processing that are especially interesting for interactive composition.

Wet/Dry Mix

All processors contain a setting that determines the wet/dry *mix,* the final mix or ratio of the level of the original signal (dry) to the level of the processed signal (wet). At 100 percent wet, all the original signal will be cut out, whereas 0 percent wet will cut all of the processed sound. Interactive control over the wet/dry mix can be very effective, adding more or less reverberation, for example, in response to velocity, register, or tempo.

Time-Delay Processes

Delay and echo record the incoming signal and play it back after a specified delay time, with a feedback or regeneration parameter that determines how many discrete repetitions will be heard. Longer delays may be used to create canons, and some processors will automatically adjust the delay time to correspond to the tempo of the incoming MIDI data so that the delay time is always synchronized with a performance tempo. This technique is also possible using tempo objects in Max to continuously reset the processor's delay time. Dense rhythmic textures may develop by synchronizing audio and MIDI delays.

Reverberation (reverb) uses multiple echoes to simulate a sound as it bounces around an acoustical space. Reverb settings attempt to simulate the size and shape of a room or hall, the location of the sound, the distance to the walls and ceiling, the density and diffusion of a sound, and a room's sound absorption and reflection properties. Parameters may include room size and reverb time (or decay time). An initial panning location determines direct sound, with time set for early reflection (or early delay) simulating the distance and location of the nearest surface, such as a wall or ceiling. Reverb density or diffusion will determine the number of copies of the sound. A parameter that filters out high frequencies over time, high-frequency damping (or high-frequency feedback), simulates the sound-reflective properties of a hall, since harder surfaces will reflect more high frequencies, and softer surfaces (such as people, chairs, and carpet) will absorb high frequencies.

Flanging, phasing, and chorusing are related effects that use short delay times coupled with a low-frequency oscillator (LFO) to modulate the sound and give it continuous movement or a diffused quality. Minimal parameters include delay time, LFO speed (LFO frequency), and modulation depth, which determine the speed and prominence of the effect. Flanging produces a sense of movement by adding to the original sound a copy of the sound with a very short time-varying delay. The delay time is controlled by an LFO. A feedback level controls the amount of the returning signal and thus the strength of the effect, which may considerably alter the timbre of the sound. Phasing and chorusing are more subtle. Phasing makes a copy and sweeps its phase relation relative to the original input signal, usually without any feedback. Chorusing mixes one or more altered versions of the original and avoids some of the extreme timbral shifts that phase cancellation causes in flanging and phasing.

Pitch-Shifting

Pitch-shifting transposes one or more copies of the original sound by changing the playback rate. The basic parameter is the transposition level, specified as a single pitch shift interval, usually in semitones. Adding delay and feedback parameters will create arpeggios of the chosen interval, at the delay speed, with the register and overall time determined by the feedback level. Some effects units, sometimes called harmonizers, contain pitch detectors that supply appropriate harmony for the incoming notes according to a preset scale or user-definable harmony map. As was seen in previous examples, harmonizing functions and harmony maps can also be created in Max and made responsive to a score or an improvisation. This process applies to both audio and MIDI data.

Vibrato and Tremolo

Tangentially related to pitch shifting is vibrato, which imparts an instrumental or vocal vibrato quality to processed sound by continuously shifting pitch up and down. An LFO creates a modulating signal, the speed determines the vibrato speed, and the modulation depth (amplitude) determines how wide the vibrato will be, that is, the amount that the final sound will vary above and below the original pitch. Vibrato is a type of Frequency Modulation (FM), a synthesis technique that creates timbral changes when the modulation speed is in the audio frequency range. Similar effects are achieved with computer control applied to pitchbend functions. The **xbendin** and **xbendout** objects represent very fine increments in pitch changes (thousands of values, as opposed to 0 to 127). **Xbendout** can be used for subtle vibrato control or for accurate pitch offset in alternative tuning systems.

Tremolo uses an LFO to create a fluctuation in amplitude level. The speed of the oscillation determines the tremolo speed; the modulation depth (amplitude) determines how loud and soft the fluctuations in amplitude will go. Tremolo is a type of Amplitude Modulation (AM), another synthesis technique that creates timbral changes (although less complex than FM) when the modulation speed is in the audio frequency range.

Filtering

Filters alter timbre by attenuating a certain portion of the frequency spectrum. Filter parameters are found on many synthesizers as synthesis parameters, as well as on a variety of signal processors. When using filters, a reference frequency, either the cutoff frequency or center frequency, tells which part of the spectrum will remain. Since filters shape and modify timbre, they can give performers interactive control over the processing of their own sound. The four basic types of filters are low-pass, high-pass, band-pass, and band-reject. More sophisticated filtering processes are included in higher-end processors (fig. 8.13).

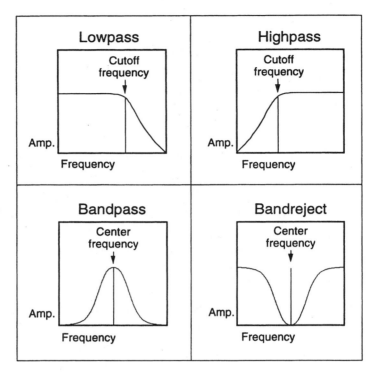

Figure 8.13
Filter types. Reprinted from Curtis Roads, *The Computer Music Tutorial,* (Cambridge, MA: The MIT Press, 1996) p. 188.

Low-pass filters cut the level of all frequencies above the cutoff frequency, allowing lower frequencies to pass through. Moving the cutoff frequency of a low-pass filter up and down (filter sweeps) is a hallmark of early electronic music, and can be controlled via continuous-controller data. High-pass filters cut the level of all frequencies below the cutoff frequency, allowing higher frequencies to pass through.

Band-pass filters cut out all frequencies above and below a specified band (range). The center frequency is the center of the band, and the bandwidth, or Q, determines the range or spread of the band. A very narrow bandwidth will emphasize a specific frequency; sweeping such a filter will create overtone melodies in most sounds with definite pitch. Band-reject filters are the opposite of band-pass filters; they cut a single band of frequencies and pass all the others. Multiple band-pass and band-reject filters may be used in a series.

Equalization is a filtering process, boosting or cutting portions of the frequency spectrum of a sound. It can be found on most mixing boards, in stand alone units, in signal processors, and as synthesis parameters.

Compositional Approaches Using Interactive Signal Processing

Several examples will help illustrate just a few of the many ways that signal processing can modify and create musical sounds and structures based on performance information. Mapping of musical gestures onto the various parameters of signal processing must be carefully planned. The output may be considered in two different ways: as an integrated component of an instrument, capable of enhancing its timbral qualities, or as a generator of new musical material, producing variations and an accompaniment based on the original input. Processing can also be used to create a single "hyperinstrument" that is closely wedded to the original instrument's sound and playing technique, greatly expanding the instrument's sonic palette and the performer's expressive role in shaping the sound. (Machover and Chung 1989). For example, in the author's work, *Snake Charmer* (1991), a solo clarinet increases or decreases the modulation speed of a chorus effect according to the continuous dynamic level. In this way, the quiet, pure sound of the clarinet is unaffected by the processor, but as the player's dynamic level increases, additional intensity is added by increasing the speed of the chorus effect, with a vibrato-like warble at medium dynamic ranges, and higher LFO speeds distorting the sound at the loudest moments (fig. 8.14).

Effects can be considered as primary musical material, not simply as an alteration of a sound. Delay and pitch-shifting are clear examples of effects that actually produce additional music (which could even be

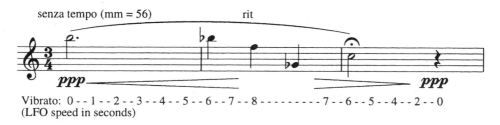

Figure 8.14
Hyperinstrument model

played by additional players). Several techniques can be combined at once using multi-effects units, or multiple signal processors, either in parallel or chained together, the output of one device being the input to the next. From a single user input, this technique allows for the creation of complex "signal-processing orchestration," producing additional notes and rhythms with a wide variety of ostinatos, arpeggios, trills, pitch-shifted melodic lines, canons, and harmonies, all from the original sound, along with effects that specifically alter the timbre, such as filtering, flanging, and distortion (fig. 8.15).

Just as the subject of a fugue must be thought of in multiple ways to consider its potential for future exploration and expansion, here, too, the composer is challenged to find musical gestures that serve the dual purpose of creating primary musical material and generating functions applicable to signal processing. For example, with **CaptureGesture**, the dynamics and timing of a lyrical arch-shaped violin phrase may be captured and used to create a function for signal processing (using **Interpolator**). The phrase function is created using a line object to inter-

Figure 8.15
Signal processing orchestration

polate between velocity values over time. The original velocity values are smoothly connected to represent the dynamic contour of the original melody (fig. 8.16). Later in the composition, while the violinist plays a different melody designed to be processed, this phrase function could be applied to control reverberation time, with the old dynamic levels used to continuously increase and decrease the reverberation time (with the identical timing as the original phrase). In this way, a performer is able to "phrase" the apparent size of the hall, imparting a malleable and musical dimension to a normally static field.

Sequences of continuous-controller information or envelope functions can be triggered by a performer, creating complex timbral changes. Pitches and other events can be matched and used to trigger stored signal-processing values or to begin processes that change over time. A simple example would use the line object to generate values between 0 and 127 over a specified amount of time. These values, routed to the **ctlout** object, could be used to control processes such as panning or changing a digital delay time from 20 milliseconds to 20 seconds. Randomizing values to **line** would produce constantly shifting and unpredictable results. Under computer control, even the ubiquitous digital delay can be used to create complex rhythmic canons, as the delay time changes in tempo according to a score. An interesting exercise would be to create a version of Robert Gibson's Canon program (chap. 7) using a signal processor and delay to alter a single acoustical sound source. Initial delay time, multiple voices, transposition level, and ramped delay time could all be implemented for automated computer control of signal-processing parameters.

Pitch shifting can be used to create doubled or tripled lines and chords from a single melody. One method demonstrated in the author's

Reverb 2 - - 4 - - 6 - - 4 - - 3 - - 2 - - - 3 - - 7 - - 12 - - - -10 - - 7 - - 4 - - 2 - - - - -
(Reverb time in seconds)

Continuously changing dynamic level is captured as a function to apply to reverb time.

Figure 8.16
Phrasing applied to signal processing

composition *Three Oboes* (1989) uses two channels of pitch shift to create three-part counterpoint from an oboe soloist by using the computer to change the intervals of transposition in time with specific notes (fig. 8.17). In this way, two melodies in contrary motion are heard along with the original solo line.

"Smart" harmonizations based on prestored pitch sets are triggered when a match note is received according to a predetermined score or improvisation. This line from *Three Oboes* shows the original oboe part and the resulting harmony that is created by the computer sending continuous controller data to offset pitch (fig. 8.18). Accompanying chords for any given note could be stored in a **coll**, the numbers representing two or three pitch-shifted notes, and indexed by incoming note numbers.

Pitch shift, coupled with delay effects, may produce interesting accompanying lines, arpeggios, or chords offset in time. In another composition by the author, *Things that Don't Belong in Houses* (1993), a solo electric double bass plays a simple half-note melody, while a signal processor produces delayed fifths in rhythm, each fifth falling on the upbeat. At the same time, another digital delay plays back an entire melody captured from the previous measures (fig. 8.19). In another section of the piece, arpeggios are generated by the signal processor for each bass note played. Changes to the processor are sent to the effects unit by a performer who uses a pedal unit that consists of four pedal controllers and switches programmable to send MIDI messages to alter

Figure 8.17
Signal processing counterpoint

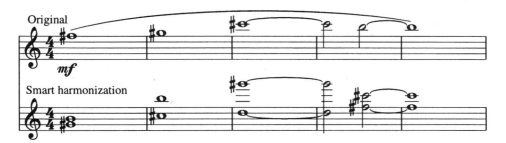

Figure 8.18
Smart harmonization

Figure 8.19
Delayed chords and arpeggios

effects parameters. The direct use of physical controllers offers a practical solution to performers who want to control signal processing without the trouble of setting up a computer system.

Composers may consider combining MIDI and acoustic instruments in an ensemble, with the MIDI instruments handling all communication to the computer. In this way, problems associated with pitch-to-MIDI convertors may be avoided, and the acoustic instruments may be processed according to a score, or more interestingly, processed depending on performance data from another musician. One scenario might have a single MIDI percussionist perform with four other musicians playing amplified acoustic instruments, with the audio signals routed to four signal processors. The percussionists could control the tempo and dynamics of composer algorithms, while sending controller data to four signal processors, altering the sounds of the acoustic instruments.

Scaling Problems and Solutions

MIDI-controllable signal processors are best suited for interactive control if they are able to alter parameters by receiving continuous controller data. Unfortunately, there is no standardization among devices for how to respond to controller data (numbers 0 to 127), which parameters are controlled by which controller numbers (often this is user-definable), or how many parameters can be changed at once.

Problems with scaling arise since these devices receive controller data from 0 to 127, but many of the parameters are scaled differently, such as 0 to 16 for panning or irregular increments for reverb time, making it necessary to create a library of translators, which take data from Max and scale them to an appropriate number before sending them to the processor. Ideally, within Max, each process should be represented to the user in the clearest possible format. Pitch-shifting is a good example. Figure 8.20 shows how arbitrary scaling functions can be. The Yamaha DMP11 uses values of -12 to $+12$ for pitch-shifting, and those are the logical values offered in the user interface. These values are

Examples of signal-processing parameters that need to be scaled. The input allows the logical numbers as they appear on the Yamaha DMP11 signal processor. The scaling algorithms convert this data to send values of 0 to 127.

Pitch Shift

Pitch shift is up or down one octave. Algorithm scales -12 to + 12 into values between 0 and 127 in increments of 5.3

Delay Time

Delay time is between 2 to 225 ms. Controller output does not take effect until it reaches 15. Algorithm scales values between 2 to 225 into values between 15 and 126, in increments of 2.

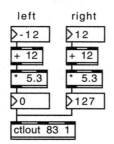

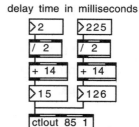

Figure 8.20
Scaling parameters

translated (scaled) using a simple algorithm into the less intuitive, but essential, 0 to 127 controller values sent via **ctlout** to the effects unit. First, 12 is added to the values to put them in a range of 0 to 24. Next, the values are multiplied by 5.3 to produce the 0 to 127 range.

Similarly, delay times, from 2 to 225 milliseconds, are scaled to send values between 15 and 126, in increments of 2. To point out the idiosyncrasies of this particular effects box, the DMP11 does not respond uniformly to controller values 0 to 127. Rather, all controller values below 15 set the same minimum delay time (which is the reason for the +14 offset).

The Future of Max: Audio Input, Signal Processing, and Sound Synthesis

Several projects have shown promising developments in signal processing. Specialized hardware, such as the IRCAM Signal Processing Workstation (ISPW), and several devices based around the Motorola DSP56000 and Silicon Graphics Workstations have demonstrated unprecedented real-time control over sound processing. Many complex processing algorithms that previously took hours to compute on a mainframe computer are already up and running in real time on these systems. The increased flexibility in speed and programming enables composers to create unique processes specifically tailored to a musical need. As this technology becomes more available via software modules, composers will be able to create processes much more closely aligned with their musical concepts, going beyond the standard choices offered by off-the-shelf effects units, such as flanging, chorus, pitch-shift, and reverb. But the current generation of processors still offers a wide range of musical possibilities, most notably the abilities to process a sound using multiple effects and to use interactive signal processing to create the essential materials of a composition.

Around 1990, the evolution of Max split off in two directions. One direction, the current one we are following, saw Max placed in the hands of Opcode, Inc., with David Zicarelli continuing the work that led to the version discussed in this book. The other path, following Miller Puckette and engineers at IRCAM, notably Eric Lindemann, developed a new system that solved many of the problems and limitations inherent in MIDI (Lindeman 1990). What they came up with was the IRCAM Signal Processing Workstation (ISPW), a high-powered accelerator board running on the NeXT computer. With the demise of NeXT as a manufacturer of computers just a few years later, researchers began working on new hardware solutions for Max at IRCAM and the Center for New Music and Technology (CNMAT) at the University of California at Berkeley. The CNMAT version uses Silicon Graphics computers combined with Macintosh computers to place Max in an integrated environment for interactive signal processing and composition. IRCAM has continued the development of "Signal Processing Max" to run on a several different computers. At the University of California at San Diego, Miller Puckette continues his work with Max on the Silicon Graphics platform.

A stable version of Max running on the ISPW for the last few years has proven to be viable as an interactive performance environment. Along with a complete set of familiar Max control objects, the ISPW version includes a large library of signal-processing objects. Along with MIDI, the board is capable of receiving several audio signals. These signals can then be sent to objects for processing. All the techniques discussed earlier involving the automated control of MIDI effects boxes, plus many more sophisticated processes not available commercially, can be achieved in a single unified software environment. The ISPW's processing capabilities go way beyond most commercial MIDI devices, since the board uses general-purpose processors that can be programmed in unlimited ways.

The two classes of Max objects, control and signal objects, create a complete software environment for interactive composition that provides unprecedented control over all aspects of the listener and composer objects. Many complex synthesis techniques, previously available only on non-real-time platforms, are available in real time on the ISPW, allowing a composer to use a single machine and a single programming language to fashion synthesis and signal-processing algorithms according to the demands of a composition rather than the limitations of MIDI gear (Puckette 1991). With this newfound freedom and capability comes a steep learning curve and the need to spend extra time programming the many details required by the system. Hopefully, the added work will pay off in the flexibility and additional options available to explore uncharted territory.

The realization on the ISPW of powerful signal-analysis techniques can eliminate much of the need for external sensing and provides an accurate description of timbre. Several people have employed real-time Fast Fourier Transform (FFT) analyses on the ISPW, which can be used to capture the subtle nuances of timbral changes always present in acoustic music (Settel and Lippe 1994). This opens up a new world of interactive possibilities. Specific harmonics can be followed and mapped to filters, for example, or the strength of upper partials can be used to influence the speed of modulation. Spectral analysis can also be used to control sound-synthesis algorithms residing in software, or via continuous-controller data sent to external MIDI gear. The workstation is fast enough to perform an FFT simultaneously with an extensive network of other signal and control processing. Through the audio signal alone, sophisticated pitch, envelope, and timbre-tracking objects recognize continuous changes during a performance. Thus, one unified system analyzes performer input, processes audio signals, synthesizes sounds, and creates music using compositional algorithms. The ISPW pointed to the future, proving the viability of a single integrated, interactive system. Similar systems are now running on other computer platforms.

9 Score Objects: Compositional Strategies, Structures, and Timing Mechanisms

Compositional Strategies

Previous chapters have shown the vast possibilities for building modules to create computer music influenced by user input. But a music composition is more than just the sum of its parts, and more than a series of isolated events. Composing is the art of combining various parts and elements to form a unified whole. How sections are delineated, how transitions are made, how ideas are presented and developed, and how sounds evolve over time are just some of the essential aesthetic questions that a composer must ask, questions not easily answered by a simple computer algorithm. Timing and scheduling of musical events and processes are crucial to the physical and emotional shape of a composition. Thus, the hardest work comes not in producing musical material, but in shaping, editing, and crafting that material into a convincing musical form, guided by a clear artistic sense of purpose.

The multitude of options available for interactive music makes the art of composing more difficult. The technical possibilities alone can be overwhelming: sampling, synthesis, and signal-processing sound sources, linear and nonlinear structures, improvisational algorithms, improvisational input, fully notated scores, sequenced computer response, and so on. Whether working from a top-down or bottom-up approach, what is needed is a strong aesthetic concept or voice that will help define the purpose, mood, limits, and scope of the work. Scientific phenomena, emotions, poetry, human relationships, narrative, musical processes, sound, and visual art are just some of the influences that may guide the modeling process. A clear concept of how musical ideas are realized through interactive relationships will also suggest how musical structures are formed. Although bottom-up approaches are essential for research and experimentation, defining the work as a whole, its essential purpose, will help inspire an appropriate compositional strategy.

Compositional strategies are plans of action for creating a work. These plans are often formulated in the precompositional stages before detailed work begins, and take the form of musical sketches, diagrams, or prose. Just as computer algorithms are step-by-step plans of action to solve problems, compositional strategies are plans to produce and integrate the disparate elements of a work. These elements include the creation of a score or other instructions for the performer, primary musical material and processes, algorithms for listener and composer objects, a model or framework for structuring the work, and the design of a user interface. Score objects and control objects synchronize the various actions required during the course of a performance—their control messages may come from the computer interface (keyboard and mouse), from the musical interface (MIDI), or from actions automated by the computer.

Compositional strategies for interactive works differ from strategies for other compositions in that they are always governed by the relationship between humans and computers. Will the computer part imitate the performer or will it have its own distinct character? If it has a distinct character, how is this character defined, how does the computer behave in response to particular input, and does that behavior change during the course of a work? Will a performer's response to the computer's music have a large influence over the course of the composition? Will the two be unified into a single grand hyperinstrument or will the computer represent a separate orchestra of intriguing sounds? The human/computer relationship is a central theme of the work; musical concepts and paradigms of interaction go hand in hand. Freedom and control, predetermined or improvisational, communication and response, participation and adaptation—these are the issues that drive interactive compositions and create the inevitable drama that unfolds by the very nature of the technology itself. Identifying the roles played by the members of an interactive ensemble, including the role of the computer, will not only help create a compositional strategy, but will suggest the implementation of appropriate *score mechanisms* and *score structures* comprising one or more *score objects*.

Score Objects

A traditional musical score is an abstract set of symbols that represent instructions for the performer to interpret and execute a series of musical events. It specifies what will be played (notes), how it will be played (dynamics, articulation, verbal instructions, etc.), who will play it (instrumentation) and when it will be played (rhythm, tempo). In other words, the score specifies the timing, coordination, and interpretation of musical events during the entire course of a performance. Similarly, the computer needs its corresponding score specifying timing, scheduling, and interpretation of events. Interactive works, especially in larger forms, contain collections of numerous composer and listener objects that are required at different times during a performance. These objects need to be linked, enabled, disabled, reset, and reconfigured during the course of a performance. The computer score is contained within, and executed by, a category of objects known as score objects.

Score objects come in many different forms; they may or may not have links to a traditional musical score. They act as the "brain" of a program and are comprised of the structures, data, and mechanisms for timing computer events. Score objects handle information passed from one object to another. They can act as interpreters between listener objects and composer objects by setting up the conditions to analyze incoming performance information, assigning composition modules to receive that information, and determining how music and signal processing will be generated based on that information. Also, they can route data, send and receive remote messages, change variables, turn on and off processes, select options, and so on.

Besides making and breaking connections between objects, score objects might contain access to all the parameters of a system, enabling a reconfiguration of the entire system all at once using stored data sets. With the knowledge of all available parameter changes, even those usually controlled by a performer can be automated via the computer. *Score mechanisms* can execute series of complex parameter changes that might be impossible or undesirable to control with the computer interface or with performer actions; they can change all the parameters quickly or slowly over time, as the music warrants.

One important advantage of automating parameter changes is that the computer can initialize the entire system at the beginning of each section, insuring that the proper variables are set even if mistakes have been made during a performance. This has the added benefit of allowing a performer to begin at any section for rehearsal purposes, without having to play through previous sections. Similarly, screen "snapshots" may be used to reset the user interface at the beginning of each section. The user interface may be used in performance to alter score objects, making and breaking connections between objects using the computer keyboard and mouse, and changing variables on the fly. Even when parameters are automated, it is useful to have important parameter changes reflected in the user interface, so that the status of a piece can be monitored.

Anatomy of a Score Object: Score Structures and Mechanisms

Score objects contain a *data structure* (storage objects) that organizes the messages and other data required for a performance, as well as the *mechanisms* (methods) for triggering and delivering these messages to the intended objects. Sometimes actions are produced when specific incoming data are matched to the same data stored in memory (a *match* score). Other times actions are produced based on a more general analysis of a performance or by automated functions. Score structures may include the actual data for producing a musical response, such as pitch information or sequences, and they may also include *control messages* or a separate *control score* to send messages that are not intended for musical output, such as reconfiguring the system by turning on and off processes, resetting parameters, or rerouting data to both listener and composer objects.

Score-object mechanisms are the techniques and methods that define the actions for advancing a computer score or altering its state. They contain the mechanics for identifying performance features via listener objects, translating composer algorithms, making and breaking connections between objects during the course of a work. These are the active sensors that drive a work, determining its form, method of

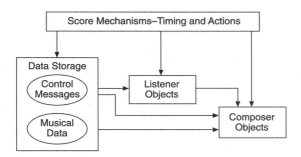

Figure 9.1
Anatomy of a score object

performance synchronization, amount of freedom or indeterminacy, and general quality of interaction (fig. 9.1).

The inevitability of performance or computer errors, and the ways to recover from them, must be considered when creating a score mechanism. Several techniques may be used to minimize errors. First, a backup method to advance the computer's score from one section to the next will allow a computer operator or performer to recover from performance errors. Second, passages where accuracy in performance is crucial to the correct synchronizing of the computer should be written in a way that gives the performer enough time and confidence to insure an accurate reading. Error-checking methods using at least two parameters instead of one, such as looking for pitch and dynamics, or pitches at specific times, also may improve the odds of the computer receiving accurate data. Error filters may also be used to throw out unwarranted double triggers (chap. 6). Finally, many of the most useful and interesting mechanisms are "errorless" in the sense that they cannot fail due to performance errors—they will always function properly no matter what a performer plays. These techniques are especially well-suited for improvisation since they will respond appropriately to any input, rather than waiting to receive expected performer data.

Triggering Changes in Sections and Events

A composition creates form, on a large scale, by the transformation of musical material and the differentiation of various sections. Score structures are often organized into sections, reflecting the processes, functions, and transformations called for in each section of a work. These sections are often musically differentiated and provide good locations for rehearsal letters or starting points. Within larger sections, smaller event-changes describe the moment-to-moment status of a program. Strategies depend on the amount and detail of parameter changes to be controlled by the performer. Score mechanisms may be as detailed as providing a one-to-one response to expected note input, or as broad as identifying a few key events that will advance larger sections, placing the performer in open "states" responsive to any input. This type of section/event structure was implemented in various score-object schemes in the late 1980s by Miller Puckette and Cort Lippe at IRCAM (which will be discussed in more detail in the section "Score Following in Max").

Regardless of the level of detail of local events, a score object usually contains a mechanism for advancing from one larger section to the next. Immediate access to all the primary sections is essential for testing and rehearsal purposes. A simple on-screen **number box** is very helpful to jump to any section of the control score, with all the parameters reset as needed at the start of each location. During a performance, the mechanism to advance the control score may be linked to a performer's score (and therefore triggered by a performer's actions), automated by the computer (as by a **timer**), influenced by improvisational conditions, or advanced by a computer operator using a mouse to coordinate actions.

Performance Synchronization Techniques

Score mechanisms look for "triggers," identifiable actions or conditions that will cause the score to change, sending messages that will alter parameters in the system. Often it is beneficial to organize these messages in data structures that represent all the instructions required for computer actions. Score changes may be triggered by any number of techniques. Those looking for specific event matches (such as expected pitch) are more prone to errors than automated score changes, such as those based on elapsed time, or those that update the computer based on current performance conditions, such as tempo, dynamics, or register. One simple and dependable solution is to dedicate a physical controller for the performer to advance the score, such as a foot pedal, data

Select notes, in order, using a chromatic scale beginning on middle C. Additional notes played between trigger notes will have no effect.

Match broken triads in C major, beginning on middle C. Match will only work if notes are played in the proper order, without others in between. Therefore, triad notes must be played in ascending order. Match is especially useful for identifying small melodic fragments.

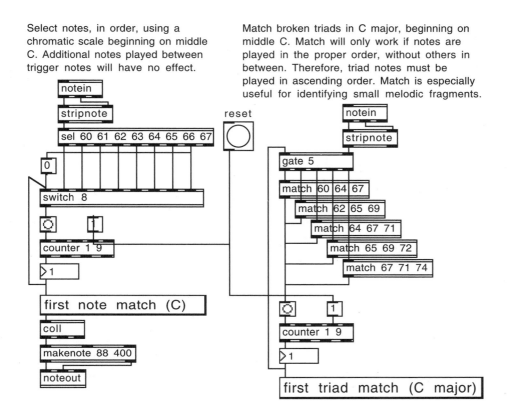

Figure 9.2
Simple score-matching mechanisms

slider, or the highest note on a keyboard, with instructions for section changes written in the score or sensitive to improvisation.

Event-matching requiring specific note input may be identified as a trigger using **select** and **match** (chap. 7). This is the basic technique used in score-following, where the performer's score (expected input) is matched to the same score stored in the computer. However, it is not always necessary to match every note played by a performer. Figure 9.2 shows two mechanisms. The left side uses **select** to hold a list of notes representing an ascending chromatic scale starting on middle C and ending on the G above (the "matching" data structure, or match score). The **switch** allows only one *bang* through at a time. It begins with the first inlet open (the **counter** sends 1 on reset), looking to match the middle C. When middle C is played, it increments the **counter**, opening up the second **switch** inlet to wait for D♯. The expected note input is displayed by indexing a **menu.** The **counter** number could easily be used to index the computer's score, typically a **coll** containing accompaniment or control data. Notice that this mechanism looks only for the next note in the list and ignores other notes played in between. Such a mechanism is a prime candidate for infrequent trigger points placed carefully in the performer's score.

Figure 9.2 uses **match** to identify a series of rolled, root position triads in the key of C major, beginning with middle C. Because **match** will respond only if the integers are received in the listed order, without others in between, it is a prime candidate for identifying melodic fragments, motives, or phrases. Caution must be used for longer phrases, since **match** is unforgiving of errors. (A match simply won't occur if every element is not played in order.) When the first triad is identified, it increments the **counter**, changing the **gate** output to route **notein** to the second **match** object, which identifies the triad, D minor.

With these and other matching methods, instructions must be given to the performer to heighten the importance of playing the proper trigger notes. Since these simple mechanisms do not compensate for performer errors, placing important triggers within difficult musical passages may result in disaster. Isolating trigger notes, or placing them in easy ranges with playable rhythms, will guarantee that the correct triggers are identified.

Similar mechanisms that are more forgiving of errors may be used to detect a range of notes or dynamics using **split, range,** < (less than), or > (greater than). More elaborate conditional statements using **if** can identify unique events or conditions. For example, the computer could trigger an event only if a crescendo is played in the upper register, only if an accelerando includes the note B♭, or only if a specific group of notes is played quietly.

Windowing

The use of **switch** and **gate** in figure 9.2 can be viewed as a series of windows, with only one window available for input. When the desired input is received, the window is closed and the next window opens up. Such *windowing* techniques often designate the span of time in which the program searches for a series of events. In Robert Rowe's Cypher program, for example, the program state is updated when a particular configuration of events is matched, and the next window is opened. (Rowe 1993) To compensate for performance errors, if the specified events are not found within the time frame of a window, the expected state change is made anyway and the next window is opened up automatically. Thus, if a cue is missed, the program will give up waiting for it and continue to the next section.

Event-Counting

Note-based matching may be replaced by or augmented with event-counting, which keeps a running count of a musical event (usually **noteins**) and responds according to the count number. Event-counting strategies are especially useful in situations where pitch data are not always reliable, such as when using a pitch-to-MIDI convertor with acoustic instruments. Even with accurate MIDI data, a performance often contains more pitch errors than rhythmic errors. Event-counting can be used equally well for both previously scored music and for improvisation, or combined with other score-matching techniques.

One basic event-counting technique, *order matching*, contains a match list based on specific event-order numbers, similar to the simple score-matching mechanisms in figure 9.3. For example, a trigger mechanism could simply count the number of notes played from the beginning of each section and trigger changes based on specific note counts, such as triggering a chord on note count three, or panning left on note count five. The **counter** could be reset automatically at the beginning of each section, or, for better accuracy, unique pitched events or physical triggers, such as foot pedals, could be used in conjunction with this method to reset the **counter** at more frequent intervals. In figure 9.3, after playing three low B♭'s in a row (identified by **match**), a **counter** begins, triggering chords on the third and fifth notes. The eighth note resets the mechanism. Delayed and timed actions could just as easily be triggered, such as fading in a synthesizer voice over ten seconds while slowly increasing the tempo. Lists of complex messages like these are best handled by **coll** or can be graphically displayed and edited with envelopes and the **timeline** object. (See below.)

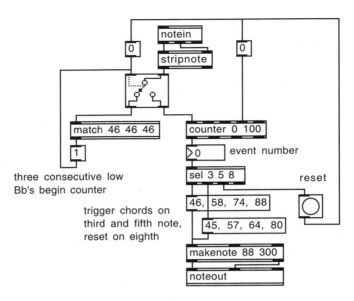

Figure 9.3
Unique event and order-matching

Continuous Updating

Continuous updating looks at the current status of one or more performance parameters and updates composer algorithms accordingly each
time a specified number of items have been identified. A new setting
could be determined by every *n*th note, such as adjusting the computer's dynamic level to match every tenth note of a performance. A
more accurate reflection of a performer's overall dynamic level would
smooth out irregularities by updating the computer's dynamic level
based on the average of the previous ten values, or a percentage of
that average. Of course, this method would not be useful for a section
requiring a sudden, dramatic change.

Figure 9.4 shows two methods for updating the tempo based on delta
time. The frequency of updating is variable. On the left, a **counter**
waits a specified number of delta times before updating the metronome. The valid delta time is the last one played before the **counter**'s
maximum. This method has a number of useful applications, such as
matching the performer's current tempo, taking control of the tempo
away from a performer by using large update numbers, or suspending

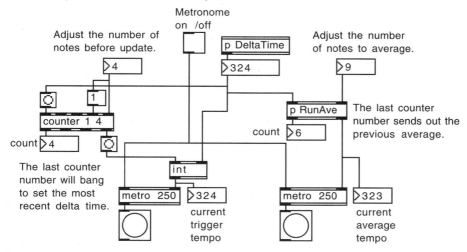

Tap the keyboard to control/adjust. The tempo will be updated with the average of a selected number of previous values.

Figure 9.4
Continuous update

computer processes until a specified number of notes have passed. However, it may be error-prone since it relies on a single delta time to accurately represents tempo. On the right side, **RunAve** (fig. 6.31) keeps a running average of a specified number of delta times. This smooths out the small variations in values, getting a general sense of how performance features, such as tempo, register, or dynamic level, change over larger periods of time.

Triggering Based on Time

Continuously updating the current status of various parameters could also take place at regular time intervals by simply replacing the **counter** in the previous examples with a **timer.** For example, every four seconds a composer algorithm could adjust its phrase length based on the previous average of incoming velocity values. Continuous updating strategies like this demonstrate "errorless" trigger mechanisms; there can be no "wrong" notes played or other performer errors that would cause the score to fail. Other events may be automated or triggered at regular time intervals using **timer, delay, pipe, clocker,** or **timeline.**

Timeline

Timeline is a dedicated and complete score-mechanism object, a time-based graphical score containing messages. It was specifically created to fulfill the need for a standardized global score object that could handle event-timing and synchronization of multiple objects. A score can be played via a tape transport interface using familiar play, stop, and rewind controls. A time ruler shows time in milliseconds, with a double arrow used as the current time indicator. Messages created in **timeline** represent the *events* comprising the score. These messages can be sent to any number of patches at specific times; as the time indicator approaches one or more events, it sends the indicated messages to the target objects. Far from being a simple playback device, **timeline** has a large list of commands that allows it to pause, start, loop, and change the clock source that determines its speed. It can be used nonlinearly to jump from one location to another with the *locate* message followed by a number representing time. A marker with a descriptive name can also be used to locate a specific point in the score using the *search* message. This is especially helpful in locating specific sections of a large work for rehearsal purposes and for dealing with nonlinear structures. All these functions can be automated or made to respond to performer input. A global **timeline** is available under the NEW menu. **Timelines** embedded in patches are also available.

Three components make up the score: the **timeline** object, events (**timeline** messages), and the target patches receiving the messages. The target patches contain the algorithms or actions that will result from the messages, usually composer objects. Each action patch will contain at least one special inlet, an object called **tiCmd** (**timeline** command), that connects specific **timeline** messages with a specific target patch. In a process similar to remote-receive messages, the connection is specified by a unique name given as the first argument of **tiCmd**. **Timeline** is aware of all the **tiCmd** names in a patch, and makes them available in a menu that appears by pressing the option key and holding the mouse down in the **timeline** window. Subsequent arguments to **tiCmd** specify the type of expected data: integer (i), bang (b), float (f), symbol (s), list (l), and all (a)—a whole message that begins with a symbol. Each specified data type will create a corresponding outlet in the **tiCmd** object. Depending on the data type, special event-

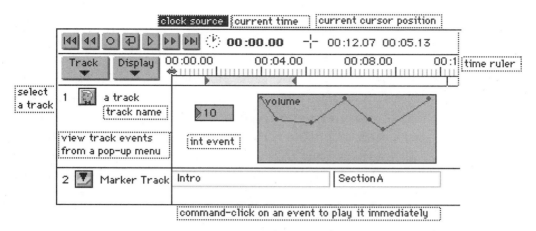

Figure 9.5
timeline

editors will appear in the **timeline** window. For example, a familiar **message box** appears for symbols. However, it begins with the name of the **tiCmd** object to which its message will be sent. The **etable** editor is one of three options that appear for editing integers. It treats the familiar **table** object as an event, with values sent out as the time indicator graphically passes corresponding addresses. **Etable** can be scaled to send out data at a faster or slower rate by clicking and dragging the bottom right corner to resize the object. Similarly, **efun** can be scaled. It is a graphic function editor, with click and drag controls to create breakpoints.

Any number of action patches can be assembled in multiple tracks of the **timeline,** with one action patch per track (fig. 9.5). Clicking on the tracks button will reveal a list of patch names stored in a special Timeline Action Folder (as specified in Preferences). Releasing on a name will create a new track. (Action patches may be stored anywhere, but only those contained in the Timeline Action Folder will appear with the tracks button.) Tracks can be resized, rearranged, and muted. QuickTime movies can be played in any track if a **movie** object is placed in an action patch. Also, a movie can be played directly from **timeline** using the **emovie** editor, without any corresponding **tiCmd** object. However, connecting a **tiCmd** inlet to a **movie** object will allow **timeline** to send it messages to read in new files, change the playback speed, start at any frame, or any of the other **movie** messages. (See chap. 10 for information on QuickTime movies.)

In addition to the use of **timeline** as a single global score control for an entire work, the exact same functions are available as a separate objects within a patch or a subpatch. In fact, multiple **timeline** objects may be used in a single program. Typing **timeline** within an object box creates a new object. **Timeline** files may be saved and automatically loaded as a first argument, with a second argument determining the number of outlets. Messages such as *play, stop, read, mute [track number]*, may be sent to the inlet of a **timeline** object within a patch. (See the Opcode's **timeline** tutorial for more information.)

In addition, the **setclock** object allows all Max's timing objects, such as **timeline, pipe,** and **metro,** to be controlled by a timing source other than the standard millisecond default. This could include an external SMPTE time-code source, or timing information from another application, such as a sequencer or digital video program. External time sources enter Max via the **timein** object. There are many other options for timing sources and synchronization.

Score Structure Examples: Models of Score Objects

The addition of **timeline** to Max version 3.0 created a much-needed score mechanism that provides an overview of timing and actions for all objects during the course of a performance. **Detonate** was shipped with Max 3.5, adding flexible graphical recording, editing, and playback of multitrack sequences and score-following functions. (**Detonate** was based on Miller Puckette's **explode** object, which has been used for many years.)

Prior to these additions, the absence of such global objects for score organization forced many composers to develop unique mechanisms tailored for their compositions, and examples of these methods are still workable and useful (and may even be incorporated into a **timeline** object). Some of these models have been generalized and reused for a number of works, with the mechanisms and data structures remaining unchanged, and new data sets loaded in for each new work.

Below are some strategies for creating and choosing appropriate score objects, followed by a description of several basic types of score objects.

This is by no means a complete list. In fact, these examples are fairly simple and generalized, presented here as models for further elaboration. New techniques are often required to create score objects dedicated to the needs of a single composition.

Sequencing Techniques

There is not much point in going through the trouble of creating and performing an interactive work if very little will change from one performance to the next. For predetermined works that require little interaction, the tape and instrument format has the practical advantages of flawless, dependable playback, portability, and easy distribution. Furthermore, well-crafted works can simulate computer/performer interaction, incorporating the performer's expected tempo changes, dynamics, timbre, articulation, and phrasing into a fixed tape part. Still, the performer's interpretation is not reflected in the tape playback, and the unresponsiveness is especially noticeable with regard to tempo. Other potential problems of synchronization arise when the tape requires stopping and starting during a performance, or, in longer works, requires locating the beginning of sections for rehearsals. In fact, much of the early research in interactive systems was in response to these problems.

One simple and elegant solution is suggested by William Kleinsasser's Sequence Control program (fig. 9.6). In effect, the program replaces the typical tape playback system found in works for acoustic instruments and tape. Numbers on the computer keyboard provide easy access to nine different sequences, with start times, order, and tempo "performed" from the front panel by a computer operator. The interface contains a large message window where preprogrammed messages automatically appear at the right time to remind the computer operator to set devices, cue performers, or begin a countdown to the next sequence. Performers can also control sequence playback using a MIDI sustain pedal to advance to the next sequence. (**Detonate** could also be used to store multitrack sequences with more flexible playback options.)

The tempo-control section takes the original tempo of the recorded sequence and scales it according to a tempo tapped on the computer's

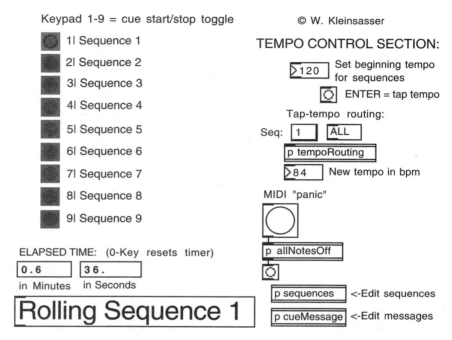

"Front-panel" for controlling the playback of multiple sequences for live performance of electro-acoustic music.

Keypad 1-9 = cue start/stop toggle

© W. Kleinsasser

1I Sequence 1
2I Sequence 2
3I Sequence 3
4I Sequence 4
5I Sequence 5
6I Sequence 6
7I Sequence 7
8I Sequence 8
9I Sequence 9

TEMPO CONTROL SECTION:

▷120   Set beginning tempo for sequences

◎ ENTER = tap tempo

Tap-tempo routing:

Seq: 1   ALL

p tempoRouting

▷84   New tempo in bpm

MIDI "panic"

p allNotesOff

ELAPSED TIME: (0-Key resets timer)

0.6   36.
in Minutes   in Seconds

p sequences <-Edit sequences
p cueMessage <-Edit messages

Rolling Sequence 1

Figure 9.6
Sequence control

enter key (keyboard delta time). As long as the initial sequences were recorded at a steady tempo, and that tempo is entered into the "set beginning tempo for sequences," the tap tempo will accurately scale the original music to the tap tempo. This gives the computer operator some control in synchronizing a performer to sequence playback and accommodating a performer's tempo changes during the course of a piece. The computer operator can, in effect, conduct the computer music playback tempo to match the performance. Similarly, the tap tempo function can be controlled by a second foot pedal, allowing the performer to set the tempo. Sequence Control was first used in Kleinsasser's *Threads of Mitoses* (1993), a work synchronizing two saxophones with sequences playing saxophone sounds stored on a MIDI sampler. Another work, *Wings of Daedalus,* uses a custom-made baton to allow a conductor to control sequence tempo and playback (Kleinsasser 1993).

Master Preset

The **preset** object has already been shown to be a useful score object (chap. 5) since it can store and recall all the settings of user interface objects within its own window, or those connected to its outlet. For larger programs, a series of **preset** objects may be used to configure, store, and recall the parameter settings needed for a performance. For ease of operation, a master **preset** may be designated as the primary object used to control other **preset** objects, or subscores, embedded in subpatches.

Master Preset (fig. 9.7) is an example of a score mechanism used in the author's FollowPlay program. A front control panel contains controls to *store, recall,* and *clear* event settings from a **preset.** Selecting a number under Store Event and hitting the **bang button** beneath, will store the current interface settings. A recall number will call back any settings stored at that number. **Master Preset** Object contains storage for hundreds of events. Preset numbers do not need to be stored or accessed consecutively; a blank address will simply not make any changes.

A composer may wish to work directly with a traditional score, circling and numbering expected score events corresponding to index numbers stored in **preset.** During a performance or rehearsal, a computer operator could follow a score, advancing the score using the advance **bang button,** or a performer could advance sections using a foot pedal. Sections may begin at any event, since the recall **number box** provides random access to all event locations. Care must be taken to insure that variables are initialized at the start of sections.

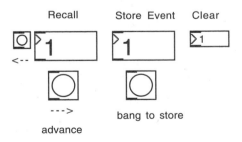

Figure 9.7
Master **preset** interface

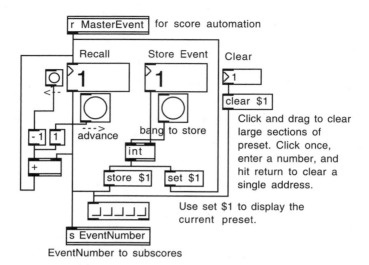

Figure 9.8
Master **preset** score object

Looking beneath the interface reveals a remote **MasterEvent** input that allows performers or score mechanisms to advance the score (fig. 9.8). The advance mechanism, to the left, could easily be replaced with the **IncDec** object. However, in the heat of a performance it is safer to have an extra large advance (increment) control that is physically separated from decrement control. The *clear $1* message will clear any information stored at the specified index number. Care should be taken when clicking and dragging, since all values will erase the corresponding **preset** contents. The store-event mechanism, in fact, is a fail-safe mechanism to prevent writing over previously stored scores by clicking and dragging.

The master-event number is broadcast to subpatches containing similar **preset** objects. These subprograms control the variables within their subpatch, and can be edited and tested on local events (within the window). Figure 9.9 shows just the interface portion of a Preset Subscore. This structure can be copied and pasted into any number of windows to allow coordination of multiple events from a single master. These imbedded **presets** are useful interactive tools for developing a work, since user interface objects enable quick experimentation with musical processes, and all the parameters can be saved at any point along the way as a screen snapshot. These controls can be hidden be-

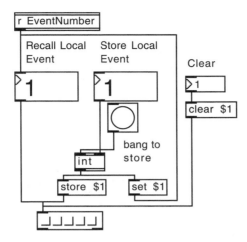

Figure 9.9
preset subscore

cause they are not needed during a performance. Thus, several large modules or subprograms contain interfaces affecting only their own internal parameter settings, while the **Master Preset** object is designed to control all the others during a performance.

Remote Parameter Lists

The original version of FollowPlay contains a score object with a "peel off" user interface, sending over sixty significant parameters fitted with corresponding remote **send** and **receive** objects to hidden subpatches. Any or all of these parameters can also be changed and automated by large lists of *send* messages. Since the **receive** objects are given descriptive names specifying their function, the lists of corresponding *send* messages are easy to read and edit, and provide an overview of the state of the entire system. These lists may be printed out and indexed to the performer's score. Computer access to all available parameters allows for complex changes that would not be possible from the interface alone. The status of parameters may be updated and viewed in the user interface. However, care must be taken to avoid remote feedback-loops, caused by sending a remote message back to the object that sent it. Figure 9.10 shows how a number box sending out remote data may be updated by remote lists using the message *set $1,* which displays the incoming data without output.

To use both interface and score objects, use set $1 to reflect automated changes in interface (without causing a feedback loop).

Figure 9.10

Updating the interface with remote messages

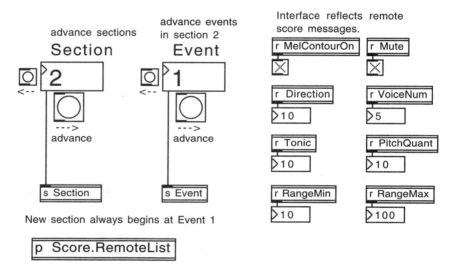

Figure 9.11

FollowPlay front panel example

Figure 9.11 shows a small model of another FollowPlay score object, with five sections and eight parameters changeable from the list. More sections, events, and parameters can easily be added to this model. (The original version of FollowPlay has over sixty changeable parameters.) The score structure is divided into sections and events (after Cort Lippe's score object). Each **Section** begins with event 1, which resets all parameters so that necessary information will be sent to FollowPlay modules and MIDI equipment. Sections can have flexible states that change parameters continuously according to performance information. After a section is initialized, changes are handled by **Events,**

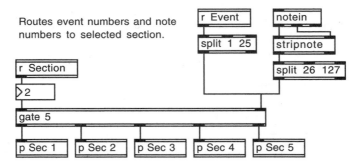

Figure 9.12
Section Control (subpatch of fig. 9.11)

which are identical to Sections, but only make the necessary parameter changes within each section. With Events, any parameter can change immediately or can be set to smoothly change from one value to another over a specified amount of time using the **line** object. This feature is an especially helpful creative tool, allowing composers to hear and experiment with time-varying compositional processes.

Various strategies can be used to advance to the next event including score-following, event-following, absolute time, or any condition set up in the performance data modules. For example, during a musical passage that contains legato and staccato passages, **Articulation-History** can be called upon to track performer articulations, and send messages to **SigPro** (signal processor) to increase reverberation time during a legato passage and decrease the time during a staccato passage. In a similar way, composer objects could receive messages to lengthen or shorten the time of accompanying phrases.

Figure 9.11 shows the interface. The previously mentioned advance and rewind buttons control the location in the computer score. Hidden remote receive boxes [**r GoToSection**] and [**r GoToEvent**], can access the main **number boxes**, making random access to events and sections possible from anywhere in the system. Parameters to the right are available to receive remote messages, reflecting any changes in the score. (For this example, these objects simply receive numbers.) The object **Score.RemoteList** contains the messages and the mechanism needed to communicate to the various parameters.

Inside **Score.RemoteList**, figure 9.12, a mechanism enables one section at a time, routing event numbers and note data to the selected

Events for section 1. Select triggers remote messages in two different ways: by receiving Event numbers from the interface or by using follow as an index to trigger events. Events and sections can be accessed remotely by sending numbers to remote receives [GoToSection] and [GoToEvent].

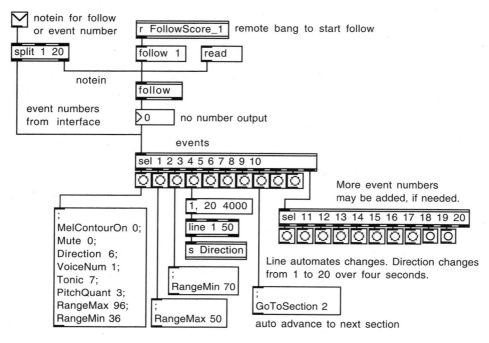

Figure 9.13
Section 1 (subpatch of fig. 9.12)

gate output. **Split** objects insure that numbers one through twenty-five are reserved for event number selection, with MIDI *notenumbers* allowed above twenty-five.

Inside each section is a series of remote lists of events, accessed by a number to **select.** An event may be triggered in three ways: by physically controlling the **Score** and **Event** interface objects in the front panel, by allowing a process or condition within the program to make a selection by sending numbers to [**r GoToSection**] and [**r GoToEvent,**] and by using the **follow** object to output trigger numbers based on incoming pitch data.

In figure 9.13, the first event sets all the variables using a remote send list. The next event changes [**r RangeMax**] to 50, and the third event changes [**r RangeMin**] to 70. Event number four starts an automated process. Using **line,** the behavior of melodic [**r Direction**] can be

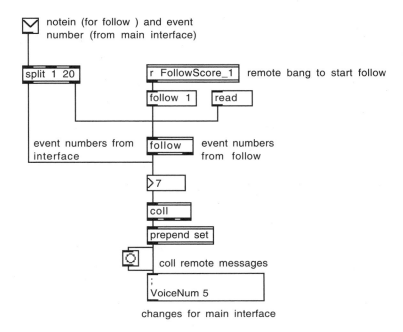

Figure 9.14
Remote score lists using **coll**

triggered to change over four seconds, from very short rapidly turning ostinati, to long, sweeping, and dramatic runs.

Figure 9.14 shows a similar score-object section using **coll** to store and retrieve lists of messages. The **coll** stores these messages neatly, and provides many features for organizing data. The previous method, while being a bit messy, is more immediate.

Score-Following Overview

Much of the early research in interactive music was fueled by a desire to solve "most of the synchronization problems inherent in taped accompaniment" (Dannenberg 1984) and "to recognize the machine's potential . . . as an intelligent and musically informed collaborator in live performance" (Vercoe and Puckette 1985). Whereas Dannenberg's earliest work concentrated on providing a computer accompanist who could synchronize with a performer, Vercoe strived to "replace any member of an ensemble by a synthetic performer (computer model) so that the others cannot tell the difference."

Since then, score-following concepts have evolved to include a group of techniques that match a performer's score to an analogous score stored in the computer. Score following is just one of many ways to organize an interactive work. Traditional score following assumes a fully notated, predetermined score, with the computer attempting to follow, linearly, the performer's note-by-note location during a performance. The computer then supplies an accompaniment by matching notes (or other expected input) from the performer to a similar score or a "match list" stored in memory. Score following can also be used as the primary synchronizing mechanism to start and stop computer processes during the course of a piece.

If note-by-note following is not essential to the realization of a work, less frequent event matches can be used to set the computer's tempo and dynamic level, or to trigger other processes. In fact, a smaller match list is usually more dependable, since it creates fewer opportunities for performance errors. A typical problem would be a trill or tremolo. In a circumstance such as this, where the follower has a high probability of failure on a note-by-note basis, simply matching the starting note and waiting for the fast notes to subside would yield a more dependable accompaniment (Puckette and Lippe 1992).

In most score-following algorithms, a series of designated "match points" enables score-following algorithms to track the location of a performer within a fully notated score. Thus, the computer is expected to synchronize itself with a performer automatically. At least three components make up a score follower: a performer's score, a computer version of the expected input from the performer (a "match" score), and an accompanying score stored in the computer that may produce music directly and/or act as a control score for other processes. The "match" score compares the performance to a score stored in memory, determining the performer's score location and tempo. The performer can speed up or slow down and algorithms compensate for errors such as wrong notes, added notes, or skipped notes. According to Vercoe's method,

the best theory of the current tempo is then used to drive a realization of an accompaniment. A pattern-matching process directs the search of a space of tempo theories. The derived tempo is used to schedule events for an accompanying part, played by the computer, whose rhythmic presentation follows the live performer—adapting its tempo to that of its human partner. The machine adjusts its speed of scheduling the accompaniment part by matching the notes arriving in real time to the score stored in the computer. (Vercoe 1984)

Rowe (1993) explains that "such applications are unique in that they anticipate what a human player will do: the derivation of tempo is in fact a prediction of the future spacing of events in a human performance based on an analysis of the immediate past."

Dannenberg and Vercoe's research caused a flurry of related developments in the mid-1980s that continues to this day. Interactor, a graphically-based programing language developed by Mark Coniglio and Morton Subotnick, provides a fast and reliable score-following mechanism by combining several techniques. First, the accurate measurement of tempo, not pitch identification, is the primary information used to follow a score. Tempo updating is not continuous, but occurs only at points in the score where a change is expected. Erroneous data is filtered out by specifying the allowable maximum and minimum tempo for each tempo change, as well as the allowable percentage of change based on the previous tempo. (See **TempoWindow** in chap. 6.) A smoothing algorithm makes less abrupt changes in tempo by combining a percentage of the old tempo with a percentage of the new. Finally, they incorporated a method first proposed by Vercoe and Puckette, whereby the computer could "rehearse" with a performer, learning the tempo at each moment, and thus being able to better predict future tempo changes.

Interactor uses eight different timing sources based on beats per minute, rather than a fixed time unit, such as milliseconds. Unique combinations of pitches and rhythms in the score are marked and used to determine the location of the performer within a score. As a demonstration, using only unique combinations of dyads and the rhythmic distance between them, the program is able to successfully synchronize the right hand of a Debussy prelude, played by the performer, with the left hand, played by the computer. Whenever a match is found, the computer jumps to the point in the score and begins playing the left-hand sequence. Once the program has located its position in the score, the computer follows the performer's tempo, and at those times is immune to errors of pitch. The match list of unique events also facilitates rehearsals by automatically orienting the computer whenever a match is found (Coniglio 1992).

Another promising method locates a performer in a score through the recognition of rhythmic patterns, with pitch information used as a backup method when temporal pattern prediction fails. This makes sense, since both rhythm and pitch are known prior to a performance and most performance errors are made in pitch, not in rhythm (Vantomme 1994). Many researchers have developed real-time beat-tracking algorithms, enabling a computer to follow the tempo of any performance, including jazz improvisation, based on algorithms that determine the most likely pulse. (For more information and a complete reference on beat tracking, see Peter Desain and Henkjan Honing's "Foot-tapping: a Brief Introduction to Beat Induction.")

Score Following Objects

Max contains a number of special objects useful in creating score-following systems. **Follow** is a score reader, allowing the computer to follow a performer's score, synchronizing computer music by matching incoming *Note-On* messages with a similar score stored as a sequence in the computer's memory. (**Detonate** takes the *follow* message, with very similar results.) Each note number in a **follow** object (the score) is paired with a consecutively ordered index number. When an incoming note is matched, **follow** sends the index number out the left outlet. The index number, representing the location in the score, may then be used to trigger events in the computer's score as the performer arrives at various locations. A typical use of the index would be to access accompaniment or send messages stored in a **coll** or other data structure.

The computer's score often requires two different types of responses. Parallel events, which occur simultaneously between the performer's score and a computer accompaniment, are easily triggered with a match number. Interim events are scheduled by the computer between notes played by the performer; for instance, the computer responds with triplets to every quarter-note played (Vantomme 1994). These interim events are most often scheduled at a percentage of the current tempo. The percentage, as well as duration, may be stored along with pitch information in a **coll.**

Follow will ignore note numbers not designated as location points. Thus, it is not often necessary to match every single note in a performer's score. The beginning of a measure or a small section may be all that is needed to trigger musical processes. To supply a note-for-note accompaniment, a more detailed match list is needed. But even then, certain playing techniques, such as trills or tremolos, should have the first note only as the identifying marker, with the indeterminate aspects ignored.

The **follow** score is a sequence recorded as either full MIDI messages using **midiin**, or as integers using **notein.** Sending the message *follow* prepares the object to begin following a performance, matching incoming pitch numbers with the recorded score. As each successive note in the score is matched, **follow** sends the corresponding index number out the left side.

Follow takes many of the same messages as **seq.** It can *read* and *write* files, and takes an optional argument specifying the name of a file stored on disk. Sequence recording and playback uses *record, bang, stop,* and *delay.* An integer included in the *follow* message, such as *follow 4,* will begin following the score at index number 4 (i.e., it will ignore indices 1, 2, and 3).

It is important that score followers accommodate typical performance errors. This is perhaps the most difficult and crucial aspect of score following. **Follow** will attempt to follow a score even if the input does not exactly match the stored score. It has a simple built-in algorithm for error detection; it first checks each incoming number with the current location in the score, and if a match is not found it looks ahead to the next two notes in the list. Therefore, if a performer misses a note or two, **follow** will look two notes ahead and jump to the point in the score where a match is found. If more serious errors are performed, **follow** can easily loose its place. Other methods may be used as backup score locators in case of such mistakes. For example, in addition to **follow,** unique matched events, foot pedals, or on-screen buttons may be used to help locate the start of each small section. Many more elaborate error-avoidance and recovery schemes have been demonstrated in other score-following systems, such as using previous rehearsals to predict the current tempo (Vercoe and Puckette 1985), using melodic segments as match elements (Baird, Blevins, and Zahler 1993) or finding the best match by computing a matrix comparing the stored score with the performance (Dannenberg and Bloch 1985; see also Stammen and Pennycook 1993; Rowe and Li 1994; Grubb and Dannenberg 1994).

Stores note numbers for match score. Indexes the computer
score in coll, with accompaniment in tempo taken from Delta.

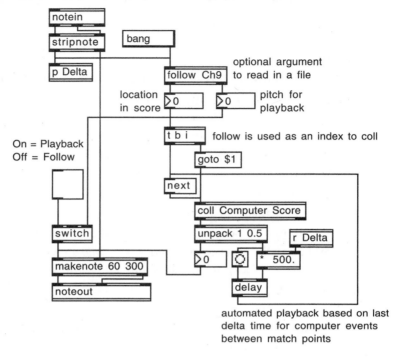

Figure 9.15
follow

However, **follow** can be useful for a variety of simple score-following purposes. In figure 9.15, the location numbers output by **follow** are used to index a computer score stored in **coll**. Simultaneous events are simply played at the index location. Each index number triggers one note number output. For computer events occurring between matches (interim events) the **coll** contains pairs of numbers representing pitch and rhythm. The rhythm is a scaling factor for the last reported delta time. For example, if the performer just played a quarter note, and the computer rhythm is a sixteenth, the scaling factor would be 0.25. Each note automatically sends a *next* message, in time, to the **coll**, thereby playing the next note in **coll**. Simultaneous events are listed in the **coll** by integers representing match points, whereas interim events are labelled as subsets [*3_2, 3_3, 3_4*]. This labeling is not a convention in Max, but is just a helpful way to remember the order of events. Typically, a composer working with a full score will label all performer match events and computer-response events before going through the trouble of creating a computer score. Opening up the **coll** reveals the contents shown in figure 9.16.

In a similar way, **follow** may be used to start and stop sequences, with the sequence playback tempo controlled by the performer. For creating the computer score, the **detonate** object is a convenient way to get large amounts of information into the computer. Techniques used in **ParamRecordColl** (fig. 7.34) can facilitate data entry into a **coll.** Using parsed MIDI files, the computer accompaniment can be first created using a notation program or MIDI sequencer before it is imported into a **coll.**

Explode is a nonsupported object designed by Miller Puckette for the purpose of score following (Puckette 1990). Over the course of many years of production at IRCAM, this reasonably sturdy score-following mechanism has proven invaluable. **Explode** is often used in conjunction with **Qlist**, a list of event messages that may be triggered when a match is found. While these two objects are not listed in the manual, they will serve as valuable models for study. **Detonate** is based on the **explode** object, with expanded graphic and editing capabilities. The score-following features and techniques described for **explode** also apply to **detonate**. **Qlist** functions can be duplicated with **coll.** (See chapter 9 disk example, **Qlist** and **coll.**)

1, 66 0.5;	On the first match note, play 66 and go to the next line in half the current delta time (eighth notes if the performer was playing quarter-note beats).
1_2, 68, 0.5;	Play 68, then go to the next line in 0.5 * delta.
1_3, 70;	Play 70, then stop and wait for the next cue.
2, 88;	On the second match note, play 88, then stop.
3, 77 0.25; 3_2, 76 0.25; 3_3, 75 0.25; 3_4, 74;	On the third match note, play 77 followed by sixteenth notes, 76, 75, and 74. Stop at 74.
4, 47;	On the fourth match, play 47, then stop.

Figure 9.16
follow coll

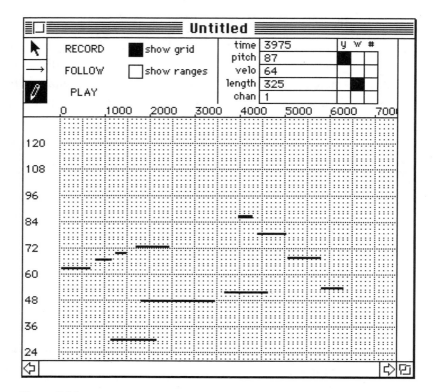

Figure 9.17
Explode: graphic editing

    Explode is a successor to **follow**, and they are similar in some ways: both record MIDI data, play it back, and accept the *follow* message to begin following a score. The five inlets and outlets of **explode** correspond to (from left to right) time, pitch, velocity, duration (length), and MIDI channel. Double clicking on **explode** reveals a flexible, multilevel graphical editor for score data. Any of the parameters mentioned can be viewed graphically or as numerical data.

    Figure 9.17 shows the **explode** editor. In the bottom grid, notes are represented in a familiar "piano roll" style editor (proportional notation). The left side of the graph (x axis) shows MIDI note numbers. Across the top (y axis) the time, in milliseconds, is displayed. Any note can be clicked and dragged to a new position. Groups of notes may be moved in a similar way using the selection tool in the upper left corner. The standard Macintosh cut, copy, and paste commands may be applied. A drawing tool (the pencil in the upper left corner) can be used to draw in new notes.

Explode contains the match score on MIDI channel 1. It can also contain an accompanimental score or a control score on other MIDI channels. When a match is made on MIDI channel one, all events on the other channels prior and up to that moment are sent out. Typically, a control score is embedded on MIDI channel 2, which outputs consecutively numbered event "hits" on a separate channel (much as **follow** outputs numbers representing successful matches). The event numbers are then indexed to a data structure that sends out control messages.

The data structure initially used for this purpose, **qlist,** was created by Miller Puckette to hold a collection of messages, either an **int** or **float,** or a list of **ints** and/or **floats. Qlist** is also designed to send remote messages by beginning a message with the name of a remote **receive** object followed by data to send. The *next* message outputs the next message in the list. The *rewind* message begins playing the messages back from the beginning. A semicolon is used as a separator between messages. **Qlist** can output a series of timed events in response to a single score match, similar to the technique using **coll** previously discussed.

Cort Lippe's score-following example uses **explode** to follow a score, and outputs consecutively numbered "event" markers when specific locations are reached (figs. 9.18, 9.19, and 9.20). These event-marker numbers serve as cues that are used to output messages in **qlist.** Thus, **qlist** holds the messages required to control the computer's score. Each section of a large work has its own **explode/qlist** configuration. More details of their use, a help file, a detailed score object, and a tutorial written by Cort Lippe can be found in the chapter 9 disk example, Explode/Qlist Score Following.

Useful score objects and score-following techniques are of high interest to computer music researchers, and are making their way into commercial products and applications. Roger Dannenberg's score-following algorithm, for example, has been licensed by Coda for a music-teaching system that provides automated, flexible computer accompaniment to students learning the standard classical repertoire. Interactive CD-ROM titles, CDI (interactive music CDs), installations, and multimedia performances are all able to take advantage of the many years of research devoted to how humans may influence the precise coordination and timing of computer events.

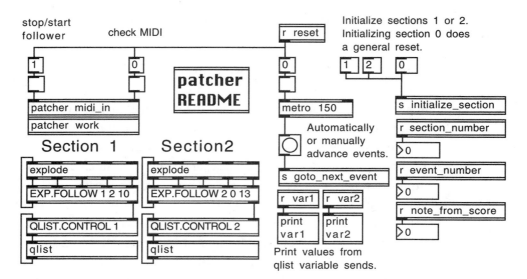

Figure 9.18
Score-following example by Cort Lippe

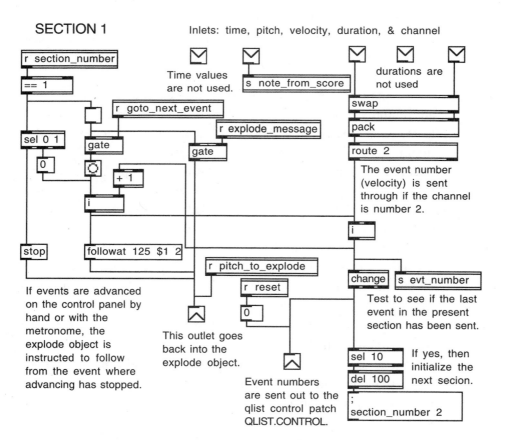

Figure 9.19
Explode-Qlist section (subpatch of fig. 9.18)

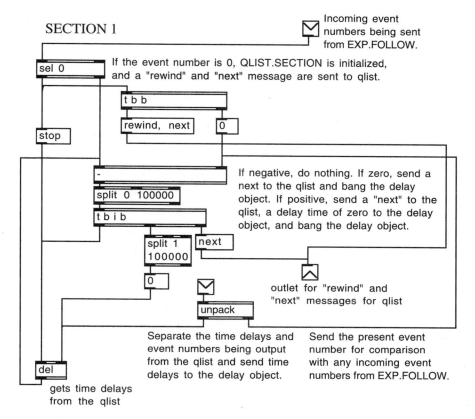

Figure 9.20
Qlist control (subpatch of fig. 9.18)

Designing Score Objects for Actions

Issues of indeterminacy and control will define the type of actions required in both the larger structure and the smaller events. Creating algorithms responsive to *any* performer input is a very different task from writing algorithms for specific, *expected* performer input. Triggering prestored sequences will require a different approach than shaping flexible, changeable compositional algorithms. As was stated in chapter 2, predetermined scores and algorithms allow composers to create detailed, polished, dependable, and repeatable works. On the other hand, introducing aspects of indeterminacy offers more freedom and spontaneity, a chance for dialog, and the excitement of the unexpected. Some of the potential scenarios for predetermined and indeterminate actions, discussed in chapter 2, are summarized below.

Predetermined Score and Predetermined Computer Sequences

The least interactive of all are models with all or most aspects of a piece predetermined. If a score and the resulting computer part are intended to be identical for every performance, then a composition for performer and tape (or tape alone) might be more appropriate. Most often, however, the composer desires to break away from the unyielding structure of tape music, calling upon the performer to supply the tempo and possibly dynamic information, the "conductor model," to impart some human expression to an expected computer accompaniment. This category is a prime candidate for score-following techniques using **detonate or follow**, where the computer contains some information about the performer's score, and matches incoming events to play a predetermined sequence of events.

Predetermined Score and Indeterminate Computer Actions

With a notated score, the computer could still be aware of the location in a score, or contain a list of expected events, and use that knowledge to trigger flexible or improvisational algorithms, start and stop events, or automated functions such as mixing or panning. Of course, expected performance information could also be sent to composer objects that generate music with any input, such as those producing arpeggios or canons. General performance features such as phrasing, register, and articulation, could also be used on a matched or non-matched basis.

Performer Improvisation and Predetermined Computer Sequences

Here an improvisation triggers predetermined sequences, with the computer looking for basic categories of actions or musical features. The order of sequences could be linear, triggered by the number of notes played, the time elapsed, or specific pitches. The order could also be nonlinear, responding to listener data such as register, dynamics, or specific notes or chords. This is the method usually used for most computer-game and CD-ROM soundtracks, where the same sampled loop or prerecorded soundfile is played back without change each time a specified situation or action occurs within a nonlinear structure. A large collection of predetermined material may add more detail and variety to the musical response, and even simulate a quasi-random result, but the material itself does not change.

Improvisation and Indeterminate Computer Actions

This option has a wide range of possibilities. In the most open examples, a performer may play anything, and the computer will respond with something that is unexpected and unrepeatable, but which, hopefully, makes sense to the performer and to the audience. With total freedom comes the possibility of producing wildly random, chaotic, and incomprehensible results. The sensibilities and skills of the performer are most crucial to the success of this type of work, as are the response capabilities of the software.

Very often performers will play guided improvisations, with musical suggestions supplied by a composer or practiced beforehand by a performer. This may take the form of a short score or a list of musical fragments, with the composer supplying the basic musical materials on which to improvise. This could be an approach similar to a typical jazz ensemble using a written lead sheet consisting of a tune and chord progression as the basis for improvisation. As was seen in chapter 7, composer algorithms may also improvise using such methods by taking basic musical material and processing it to create elaborate variations.

Finally, there are no rules governing the use or combination of the methods described above—all have merits that composers will find useful. Sore objects are as varied as the compositions they create; they will inevitably reflect the musical concepts and the structure dictated by the demands of the composition and the desired quality of interaction. Strictly notated sections may be followed by improvisational "states," with prewritten performer cues used to advance to the next section. The score object might give or take away the ability of performers to control algorithms at any time, replacing improvisational computer events with sequences. Thus, the actions permitted the performer and computer through these score objects define their relationship and prospective roles. The most efficient techniques are those tailored to the required actions. Often a simple solution is overlooked in favor of a complex one with identical results. However, the best solutions offer elegance and clarity using a minimal amount of technology.

10 *Interactive Multimedia and New Controllers*

It is hard to believe that creating music with computers was only recently considered an esoteric subject. From the invention of the first computer music by Max Mathews in 1958, the field developed slowly at first at just a handful of research centers and universities. The pace of development has increased exponentially in the last ten years, paralleling breakthroughs in computer science and the wide availability of sophisticated technology. Music has lead the way among the arts in providing inexpensive tools capable of professional production work, mainly because it has minimal computing requirements. In fact, digital recording and other computer music techniques have become the primary means of producing, editing, and distributing music. Most music, if not originally produced with a computer, is at least recorded and played back in digital form. Besides compact disk titles, computer music finds its way into computer games, multimedia educational titles, CD-ROM, the Internet, and even class papers (sound clips may be included in standard Microsoft Word files, for example). Techniques involving digital recording, sound synthesis, and signal processing are no longer the exclusive domain of high-priced studios, but are available on most personal computers. Recently, prices for high quality digital video and graphics capabilities have fallen rapidly to the point where most computers are now sold with "multimedia" features, which may include "CD quality" digital audio and 24-bit video and graphics. As these features become as ubiquitous as the mouse, the nature of personal computing is shifting from a text-based medium to a language that incorporates the richness of images and sound.

The convergence of various artistic disciplines, united in the digital domain, has had a tremendous impact on all the arts. Many of the techniques outlined in previous chapters may be adapted for use in interactive multimedia work. Max can be used to create stand-alone applications for screen-based work, or to create complex multimedia systems for live performance. Many composers, already experienced with creating artistic work using the computer, will find that expanding music into the multimedia realm is a natural extension of their work. Because music is fundamentally a time-based art, composers are well-trained to deal with the aesthetic issues surrounding time—tempo, pacing, transitions, structure, and editing—all of which have counterparts in the film and video world. Since Max has been optimized for the reliable real-time responses required by music, it offers rich opportunities to experiment with the creation of *new media,* emerging communication and art forms that combine text, graphics, video, animation, and music. The expansion of interactive music techniques into the visual domain holds great promise for future developments in multimedia performances, art installations, and screen-based multimedia works, such as CD-ROM titles. Since Max supports video and image playback through the Apple QuickTime standard, it is rapidly becoming an alternative language for visual artists and musicians who wish to incorporate multimedia elements into their work, offering a fascinating environment in which to explore combinations of sounds and images that are immediately responsive to human gesture.

Interactive Music in Screen-Based Works

In art work and titles viewed on the computer, the user (the "performer") may control aspects of music selection and compositional processes using the computer keyboard and mouse, or alternative input devices designed to translate human movement into computer data. Thus, while most of the research and concepts discussed in this book have related directly to musical performance, the idea of a performer may be expanded to include anyone capable of influencing artistic decisions in computer-based art work. Algorithms similar to Listener Objects can be used to identify such things as keystrokes, typing speed, mouse movements, and other physical gestures. Interactive music techniques add realism and elements of participation to screen-based works, creating effective soundtracks by using compositional algorithms that change continuously in response to a story or in response to a user's actions. Continuous control over musical parameters adds a level of variety and interaction not usually seen in commercially available titles. In addition, constrained random values can be used to create endless variations automatically so that the music is different with each viewing. This technique might create music for a scene that changes but retains the stylistic consistency required of the dramatic structure. Such variations could enliven the short repetitive musical sequences that usually characterize computer entertainment soundtracks.

CD-ROM titles based on the Hypercard paradigm usually present static scenes that offer user interaction in the form of mouse-clicking to select one of several options. Repetition seems inevitable in these situations as the user stumbles back to previous scenes. The success of the commercial title Myst demonstrates how two devices can make this repetition bearable and even interesting. First, the images and sounds can be complex and highly detailed, so that on a second or third look new aspects are discovered. Second, upon returning to scenes that appeared to be static, images and sounds can be transformed to reflect changes in the story. The next step, continuous control of parameters, has already taken place in the visual domain, with continuous 360-degree viewing available using Apple's QuickTime Virtual Reality (VR) extension.

Giving audio tracks and soundtracks such flexibility would add a great deal of interest. For example, the timing of decision-making, mouse movements, or keyboard strokes, could be linked to control the tempo of the music, or clicking and dragging an object downward might cause the pitch to go lower or the timbre to get darker. Parameter changes could also be controlled by the time spent within a single scene, so that the music would intensify as the viewing continued. Although Max has only occasionally been used for screen-based work, its ability to show video clips, text, and images in a structure that is completely open to the artist's conception, makes it an interesting alternative to feature-rich multimedia scripting languages, such as Macromedia's Director. Clearly, music, sound, and images responsive to user input will increase the user's level of interest and the feeling of participation.

Interactive Music in Multimedia Performance Works

Max's greater strength, however, is as a multimedia authoring language in works intended for performance or in large-scale art installations that use video projectors or large monitors to incorporate sound with text and images. Emergency Broadcast Network (EBN) is a music/performance art group that uses multiple video monitors and video projections in conjunction with a dynamic singer/actor accompanied by a disc jockey. Two additional performers trigger a vast collection of video clips, using two MIDI keyboards and Max to play video stored on disk. The keyboards are used solely as live video controllers to allow the performers to synchronize and improvise video samples with the rest of the "band."

In addition, Max has also been used in conjunction with MIDI-to-voltage converters to control complex stage lighting systems, robots, and other mechanical devices. Some examples include Steve Ellison's Max-based theater control system, currently in use by large theaters to control lighting, curtains, and arrays of up to twenty speakers. Canadian artists Louis-Phillippe Demers and Bill Vorn have mounted several installations using Max to control interactive robotics, sound, and light. For example, in *Espace Vectoriel,* robotic tubes projecting light and sound move within a dark, hazy space, and the viewer is invited to become immersed in a simulated world that represents a robotic ecosystem, a habitat made only for robotic organisms. These organisms have well-defined behaviors represented by algorithms in Max, which controls samplers, MIDI lighting dimmers, DC servo controllers, sonar-to-MIDI transducers, pneumatic valves, solenoids, strobe lights, and a smoke generator. Ultrasound sensing devices detect a viewer's presence and movement. Rather than giving control of the system to the viewer, the artists have allowed this habitat to have its own inherent flocking and propagating behavior, which reacts to the presence of viewers in the unfolding of higher-level events. "In many ways this communication scheme seems closer to the relationship between living organisms and their environment compared to the usual interactive model found in hypermedia where the system is usually waiting for a command from the user in order to react" (Demers and Vorn 1995).

These original works of art show that Max's flexibility and intuitive interface provide readily available tools for artists and composers creating emerging art forms. Understanding Max's QuickTime capabilities is a good starting point for such explorations.

Displaying Graphics in Max

The addition of Apple's QuickTime features to Max allows the playback of digitized video, computer animation, and digitized sound, and the display of still pictures and text. QuickTime is a standard multimedia format that is used on many computer platforms today, including Apple and IBM computers. A more complete definition given by Apple describes QuickTime as "a new architecture for the integration of dynamic data types." (Dynamic data is anything that changes over time.) QuickTime enables various media types to be stored and played with a minimum of memory requirements by applying various data-compression routines.

While a comprehensive look at QuickTime is beyond the scope of this book, a brief look at Max's QuickTime capabilities will suggest ideas for further multimedia exploration. QuickTime is a system extension that enables the computer to recognize various file types and hardware. Advanced applications require the related utilities and software programs that perform very specific operations, such as data compression, image processing, and video editing. Many software applications for video editing take various types of video, picture, sound, or animation files and convert them to a QuickTime-compatible format.

QuickTime has several file types, some of which have their own data-compression routines. A QuickTime *movie file* plays back time-based files: video, animation, and sound. A *PICT file* displays a single image. PICT is the standard QuickTime format for storing high quality still images; almost all Macintosh graphics applications can save and store images in PICT format. QuickTime movie files can also show a single image by displaying a single frame of video or animation. Text can also be displayed in either file format.

A standard QuickTime movie with video and sound is composed of one video track and one audio track. A QuickTime movie can include multiple audio or video tracks, or a single track of either type (video only or sound only). In addition, there is a text track, a music track (for MIDI), and a time-code track. QuickTime Interactive is a format that lets users click on "hot spots," locations on the video image that produce interactive results. Max already has this capability since invisible buttons (**ubuttons**) can be imbedded on-screen to produce *bangs* when clicked. These can be in effect while the video is running. Also, the **movie** object, described below, outputs the X, Y location of the mouse within the video-image window, so decisions can be made based on where the mouse is pointing at a given time.

Of particular interest to composers is the option of playing Sound Only QuickTime movies. Audio Interchange File Format (AIFF) is a standard Macintosh file format for storing digital audio; most digital audio applications can save files in AIFF format. Opening an AIFF file with QuickTime is easy since there is no file conversion; QuickTime simply references the original sound file. This is another way to play sound files directly from the hard disk, in addition to the **snd** and **Aiff-Player** objects described in chapter 8. Many audio applications have the ability to capture files from audio CDs via the CD-ROM drive and to write these files to disk. CD audio can be converted into AIFF files or directly to QuickTime movies.

The QuickTime *music file* format can connect a QuickTime movie to a synthesizer to save memory and increase sound capabilities. The **qtmusic** object plays sounds from the QuickTime Musical Instrument extension, a software-based synthesizer that generates a variety of sounds from the computer without the need for a MIDI module.

PICS is a format used for animation. A PICS file is essentially a series of PICT images that make up the multiple frames that are played back sequentially to create an animation. Because PICS files are made up of a series of uncompressed PICT files, they require a lot of memory. PICS files can be converted to QuickTime movie format (PICS is not part of QuickTime), which will not only dramatically reduce the amount of memory needed, but will also make them easier to use. Most animation programs can export files in QuickTime format.

The Graphic Window

Though users can simply paste a PICT file using Paste Picture from the edit menu, there are objects that can interactively draw and display graphics and video that require the use of the **graphic** object. With a few exceptions, notably the **lcd** object (see below), Max cannot draw any type of graphic inside a patcher window. Instead, special windows are created specifically for drawing and displaying graphics. The **graphic** object inlets receive messages to *open* or *close* such a window. Double-clicking on any **graphic** window will also open it. Since many of these examples require that a control window and a display window function simultaneously, All Windows Active must be checked in the Max options menu. Otherwise, only one window can be used at a time.

Graphic has one required argument, the name of the window to be created, and other objects that draw inside this window will need to refer to it by name. Four additional arguments specify the on-screen location of the four sides of the window, which determines both the location and the size of the window. If no arguments are specified, a default window with a title bar will appear on screen. A **graphic** window with a title bar behaves like other Macintosh windows. Clicking in the lower corner and dragging will resize the window. Clicking and dragging on the title bar will reposition it on the screen. If a window is moved around with the mouse, its locations will be saved with the file, and will default to that location the next time the file is opened. An optional nonzero argument, inserted just after the name, will create a window without a title bar. This option should be used only when the programmer wishes to have a permanent size and location for visual elements since the window cannot be resized and will appear in the same location each time the program is loaded (command-click on the window to drag it).

The location of the sides of the windows is specified in pixels. The arguments are: x-coordinate of left side, y-coordinate of top, x-coordinate of right side, and y-coordinate of bottom. The upper left-hand corner of the main monitor is (0, 0). On a standard 14″ monitor, the lower right corner will be (640, 480). Windows, which may appear anywhere on larger screens, can be positioned to be displayed on more than one monitor by giving them coordinates off the main screen. Because coordinates are always measured in pixels from the main monitor, a second monitor placed to the left of the main screen will have negative x-coordinates. This method is also used for projecting images with an LCD panel or data projector.

In figure 10.1, the first **graphic** object, **demo1**, creates a square window, 100 pixels wide and tall, with the left side at 0 (far left), the right side at 100, the top at 40, and the bottom at 140. The y-coordinate for the top is 40, not zero, in order to compensate for the room that the

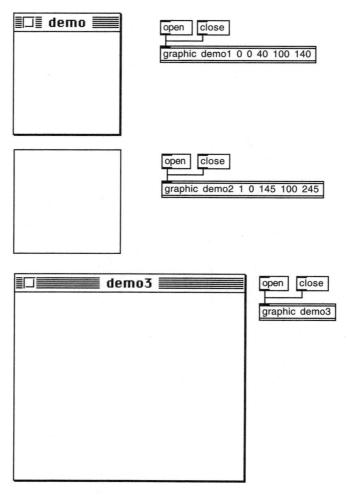

Figure 10.1
graphic

menu bar takes up at the top of the monitor. If this window is moved with the mouse and the document is saved, it will re-open in the new position, not the one specified by the arguments. (The second argument, 0, creates a title bar, but is unnecessary since this is the default when no argument is specified.)

Demo2 creates another 100-pixel square 200 pixels below the first one. This one does not have a title bar because the second argument is 1, so the window cannot be resized or closed with the mouse and will always remain in the same location when the program is loaded.

Demo3 creates a default graphic window whose size and location can be adjusted.

Drawing Tools

Max has four objects to draw basic shapes: **oval, ring, rect,** and **frame** (hollow rectangle). These tools can create pictures in Max without importing them from another program (fig. 10.2). A **graphic** window must first be created. Clicking on the *open* box in the upper right corner of the patch shown in figure 10.2 will open [**graphic draw**]. A black circle, which was produced by the oval object, appears in the window. Notice that the *draw* argument is given to the **oval** object, so that Max knows which **graphic** window to draw the oval in. All drawing objects have the same inlets. The first four are coordinates for the left, top, right, and bottom sides of the shape. The coordinates shown specify a circle, 100 pixels in diameter.

The oval shape and size can be altered by changing the four coordinates with the number boxes above the image. The coordinates are

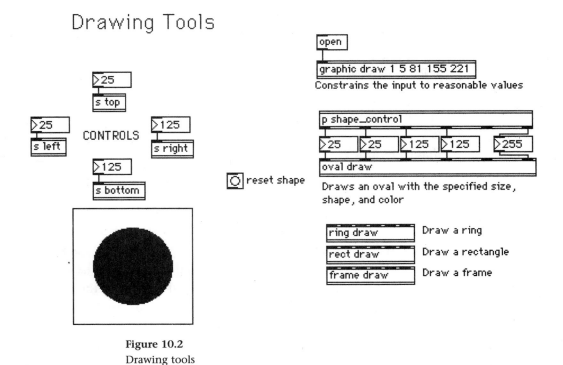

Figure 10.2
Drawing tools

sent to the respective inlets of the [**oval draw**] object. The patcher **shape_control** prevents the oval from disappearing when coordinates are entered that would force the top and bottom or the left and right sides to cross each other; it also forces the oval to redraw every time a coordinate changes. The sixth inlet of all drawing objects specifies color. Numbers sent to this box correspond to colors in the system palette. For example, the number 255 causes the oval to be black, and the number 241 will cause it to become white. All other numbers between 0 and 254 will cause the oval to become different colors or shades of gray if the monitor is set to display 256 colors.

The **oval** object pictured in figure 10.2 can be changed into one of the other types of drawing objects by replacing the word **oval** with **ring, rect,** or **frame.** Notice that each example is using the same graphic window, *draw,* to display the image. Replacing the object name **oval** with another shape name and then hitting the Reset Shape button will change the display.

The **lcd** object adds animation and automated drawing capabilities using standard Macintosh QuickDraw commands, such as PaintRect (paint a rectangle) and frameRect (draw the outline of a rectangle). It can take elaborate messages describing how to draw graphics and display text in a patcher window and it works without using a corresponding **graphic** object. A user may also click and drag inside the **lcd** window to draw a shape or picture, with the coordinates of the mouse sent out the left outlet. In this way, **lcd** may be used as input to a **table** to draw functions from the interface.

QuickTime Movies

There are two similar objects for playing QuickTime movies in Max: **imovie** and **movie.** The **imovie** object is probably the quickest and easiest way to play video or animation in Max since it plays movies directly within a patch without having to specify a separate graphics window (fig. 10.3). **Imovie** is a graphical interface object available from the tools palette. (The icon looks like a film strip.) When the **imovie** object is placed into a patch, it creates its own graphic window embedded directly within the patch itself. This window can be resized by clicking and dragging in the lower right corner. One of the more subtle

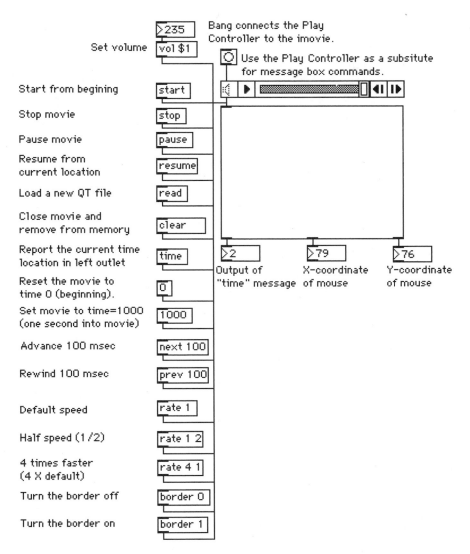

Set volume

Start from begining

Stop movie

Pause movie

Resume from
current location

Load a new QT file

Close movie and
remove from memory

Report the current time
location in left outlet

Reset the movie to
time 0 (beginning).

Set movie to time=1000
(one second into movie)

Advance 100 msec

Rewind 100 msec

Default speed

Half speed (1/2)

4 times faster
(4 X default)

Turn the border off

Turn the border on

Bang connects the Play
Controller to the imovie.

Use the Play Controller as a subsitute
for message box commands.

Output of
"time" message

X-coordinate
of mouse

Y-coordinate
of mouse

Figure 10.3
imovie

effects of **imovie** is the *border* message, allowing the black rectangle surrounding the movie to appear and disappear.

The procedure to load a movie into this window permanently begins by selecting the object and choosing GET INFO from the Max menu. This opens a standard dialog box that asks the user to choose a QuickTime file stored on disk. (This file name can be stored with the program.) Similarly, **movie** can take a filename as an optional argument. The *read* message can be used to load one or more movies. The names of the currently loaded movies that are saved with the program will be loaded the next time the patch is opened. Any currently loaded movie can be purged from memory at any time with the *dispose* message.

The **imovie** and **movie** objects can be controlled with the standard messages shown to the left of the example below, or with a standard **QuickTime Play Controller** graphical object, available in the Max toolbar at the top of the screen. Clicking on the **bang button** will connect the QuickTime Play Controller to the **imovie**. Its function is to play, pause, resume, and change the location of the movie. (Notice that it gives real-time feedback of the movie's current location.) External sources can be used to send numbers to locate and playback any section of a movie, or even to display a single frame. (Although the quality isn't as good as PICT, QuickTime movies are very efficient when it comes to displaying a still image.) The rate message or a timing source within Max may be used to change the frame rate (playback speed).

The x- and y-coordinates of the mouse relative to the **imovie** object are reported from the middle and right outlets whenever the mouse is down. This gives accurate location within the image and, coupled with timing information, can be used to create interactive multimedia pieces where text, music, and video can be altered by the click of a mouse. **Ubuttons** can also be used for a similar effect, embedding invisible buttons anywhere in a movie. These interface devices can be combined with QuickTime's text capabilities to produce interesting queries or animated menus.

The **movie** object is almost identical to the **imovie** interface object with two main exceptions: It creates its own graphics window to function, and it takes one argument, the QuickTime filename, that it loads on start-up.

PICS Animations

PICS files that were created using another application may be played in Max. The **pics** object will load a PICS file into memory and display it in a **graphic** window. A PICS file is a group of pictures stored as a series of frames and needs to be created with an animation program or other graphic program. This is the simplest form of animation on the Macintosh because it does not use any form of compression or time code like QuickTime does. Because there is no compression involved, a PICS file will generally require more RAM to play than a comparable QuickTime file. (Many graphics programs will convert a PICS file to a QuickTime file.) The Max window contains a list of each individual frame in a PICS file, including how much memory it occupies. Since PICS files are uncompressed, they usually have a better image quality than compressed QuickTime files, and because PICS files are simply a series of frames, they can be accessed easily by individual frame numbers. **Pics** would be an ideal way to access numerous high quality PICT files for a slide-show type presentation. Unlike QuickTime movies, which have a built-in player and default speed, a patch using **pics** must incorporate some type of time-based driver (such as a **counter** or **line** object) to supply timed integers to represent frame numbers to make a movie play or show images. Finally, PICS files cannot incorporate sound, unlike QuickTime movies.

In figure 10.4, clicking on Open opens the **graphic** window *picsdemo*. A **graphic** window must be specified for Max to draw the PICS animation in. Clicking on 0 will display the first frame (frame 0) of the PICS file. Since **pics** does not have a default playback mode, a timing source needs to be supplied from Max for an animation. Clicking on the message box [0, 15, 1000] connected to the **line** object's inlet will cause **line** to count from 0 to 15 in one second (hence, 15 frames per second). This will cause the animation to play all the way through, since there are only fifteen frames in the file *Demo.PICS*. A *bang* advances the animation one frame at a time. A nice feature of the **pics** object is its ability to randomly access frames by number. Clicking on the *0* message will display the first frame. Clicking on the *7* message will display the eighth frame. (Max always starts counting from 0.) Clicking and dragging on the number box will play the movie continuously in either direction. Similar random-access techniques can be used with **movie**

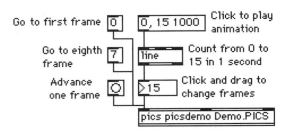

Figure 10.4
pics

and **imovie** as well, by sending an integer to the left inlet that specifies time in milliseconds. (It will call up the single frame associated with that time.)

PICT Files

The simplest way to display a single image in Max is to use a PICT file. In addition to movies and animations, Max can display single images stored in PICT format. Images created with other Macintosh graphics applications and saved or "exported" as PICT files can greatly enhance the aesthetics and functionality of the user interface design. PICT files have excellent image quality, but some files can use up a lot of RAM.

Max's three ways to display PICT files may be a bit confusing. The simplest way is to simply copy an image from one source, and paste it into a Max window using Paste Picture in the edit menu (which is highlighted whenever a PICT file is on the clipboard) or the usual keyboard shortcut for paste, command-v. The PICT file will be saved with the program and may be moved around on the screen.

To save memory and make a patch more efficient, the **fpic** interface object is recommended. It is identical to Paste Picture, except that it references the PICT file on disk rather than saving it with the Max program, and it pastes it into its own box. This can save memory and speed up load and save times. Selecting GET INFO on **fpic** creates a link to a file stored on disk. The name of the last PICT file read in will be remembered when the program is saved, and automatically called up when the program is reloaded. (The PICT file must be placed in a folder where Max can find it; see *file preferences*.) **Fpic** can call up various images at any time with message *pict*, followed by the name of a PICT file. As was mentioned in chapter 5, these images can be made to control computer functions when combined with the **ubutton** object, which acts as an invisible **bang button** or **toggle switch** when placed on top of an image.

In figure 10.5 the *open* message will open the **graphic** window *pictwin*; a *bang* to the PICT object will display the PICT file *Demo.pict* in *pictwin*. As with **file** and **table**, Max automatically calls up the file name given as an argument. Monitors set to display "thousands" of colors

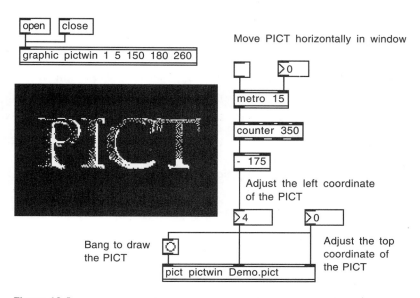

Figure 10.5
pict

will give the best results. The position of the PICT file in a **graphics** window can be adjusted by changing the value of the two right inlets. Simple animations can be created simply by changing these two numbers. In this example, the counter object makes the image scroll horizontally across the window. The second two inlets are also useful for positioning a PICT file to display a portion of the image.

Videodisk Playback

The **vdp object** is designed to control a Pioneer 4200 or 8000 laser disk player from Max and can be used to display high quality video and graphics in a concert setting or installation. **Vdp** is similar to the **cd** object in that it can respond to performer or automated information in Max to locate and play back images on laser disks from an external device. These random-access media devices are less responsive than MIDI data, since there are unavoidable delays searching specific locations within a disk (Freed, Wessel, Zicarelli 1991). Vdp takes input messages and integers corresponding to videodisk operations. The message *control 1,* for example, will eject the disk; *play* will play from the current location; and *fps slow* will cause the videodisk to play back at half the normal speed (fifteen frames per second instead of thirty). Each command sends a stream of numbers out the object's left outlet that then needs to be connected to the **serial** object (fig. 10.6). The **serial** object, in turn, sends characters to the serial port. The serial object can be used to send and receive characters from the two built-in serial ports (printer and modem) or from installed cards that contain serial ports. Control of a serial port may be useful in controlling a host of external devices, such as a modem. (See the Max manual for more details.)

Optimizing Graphics and Memory Management

Graphics objects and graphical interface objects tax the computer by requiring the screen to be redrawn each time a change is made. If graphics are drawn while a complex program is creating music, there is a chance that the music will be interrupted. Overdrive mode, available in the options menu, gives priority to the time-critical computations that will affect music. Objects such as **sliders, bang buttons, toggle switches, animations,** and **movies** appearing on the screen in

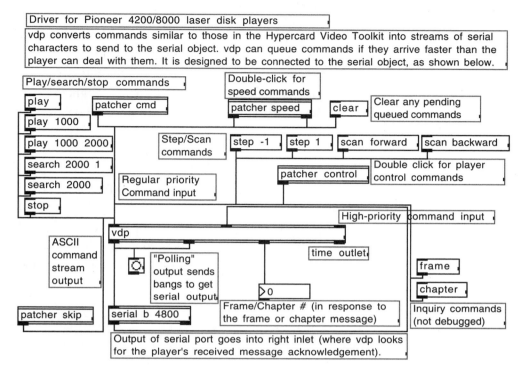

Figure 10.6
vdp (video disk playback)

Overdrive mode will be handled after all other computations, and may appear jerky or distorted since frames will be skipped to keep up with the music. Therefore, Overdrive should be turned off when graphics performance timing is critical, especially when displaying movies or animated PICS files. The capabilities of simultaneous playback of sound and graphics will depend on the speed of the computer and the amount of available internal memory (RAM).

In order to get the most out of Max's multimedia capabilities, it is important to understand and optimize limited RAM. The examples of movies, images, animations, and sound included on this disk have been specifically designed not to use up too much RAM. However, larger files may put a greater demand on memory. The **pics**, **movie**, **imovie**, **snd**, and **AiffPlayer** objects all function by loading a file, or a portion of a file from disk, directly into RAM. This allows the files to play as fast as possible without sacrificing the timing in the rest of the patch; however, these files tend to be large and quickly use up available

RAM. The key to working with movie and sound files effectively is to keep them as small as possible, and to purge them out of memory whenever they are not needed. Techniques for controlling the size of files will vary for each situation. Often there is a trade-off between the quality of digitized images and sounds and the file size. Higher resolution means larger files. The following guidelines should be helpful.

Movies and PICTs

1. QuickTime files are almost always smaller than PICS files.

2. In most applications, various parameters for compression are applied to QuickTime files. Depending on the speed of the computer and the speed of the hard disk the compression setting should be adjusted as high as possible while maintaining the desired image quality. Creating QuickTime movies at half screen size (instead of full screen) and at 15 frames per second (instead of 30) may be necessary to reduce the file size.

3. Color depth is crucial. Color depth determines how many colors are available to each pixel on the screen. More colors need to be represented by more numbers. Eight-bits can only represent binary numbers from 0 to 256. Therefore, images stored in 8-bit color will have 256 available colors for each pixel. Images stored in 32-bit color will have much larger files than those stored in 8-bit color. For many projects, color depths of 8-bits or less are sufficient. Always work in the lowest depth possible.

4. QuickTime files can be purged from RAM when not needed with the *dispose* or *clear* messages. The file(s) will need to be read in again in order to play. PICS and PICT will remain in RAM until the Max file containing the object is closed. In some cases, RAM can be conserved by using a 1-frame QuickTime file instead of a PICT, or showing a series of PICT files as still frames in a movie (although the quality will not be as good).

Sound Files

1. Make sure that sound files do not contain any blank space. A 2-sec recording of a 1-sec sound will lose RAM for the second of silence.

2. Many sound-editing programs allow sounds to be sampled or resampled at a lower sampling rate. 22 kHz will often be as usable as a standard 44.1 kHz file. File size may be further reduced by using 8-bit

sounds, with some grainyness added to the sound. This is the equivalent of saving graphics files at a lower color-depth. Although CD-quality sound is usually desirable, it is not always crucial to a project. Therefore sampling sound files at the lowest possible rates while maintaining the desired quality will greatly reduce the file sizes.

New Controllers and Multimedia Performance Systems

Musical instruments continuously evolve in response to available technology. The modern trumpet valve system, the structure of the piano, and the electric guitar were all inspired by technological advances. Musical thought evolves to incorporate expanding resources and pushes further instrument development. The invention of the modern piano, for example, quite an impressive feat of engineering for its day, fueled the imagination and technique of nineteenth-century Romantic composers, offering both intimate moments and huge thundering sounds that filled the concert halls of major cities. The aesthetic and the instrument were wedded. The conclusion of this book examines how new instruments inspire artistic thought, and how the demands of interactive music technology foster the development of new controllers.

The first expressive and commercially viable electronic musical instrument was invented in 1919 by Leon Theremin. His invention, the Theremin, foreshadowed the development of music produced by electrical means and is even more remarkable as the first musical instrument performed without physical touch. Rather than create this new instrument on an acoustic model, he invented a new way to perform electronic music by moving each hand in the air closer or farther from two radio antennas that controlled the frequency and amplitude of a simple electronic oscillator. The results produced by moving the hands in space were surprisingly subtle and varied because the sound reflected the expressive quality of human movement.

The world caught up with Leon Theremin in the 1960s and 1970s when several composers rediscovered the use of movement to create electronic music. Of particular note is *Variations V* (1965), a collaborative work featuring music by John Cage and choreography by Merce Cunningham, with a system designed by Gordon Mumma and David Tudor to derive sounds from the movements of dancers, who produced music based on their proximity to several electronic sensors placed on stage. Thus, the entire floor was transformed into a musical instrument responsive to movement throughout the space (Nyman 1980). (Theremin had previously experimented with a smaller platform system for dance.)

Since the 1980s, the sophistication and accuracy of digital technology has brought opportunities for the development of new musical instruments and motion-based controllers. Researchers in both dance and music have created numerous systems showing the viability of using computers to interpret data from motion detectors and body sensors, as well as new instruments capable of utilizing unique playing techniques designed specifically for the digital medium. Of particular interest is ongoing work at STEIM in Amsterdam, a studio committed to custom instrument design and research. Corporate interests are now pushing their own research and we will soon be inundated with body suits, gloves, motion detectors, and other devices for virtual reality environments. While these physical computer-input devices may not be intended specifically for music, and therefore may lack some of the subtle idiosyncrasies of musical instruments, many have been used to perform or shape sound and music. A few examples in this book have shown the viability of using controllers such as a foot pedal or a computer mouse as instruments. In fact, any device that translates physical movement into numbers is fair game for an interactive musical performance.

The analysis and interpretation of movement data holds great promise for interactive composition, dance, and creating responsive music in virtual reality systems. While MIDI keyboards and other instruments based on acoustical models enable experienced musicians to take advantage of years of training, there are many instances where a specially built instrument is more suitable to performing and shaping interactive computer processes. New performer requirements, such as influencing aspects of multimedia systems or shaping signal-processing parameters, have spawned the invention or adaptation of new controllers. Whereas older instrument designs are based on their sound-producing mechanism, new controllers have no such limitations and therefore may be optimized to use pure physical gestures as primary compositional constraints.

Data describing movement can produce musically satisfying results by their impact on sound and musical processes. Physical-gesture data may be interpreted by software as primary compositional constraints in interactive music systems, effectively replacing the usual role of musical-performance data. Movement data might not be note oriented, but instead use timing, placement, and force as relevant listener parameters. A performer's actions may translate into immediate musical results; they may have delayed reactions, or they may be analyzed over longer spans of time for direction, repetition, and other patterns. Influences may be used in a less obvious manner when applied to the unfolding of higher-level events in more fully developed musical environments. With more parameters available for change, highly interactive schemes require performers to spend additional practice time learning the idiosyncrasies of a system capable of intricate connections between movement and music.

Controller Types

Controllers can be roughly divided into four categories, although these categories are by no means mutually exclusive. Acoustic models are controllers designed to take advantage of a preexisting instrumental technique, such as a MIDI keyboard, or MIDI guitar. New instruments are devices designed with the physical limitations and technical expertise required of acoustic models. As with acoustic instruments, new instruments make music by exciting physical devices that produce sound or MIDI data. Physical energy is transformed into sound through a musical-instrument mechanism. The modulation wheel could be viewed as a simple example of a new instrument. More evolved models include Donald Buchla's Thunder, a device comprised of twenty-five small touch-sensitive pads arrayed in a pattern resembling two hands side-by-side. The pads are sensitive to touch and velocity and may be programmed to send out a variety of MIDI messages (Pressing 1992). The Web, an instrument developed at STEIM, resembles the spokes of a bicycle wheel, or a spider's web, with a series of strings mounted on a circular frame. The performer grasps and pulls the strings to generate or manipulate channels of continuous controller data, offering a unique playing method for the coordination of numerous parameters (Ryan 1992).

The two other types of controllers are designed to measure human movement directly. Although the wide variety of devices for detecting movement have unique sensing apparatuses, capabilities, and features, many share common attributes. Spatial sensors detect location in space, by proximity to hardware sensors or by location within a projected grid. Body sensors measure the angle, force, or position of various parts of the body, such as hand movements or leg position. These two methods are by no means mutually exclusive.

Spatial Sensors

Spatial sensors respond to the location and movement of a performer in space, often without the performer touching any hardware devices. Several performers have used off-the-shelf motion detectors and inexpensive pressure triggers, as well as custom-designed hardware, to map body location within a space into MIDI data.

David Rokeby's Very Nervous System tracks a person's movements in a large space using a video camera to send images to a computer that analyzes consecutive frames to detect motion. Using Max software to create music, the system allows dancers and other participants to influence compositional processes based on their location and movement in a room. The same system has been used for video artist Paul Garrin's interactive video installation, White Devil, in which the menacing image of a white pit bull roams across twelve large video monitors, tracking and responding to a viewer's movement (Cooper 1995). Another technique that analyzes movement with video cameras is Rob Lovell and John Mitchell's Virtual Stage Environment, which identifies hot spots demarcating areas within a video camera's viewing field. Actions within these areas are interpreted by Max to control musical process and playback of a video disk player (Lovell and Mitchell 1995).

Max Mathew's Radio Drum (or Radio Baton) is a spatial controller that consists of two radio-frequency transmitting batons moved above a rectangular drum surface consisting of an array of radio receivers (Mathews and Schloss 1988). Each baton sends continuous data in three dimensions. Mathew's early demonstrations show effective conducting techniques, with one baton controlling the tempo of a score stored in the computer, and the other baton controlling dynamics and/or timbre. More complex interactive systems using the Radio Drum can be seen in performances by composers Andrew Schloss and Richard Boulanger. The **drum** object is a custom Max object designed for the Radio Drum, receiving stick-position data, trigger-plane hits, and velocity (Freed, Wessell, and Zicarelli 1991).

Donald Buchla's Lightning uses an infrared signal to locate a performer within a user-definable two-dimensional grid. In one of Buchla's theatrical demonstrations, a percussionist plays a large assortment of instruments on stage. As he or she plays, two "thieves" approach and one by one steal all the instruments. However, the percussionist is able to return to the exact location of the instrument and continues to play in the air! As it turns out, the drumsticks contained the infrared source and triggered all the sounds from a sampler, with the location of the original instruments triggering the expected percussion sample (i.e., the location of the cymbal triggered the cymbal sample). When the instruments were removed, the same samples continued to be triggered. Among other things, Lightning has been used as a conducting system to coordinate musicians while sending tempo and dynamic information to Max (Lee, Garnett, and Wessel 1992).

Body Sensors

Body Sensors are hardware devices attached to the performer that directly measure movement of parts of the body. These instruments have been developed to measure such things as the movement and position of the arms, legs, and especially hands and fingers. Michel Waisvisz's The Hands is one of the first such devices (Waisvisz 1985). It looks like a pair of oversized gloves with switches and fits on both hands, translating finger position, hand proximity, and wrist motion into MIDI data. Other hand-modeled devices include Tod Machover's adaptation of the Dexterous Hand Master to shape timbre in his composition *Bug-Mudra* (Machover 1989). A good example of how a non-musical device may be adapted for musical production is the Mattel Power Glove, a controller for the Nintendo Entertainment System. The GoldBrick interface allows the Power Glove to communicate to the computer through the Macintosh ADBport (the same plug that is used by the mouse). The **glove** object receives eight gestural variables from the Power Glove, including X, Y, and Z location, rotation, and bend of the thumb and fingers. The object reports these values whenever it receives a *bang* (Freed, Wessel, and Zicarelli 1991). Numerous compositions have successfully utilized gestural information from the Power Glove (Boulanger and Smaragdis 1995).

Mark Coniglio's MIDI Dancer is a wireless device consisting of thin plastic strips that measure the bending of body parts. The device uses Coniglio's Interactor software to create music based on a dancer's body shape. A suit fitted with several sensors measures the angle and movement of primary limb joints, such as arm and leg position, motion, and speed. In his recent piece, *In Plane,* a solo dancer's role is expanded to control video playback, a lighting board, and the position of a video camera on a 24-foot robotic platform. In one section of the work, the computer analyzes the dancer's shape and looks for matches in the computer in a library of prestored body-shape data. When a match is found, the computer projects an electronic video image that mimics the dancer.

A subset of body sensors, *bio sensors* use medical testing equipment to monitor internal human biological functions, such as brain wave activity or muscle activity. Data from these devices are used to affect musical production. In Alvin Lucier's *Music for a Solo Performer* (1965), a performer's scalp is wired with electrodes that pick up alpha brain waves which are amplified and processed; they are then sent to numerous speakers around the hall, which causes the adjacent percussion instruments to vibrate. Several composers, such as David Rosenboom and Sylvia Penguilly, have continued these explorations, using EEG devices to generate music (Schaefer 1987; Penguilly 1995).

Several engineers have created movement-directed music systems using medical devices that measure low-level voltages produced by the force of muscle contraction. The myoelectrically-activated dance-directed music system (MADDM) is described as a wireless system that uses electrodes placed on two opposing muscle groups to transmit the velocity and direction of a dancer's movements (Gillet, Smith, and Pritchard 1985). Currently, composer Atau Tanaka performs with the BioMuse system (Knapp and Lufsted 1990), using similar devices to measure the amount of muscle activity in each arm, and translating the information into MIDI continuous controller data for processing in Max. His work *OverBow* explores the possibility of direct bodily control over sound synthesis. Even though control is limited to the equivalent of three continuous controllers, the success of the work lies in the fact that exertion and recuperation is viewed by the audience, felt by the performer, and directly reflected in the spectrum of the sound (Tanaka 1993). His new works incorporate the direct control of video processing, as well.

Making Music through Movement

Does human movement have constraints similar to those of musical instruments, which might suggest something akin to idiomatic expression? Is there a distinct character to the movement of the hands? What is finger music? What is running music? What *is* the sound of one hand clapping? These questions may be answered by allowing the physicality of movement to impact musical material and processes.

These relationships may be established by viewing the body and space as musical instruments, free from the associations of acoustic instruments, but with similar limitations that can lend character to sound through idiomatic movements. Traditional studies in orchestration, as well as studies in sound synthesis, begin by examining the physical properties of instruments and their methods for producing sound. Physical constraints produce unique timbral characteristics and suggest musical material that will be idiomatic or appropriate for a particular instrument's playing technique. These reflect the weight, force, pressure, speed, and range used to produce sound. In turn, the sound reflects, in some way, the effort or energy used to create it. A classic example is the fact that as brass tones grow louder they increase the strength of the upper partials, which produces a brighter sound.

Each part of the body has its unique limitation in terms of direction, weight, range of motion, speed, and force. In addition, actions can be characterized by ease of execution, accuracy, repeatability, fatigue, and response. The underlying physics of movement lends insight into the selection of musical material. Thus, a delicate curling of the fingers should produce a very different sonic result than a violent and dramatic leg kick, since the size, weight, and momentum alone would have different physical ramifications. To demonstrate this, physical parameters can be appropriately mapped to musical parameters, such as weight to density or register, tension to dissonance, or physical space to simulated acoustical space, although such simple one-to-one correspondences are not always musically successful. The composer's job, then, is not only to map movement data to musical parameters, but to interpret these numbers with software to produce musically satisfying results.

The stage, room, or space also has its boundaries, limiting speed, direction, and maneuverability. Psychological intensity increases or decreases with stage position. An audience perceives more energy and focus as a performer moves upstage, whereas apparent gravity pulls a performer downstage with less effort, in a way similar to the very real pull of vertical downward motion. Intensity may also vary with the amount of activity confined to a given space. These physical and psychological properties of space are ripe for musical interpretation.

Being aware of the underlying physics of movement does not necessarily imply an obvious musical solution. Indeed, since computers are only simulating real-world events, tampering with the apparent laws of physics is a luxury made possible in virtual environments. By being aware of these laws, it is possible to alter them for provocative and intriguing artistic effects, creating models of response unique to the computer. More furious and strenuous activity, for example, could result in quieter sounds and silence. At the same time, a small yet deliberate nod of the head could set off an explosion of sound. Such unnatural correlations make motion all the more meaningful. Thus, success for performers, as well as enjoyment for the audience, is tied to their ability to perceive relationships between movement and sound.

Interpreting Movement Data

With many of the technical difficulties of movement analysis successfully solved by researchers, some attention can now be shifted away from instrument building and toward musical performance and composition. Specifically, how can performers shape and structure musical material through their physical gestures?

It is doubtful that such movement data can be simply applied to preexisting compositional models. An examination of the physical parameters of movement, their limitations, and the methods used for their measurement, will yield clues to an appropriate musical response, one where imaginative connections engage performers by their power to shape sound. In his insightful essay, "Effort and Expression," Joel Ryan states that "in fact, the physicality of the performance interface gives definition to the modeling process itself" (1992). Interactive music systems can be used to interpret these data, extending the performer's power of expression beyond a simple one-to-one relationship of triggered sound to include the control of compositional processes, musical structure, signal processing, and sound synthesis.

Regardless of sensor type, it is important to recognize not only what is being measured, but how it is being measured. Many of these devices, like a MIDI foot pedal, specify a limited range of motion (left-right, high-low, open-closed) and divide that range into a limited number of steps, with data sent out more or less continuously along this range. Numbers, often represented as MIDI continuous controller values between 0 to 127, determine location over time within this predefined range. The resolution or scale of these steps, as well as the device sampling rate (how often a new position is reported), will be factors in musical interpretation. More programmable devices allow any location within this range to send out any type of MIDI data. Other devices, like a computer keyboard, may have less continuous reporting, sending out nonlinear discrete data that represent predetermined trigger points. As with musical instrument data, these numbers may be filtered, scaled, selected, or otherwise processed to prepare them as parameter input to compositional algorithms.

These numbers determine the location or body position of a performer over time within a predefined range. Timing and location may be used to determine the speed or force of an action, using tempo-following algorithms from chapter 6. Software can interpret this data to create music based on either a performer's exact location or position, or by movement relative to a previous location or position. The number of parameters transmitted by a device also defines some of its musical capabilities. Spatial sensors work in one, two, or three dimensions. Body sensors may track one or more parts of the body.

The techniques and ideas presented here point to things to come: the evolution of new genres of music; new physical interfaces; interactive soundtracks for movies, CD-ROM titles, and web sites; more tangible real-time manipulation of sound; and the development of new forms of art and communication. Now that most basic computers have built-in multimedia capabilities, computing has changed from a print-only medium to one that incorporates picture and sound. These available technologies offer opportunities for composers and sound designers to create a richer everyday experience by the deft use of interactive music techniques. At the same time, these new concepts will continue to challenge our most highly esteemed musicians to discover unique forms of expression through digitally enhanced performance.

Appendix

Master List of Figures and Examples (*continued*)

Printed Figures	Disk Examples	Related Opcode Objects
3.13 Objects and messages: MIDI studio, 59	—**Diagram**	
3.14 Interface objects and message equivalence, 60	Interface Objects and Message Equivalence	**float, int**
3.15 Multiple ways to send the same message, 61	Multiple Ways to Send the Same Message	**metro**
3.16 Get Info, 62	—None, general Max feature	**(keyboard, table, menu)**
3.17 Right-to-left order, 63	Right-to-Left Order	
3.18 Anatomy of a MIDI message, 64	—**Diagram**	
3.19 MIDI Channels, 65	Max and MIDI/MIDI channels	**pipe**
3.20 **notein** and **noteout**, 66	Max and MIDI/Notes In and Out	**notein, noteout, makenote, stripnote**
3.21 MIDI controllers, 67	Max and MIDI/MIDI Controllers	**ctlin, ctlout**
3.22 Pitchbend and aftertouch, 68	Max and MIDI/MIDI Controllers	**bendin, bendout, touchin, touchout**
3.23 Program change messages, 69	Max and MIDI/Program Change Messages	**pgmin, pgmout**
3.24 **midiin** and **midiout**, 70	Max and MIDI/midiin midiparse midiformat midiout	**midiin, midiparse, midiformat, midiout**
Chapter 4 Text Figures	Chapter 4 Disk Examples	Chapter 4 Opcode Objects
4.1 Top-down design: FollowPlay interface prototype, 75	—None	**loadbang, flush, split**
4.2 **int**, 80	Data Structures/int	**int**
4.3 **int** and order of operation, 81	Data Structures/int/int and Order of Operation	**gate**
4.4 **table**, 82	Data Structures/table	**table**
4.5 **table** graphic editing window, 83	Data Structures/table	

Master List of Figures and Examples (*continued*)

Printed Figures	Disk Examples	Related Opcode Objects
4.6 **table** music, 84	Data Structures/table/table music	**counter**
4.7 **coll**, 84	Data Structures/coll	**coll**
4.8 Contents of **coll**—lists, 85	Data Structures/coll	
On disk only	Data Structures/coll/Another Coll Example	
4.9 **seq**, 86	Data Structures/seq	**seq**
4.10 **detonate**, 87 on disk only (other data structures)	Data Structures/detonate Data Structures/funbuff and bag	**detonate** **funbuff, bag**
4.11 Message types and display, 89	Messages	
4.12 Message lists, 90	Messages/message lists	
4.13 Message lists to **table:** a little list tune, 91	Messages/message lists AND/A Little List Tune	
4.14 Message arguments, 92	Messages/message arguments	**sprintf**
4.15 **pack** and **unpack**, 93	Messages/pack and unpack	**pack, unpack**
4.16 Manipulating messages, 94	Messages/manipulating messages	**prepend, append, iter, thresh** (sort)
4.17 Order of operation, 95	Data Flow/Order of Operation	
4.18 Order control: bangbang and trigger, 96	Data Flow/Order of Operation/bangbang AND trigger	**bangbang, trigger**
4.19 **swap**, 97	Data Flow/Order of Operation/swap	**swap**
on disk only	Data Flow/Order of Operation/buddy	**buddy**
4.20 **gate**, 98	Data Flow/Order of Operation/gate	**gate**
4.21 **switch**, 98	Data Flow/Routing/switch	**switch**
4.22 **Ggate** and **Gswitch**, 99	Data Flow/Routing/Ggate and Gswitch	**Ggate, Gswitch**

Master List of Figures and Examples (*continued*)

Printed Figures	Disk Examples	Related Opcode Objects
4.23 **route**, 100 on disk only	Data Flow/Routing/route Data Flow/Routing/grab	**route** **grab**
4.24 Remote messages, 101	Data Flow/Remote Messages	**send, receive**
4.25 **value**, 102	Data Flow/Remote Messages/Value	**value**
4.26 Remote table and coll, 102	Data Flow/Remote Messages/Remote Table and Coll	
4.27 **split**, 103	Data Flow/Remote Messages/Split	**split**
4.28 **sel** (select), 104	Data Flow/Remote Messages/Select	**select**
4.29 **if**, 106	Programming Statements	**if**
4.30 **expr**, 107	Programming Statements	**expr** **print, capture, trace**
Chapter 5 Text Figures	Chapter 5 Disk Examples	Chapter 5 Opcode Objects
5.1 Controlling numbers, 115	Controlling Numbers	all **sliders, dial**
5.2 More number control: **IncDec** and **multiSlider**, 115	Controlling Numbers/More Number Control	**IncDec, multiSlider**
5.3 **preset**, 116	preset	
5.4 **preset** messages, 117	preset /preset messages	**speedlim**
5.5 **menu**, 118	menu	
5.6 **menu**:Get Info, 118	menu/get info	
5.7 **menu** displaying message, 120	Interface Feedback/Example #1	
5.8 **menu**: displaying remote messages, 120	Interface Feedback/Example #2	**snd**
5.9 Timing feedback, 121	Interface Feedback/Example #3	
5.10 **DisplayTime** (subpatch of fig. 5.9), 122	Interface Feedback/Example #3/DisplayTime	
5.11 **SeqControl** (subpatch of fig. 5.9), 123	Interface Feedback/Example #3/SeqControl	

Master List of Figures and Examples (*continued*)

Printed Figures	Disk Examples	Related Opcode Objects
5.12 **dialog** (Opcode's help file), 124	Interface Feedback/dialog	**dialog**
5.13 Using the mouse: MouseState, 125	Using Mouse	**MouseState**
5.14 Grid (graphic) showing mouse control, 125	Using Mouse	
5.15 **key** and **keyup**, 127	Using Keyboard, 126	**keyup, keydown**
5.16 Screen Graphics 1: A very messy patch, 128	Clean Up/Example 1	
5.17 Screen Graphics 2: Reposition objects and segment chords, 129	Clean Up/Example 2	
5.18 Screen Graphics 3: Encapsulate algorithms, 130	Clean Up/Example 3	
5.19 Screen Graphics 4: Comment the patch, 131	Clean Up/Example 4	
5.20 Screen Graphics 5: Encapsulate the main algorithm, 132	Clean Up/Example 5	
5.21 Screen Graphics 6: Build the performance interface, 132	Clean Up/Example 6	
on disk only	Automation, Object Design	
Chapter 6 Text Figures	Chapter 6 Disk Examples	Chapter 6 Opcode Objects
6.1 **metro**, 138	Max Timing Objects/ metro	**metro**
6.2 **tempo**, 139	Max Timing Objects/ tempo	**tempo**
6.3 **timer**, 139	Max Timing Objects/ timer	
6.4 **clocker**, 140	Max Timing Objects/ clocker	
6.5 Converting milliseconds to beats per minute (BPM), 141	Max Timing Objects/ Millisecond to BPM	

Master List of Figures and Examples (*continued*)

Printed Figures	Disk Examples	Related Opcode Objects
6.6 Note duration, 141	Timing Analysis	
6.7 Delta time, 142	Timing Analysis	
6.8 Foot tempo, 143	Timing Analysis	
6.9 Get tempo, 143	Timing Analysis	
6.10 Timing analysis with Borax, 144	Timing Analysis/Borax	**Borax**
6.11 Tempo follower 2, 146	Tempo Follower/Tempo Follower	
6.12 **BeatConfig:** determining rhythmic values (subpatch of fig. 6.11), 147	Tempo Follower/Tempo Follower/BeatConfig	
6.13 **RanMinorMel:** algorithm to produce a minor melody (subpatch of fig. 6.11), 148	Tempo Follower/Tempo Follower/RanMinorMel	
6.14 Restricting tempo changes, 148	Tempo Follower/ TempoWindow Example	
6.15 **TempoWindow** (subpatch of fig. 6.14), 149	Tempo Follower/ TempoWindow Example/ TempoWindow	**if**
6.16 Simple rhythm analysis, 151	Rhythm Analysis	
6.17 **GetRhythm** (subpatch of fig. 6.16), 152	Rhythm Analysis/Get Rhythm	
6.18 **PlayRhythm** (subpatch of fig. 6.16), 153	Rhythm Analysis/Play Rhythm	
6.19 Improving listener data, 153	Improving Listener Data	**speedlim**
6.20 **ErrorFilter** (subpatch of fig. 6.19), 154	Improving Listener Data/ ErrorFilter	
6.21 Pitch analysis, 156	Pitch Analysis	**%**
6.22 Chord Analysis: intervals and order, 158	Chord Analysis/Intervals and Order	
6.23 Chord analysis: chord type, root, inversion, 159	Chord Analysis/Chord Type	**thresh, sort**

Master List of Figures and Examples (*continued*)

Printed Figures	Disk Examples	Related Opcode Objects
6.24 **TriadAnalysis** (subpatch of fig. 6.23), 160	Chord Analysis/Chord Type/Triad Analysis	**if**
6.25 **GetRootBass** (subpatch of fig. 6.23), 160	Chord Analysis/Chord Type/Triad Analysis	
6.26 **select**, 162	Other Max Analysis Objects/select	**select**
6.27 **match**, 162	Other Max Analysis Objects/match	**match**
6.28 **past**, 163	Other Max Analysis Objects/past	**past**
6.29 **peak**, 163	Other Max Analysis Objects/peak	**peak, trough**
6.30 **histo**, 164	Other Max Analysis Objects/histo	**histo**
6.31 **RunAve** (running average), 166	Changes Over Time/ RunAve	
6.32 **Compare2** (subpatch of fig. 6.31), 167	Changes Over Time/ RunAve/Compare2	
6.33 Velocity histo, 168	Changes Over Time/ VelHist	
6.34 Duration histo, 170	Changes Over Time/ DurHist	
Chapter 7 Text Figures	Chapter 7 Disk Examples	Chapter 7 Opcode Objects
CHAPTER 7 PART 1 EXAMPLES	CHAPTER 7 PART 1 EXAMPLES	
7.1 Random melody, 177	Random Melody	
7.2 **RandomPitchRange** (subpatch of fig. 7.1), 177	Random Melody/ RandomPitchRange	
7.3 Range loop, 179	Range/RangeLoop	
7.4 Constrained arpeggio, 180	Range	
7.5 **RangeMod** (subpatch of fig. 7.4), 181	Range/RangeMod	

Master List of Figures and Examples (*continued*)

Printed Figures	Disk Examples	Related Opcode Objects
7.6 **AddArepeggio** (subpatch of fig. 7.4), 182	Range/AddArepeggio	
7.7 Scaling, 183	—Printed example only	
7.8 Select scale, 184	SelectScale	**select**
7.9 Modulation wheel melody, 185	ModWheelMelody	**speedlim**
7.10 Rest Example, 186	Rest Example	
7.11 Rest (subpatch of fig. 7.10), 187	Rest Example/Rest	
7.12 Interpolator, 188	Interpolator	**line**
7.13 Canon by Robert Gibson, 189	Canon	
7.14 Cypher Interface by Robert Rowe, 191	—printer interface only	
7.15 Midi reMap by Allen Strange, 192	separate example on disk	
7.16 **Tonicize** tutorial, 193	Tonicize Tutorial, 193	
7.17 **Tonicize** (subpatch of ex. 7.16), 194	Tonicize Tutorial/ Tonicize	
7.18 **PitchQuant** tutorial, 195	PitchQuant Tutorial	
7.19 **PitchQuant** (subpatch of ex. 7.18), 196	PitchQuant Tutorial/ PitchQuant	
7.20 **Scale** tutorial, 197	Scale Tutorial	
7.21 Scales stored in first **coll**, raw storage, 198	Scale Tutorial/Scale/coll Scales	
7.22 Scales stored in second **coll**, usable for mapping, 198	Scale Tutorial/Scale/coll (mapped scale)	
7.23 **Scale** (subpatch of fig. 7.20), 198	Scale Tutorial/Scale	
7.24 Melodic Contour: the easy version, 200	Melodic Contour Easy	
7.25 **GetInterval** (subpatch of fig. 7.24), 201	Melodic Contour Easy/ Get Interval	

Master List of Figures and Examples (*continued*)

Master List of Figures and Examples (*continued*)

Master List of Figures and Examples (*continued*)

Printed Figures	Disk Examples	Related Opcode Objects
Chapter 9 Text Figures	Chapter 9 Disk Examples	Chapter 9 Opcode Objects
9.1 Anatomy of a score object, 263	**Diagram**	
9.2 Simple score-matching mechanisms, 265	Select and Match	**select, match**
9.3 Unique event and order-matching, 268	Unique Event and Order Matching	
9.4 Continuous update, 269	Continuous Update	
9.5 **timeline**, 271	timeline	**Timeline**
9.6 Sequence control, 274	Sequence Control	
9.7 Master **preset** interface, 275	Master Preset Score Object	
9.8 Master **preset** score object, 276	Master Preset Score Object	
9.9 **preset** subscore, 277	Master Preset Score Object/Preset Subscore	
9.10 Updating the interface with remote messages, 278	Remote Message/Remote Message Updating	
9.11 FollowPlay front panel example, 278	Remote Message/ FollowPlay Remote Panel	
9.12 Section control (subpatch of fig. 9.11), 279	Remote Message/ FollowPlay Remote Panel/SectionControl	
9.13 Section 1 (subpatch of fig. 9.12), 280	Remote Message/ FollowPlay Remote Panel/SectionCnontrol/ Section 1	
9.14 Remote score lists using **coll**, 281	Remote Message/	
9.15 **follow**, 286	Follow	**follow, detonate**
9.16 **follow coll**, 287	Follow/Follow Coll (Table)	

Master List of Figures and Examples (*continued*)

Printed Figures	Disk Examples	Related Opcode Objects
9.17 **Explode:** graphic editing, 288		**detonate**
9.18 Score-Following Example by Cort Lippe, 290	Explode-Qlist Score	
9.19 **Explode-Qlist** section (subpatch of fig. 9.18), 290	Explode-Qlist Score/ Explode-Qlist Section	
9.20 **Qlist** Control (subpatch of fig. 9.18), 291	Explode-Qlist Score/Qlist Control	
Chapter 10 Text Figures	Chapter 10 Disk Examples	Chapter 10 Opcode Objects
10.1 **graphic**, 302		**graphic**
10.2 Drawing tools, 303		**oval, ring, rect, frame, lcd**
10.3 **imovie**, 305		**imovie, movie**
10.4 **pics**, 308		**pics**
10.5 **pict**, 309		**pict**
10.6 **vdp** object (video disk playback), 311		**vdp**

References

Allen, P., and R. Dannenberg. 1990. "Tracking Musical Beats in Real Time." In *Proceedings of the 1990 International Computer Music Conference*. San Francisco: International Computer Music Association, 140–43.

Baird, B. 1989. "The Artificially Intelligent Computer Performer on the Mac II. and a Pattern Matching Algorithm for Real-Time Interactive Performance." In *Proceedings of the International Computer Music Conference*. San Francisco: International Computer Music Association, 13–16.

Baird, B. 1991. "Artificially Intelligent Computer Performer and Parallel Processing." In *Proceedings of the ICMC*. San Francisco: International Computer Music Association, 340–43.

Baird, B., D. Blevins, and N. Zahler. 1993. "The Artificial Intelligence and Music: Implementing an Interactive Computer Performer." *Computer Music Journal* 17.2: 73–79.

Bate, J. 1992. "MAX + UniSon—Interactive Control of a Digital Signal Multiprocessor." In *Proceedings of the International Computer Music Conference*. San Francisco: International Computer Music Association, 356–57.

Beck, S. 1991. "Strange Attractors: Virtual Instrument Algorithm for Acoustic Instruments." In *Proceedings of the International Computer Music Conference*. San Francisco: International Computer Music Association, 332–35.

Belkin, A. 1991. "Who's Playing? The Computer's Role in Musical Performance." In *Proceedings of the International Computer Music Conference*. San Francisco: International Computer Music Association, 131–34.

Bilmes, J. 1992. "A Model for Musical Rhythm." In *Proceedings of the International Computer Music Conference*. San Francisco: International Computer Music Association, 207–10.

Boulanger, R., and P. Smaragdis. 1995. "Symbiotic Systems: Max Performance Software for Radio Baton, MIDI Power Glove, and Acoustic Instrument." In *Proceedings for the Fifth Biennial Symposium for Arts and Technology*. New London: Connecticut College, 298–302.

Chadabe, J. 1989. Interactive composing: an overview. In *The Music Machine,* edited by Curtis Roads. Cambridge: MIT Press.

Coniglio, M. 1992. "Introduction to the Interactor Language." In *Proceedings of the International Computer Music Conference.* San Francisco: International Computer Music Association, 170–73.

Cooper, D. 1987. *Cooper's Condensed Pascal.* New York: W.W. Norton.

Cooper, D. 1995. Very nervous system. *Wire Magazine* 3(3): 134–70.

Cope, D. 1977. *New Music Composition.* New York: Schirmer Books.

Cope, D. 1991. *Computers and Musical Style.* Madison, Wis.: A-R Editions.

Dannenberg, R. 1984. "An On-Line Algorithm for Real-Time Accompaniment." In *Proceedings of the International Computer Music Conference.* San Francisco: International Computer Music Association, 193–98.

Dannenberg, R. 1988. "New Techniques for Enhanced Quality of Computer Accompaniment." In *Proceedings of the International Computer Music Conference.* San Francisco: International Computer Music Association, 243–49.

Dannenberg, R. 1989. Real-time scheduling and computer accompaniment. *Current Directions in Computer Music Research,* edited by M. V. Mathews and J. R. Pierce. Cambridge: MIT Press.

Dannenberg, R., and J. Bloch. 1985. "Real-Time Computer Accompaniment of Keyboard Performances." In *Proceedings of the International Computer Music Conference.* San Francisco: International Computer Music Association, 68–72.

Dannenberg, R., and K. Bookstein. 1991. "Practical Aspects of a MIDI Conducting Program." In *Proceedings of the International Computer Music Conference.* San Francisco: International Computer Music Association, 537–40.

Dannenberg, R., and B. Mont-Reynaud. 1987. "Following an Improvisation in Real Time." In *Proceedings of the International Computer Music Conference.* San Francisco: International Computer Music Association, 241–48.

Demers, L-P., and B. Vorn. 1995. "Real Artificial Life as an Immersive Media." In *Proceedings for the Fifth Biennial Symposium for Arts and Technology.* New London: Connecticut College.

Desain, P. 1992. "Can Computer Music Benefit from Cognitive Models for Rhythmic Perception?" In *Proceedings of the International Computer Music Conference.* San Francisco: International Computer Music Association, 42–45.

Desain, P., and H. Honing. 1991. "Tempo Curves Considered Harmful." In *Proceedings of the International Computer Music Conference.* San Francisco: International Computer Music Association, 143–49.

Desain, Peter, and Henkjan Honig. 1994. "Foot-tapping: A Brief Introduction to Beat Induction." In *Proceedings of the International Computer Music Conference.* San Francisco: International Computer Music Association.

Dobrian, C. 1995. *Max Manual*. Mountain View, Cal.: Opcode Systems.

Dodge, C., and T. Jerse. 1985. *Computer Music*. New York: Schirmer Books.

Driesse, A. 1991. "Real-Time Tempo Tracking Using Rules to Analyze Rhythmic Qualities." In *Proceedings of the International Computer Music Conference*. San Francisco: International Computer Music Association, 578–81.

Emmerson, S. 1991. "Computers & Live Electronic Music: Some Solutions, Many Problems." In *Proceedings of the International Computer Music Conference*. San Francisco: International Computer Music Association, 135–38.

Freed, A., D. Wessel, and D. Zicarelli. 1991. "MAX Objects for Media Integration." In *Proceedings of the International Computer Music Conference*. San Francisco: International Computer Music Association, 397–400.

Garnett, G. 1992. *Program Notes for the 1992 International Computer Music Conference*. San Francisco: International Computer Music Association.

Garton, B. 1992. "Virtual Performance Modeling." In *Proceedings of the International Computer Music Conference*. San Francisco: International Computer Music Association, 219–22.

Gillet, R., K. C. Smith, and B. Pritchard. 1985. "MADDM—Dance-Directed Music." In *Proceedings of the International Computer Music Conference*. San Francisco: International Computer Music Association, 132–36.

Griffiths, P. 1981. *Modern Music: The Avant Garde Since 1945*. New York: George Braziller.

Grubb, L., and R. Dannenberg. 1994. "Automating Ensemble Performance." In *Proceedings of the International Computer Music Conference*. San Francisco: International Computer Music Association, 63–69.

Hiller, L., and L. Isaacson. 1959. *Experimental Music*. New York: McGraw-Hill.

Keane, D., and K. Wood. 1991. "The MIDI Baton III." In *Proceedings of the International Computer Music Conference*. San Francisco: International Computer Music Association, 541–44.

Knapp, B., and H. Lusted. 1990. A bioelectrical controller for computer music applications. *Computer Music Journal* 14(1): 42.

Laurel, B. 1993. *Computers as Theatre*. Reading, Mass.: Addison-Wesley.

Lee, M., G. Garnett, and D. Wessel. 1992. "An Adaptive Conductor Follower." In *Proceedings of the International Computer Music Conference*. San Francisco: International Computer Music Association, 454.

Lewis, G. 1994. Personal paper and conversation.

Lindeman, E. 1990. "The IRCAM Musical Workstation: Hardware Overview and Signal Processing Features." *Proceedings of the International Computer Music Conference*. San Francisco: International Computer Music Association, 132–135.

Lippe, C., and M. Puckette. 1991. "Musical Performance using IRCAM Workstations." In *Proceedings of the International Computer Music Conference*. San Francisco: International Computer Music Association, 533–36.

Lovell, R., and J. Mitchell. 1995. "Using Human Movement to Control Activities in Theatrical Environments." In *Proceedings for the Fifth Biennial Symposium for Arts and Technology*. New London: Connecticut College.

Machover, T. 1991. *Program Notes for the 1991 International Computer Music Conference*. San Francisco: International Computer Music Association.

Machover, T., and J. Chung. 1989. "Hyperinstruments: Musically Intelligent and Interactive Performance and Creativity Systems." In *Proceedings of the International Computer Music Conference*. San Francisco: International Computer Music Association, 186–87.

Mathews, M., and A. Schloss. 1989. "The Radio Drum as a Synthesizer Controller." In *Proceedings of the International Computer Music Conference*. San Francisco: International Computer Music Association, 42–45.

McMillen, K., D. Wessel, and M. Wright. 1994. The ZIPI music parameter description language. *Computer Music Journal* 18(4): 47–96.

Meyer, L. 1989. *Style and Music*. Philadelphia: University of Philadelphia Press.

Moore, F. R. 1987. "The Dysfunctions of MIDI." In *Proceedings of the International Computer Music Conference*. San Francisco: International Computer Music Association, 256–63.

Moore, F. R. 1990. *Elements of Computer Music*. Englewood Cliffs, N.J.: Prentice Hall.

Morita, H., S. Ohteru, and S. Hashimoto. 1989. "Computer System which Follows Human Conductor." In *Proceedings of the International Computer Music Conference*. San Francisco: International Computer Music Association, 207–10.

Motil, J. 1984. *Programming Principals*. Boston: Allyn and Bacon.

Nelson, G. 1989. "Algorithmic Approaches to Interactive Composition." In *Proceedings of the International Computer Music Conference*. San Francisco: International Computer Music Association, 219–22.

Norman, D. 1988. *Psychology of Everyday Things*. New York: Basic Books.

Nyman, M. 1980. *Experimental Music: Cage and Beyond*. New York: Schirmer Books.

Oppenheim, D. 1991. "DMIX: An Environment for Composition." In *Proceedings of the International Computer Music Conference*. San Francisco: International Computer Music Association, 226–33.

Pelz-Sherman, M. 1992. "Some Formalisms for Generating Expression in Melodies Performed by Computers." In *Proceedings of the International Computer Music Conference*. San Francisco: International Computer Music Association, 408–9.

Pennycook, B., and D. Stammen. 1994. "The MIDI Time Clip: A Performer/Machine Synchronization System for Live Performance." In *Proceedings of the International*

Computer Music Conference. San Francisco: International Computer Music Association, 181–182.

Penguilly, S. 1995. "The Ultimate Convergence: Music from the Mind." In *Proceedings for the Fifth Biennial Symposium for Arts and Technology.* New London: Connecticut College.

Pierce, J. 1983. *The Science of Musical Sound.* New York: Scientific American Books.

Polanski, L. 1991. "Live Interactive Intelligent Computer Music in HMSL: Notes on Pieces 1984–1991." In *Proceedings of the International Computer Music Conference.* San Francisco: International Computer Music Association, 37–44.

Polansky, Larry, D. Rosenboom, and P. Burk. 1987. "HMSL: Overview (Version 3.1) and Notes On Intelligent Instrument Design." In *Proceedings of the International Computer Music Conference.* San Francisco: International Computer Music Association, 220–227.

Pope, S. T., ed. 1991. *The Well-Tempered Object: Musical Applications of Object-Oriented Technology.* Cambridge: MIT Press.

Pressing, J. 1992. *Synthesizer Performance and Real-Time Techniques.* Madison, Wis.: A-R Editions.

Puckette, M. 1990. "EXPLODE: A User Interface for Sequencing and Score Following." In *Proceedings of the International Computer Music Conference.* San Francisco: International Computer Music Association, 259–61.

Puckette, M. 1991. "Something Digital." *Computer Music Journal* 15(4): 66.

Puckette, M., and C. Lippe. 1992. "Score Following in Practice." In *Proceedings of the International Computer Music Conference.* San Francisco: International Computer Music Association, 182–85.

Rich, R. 1991. Buchla lightening MIDI controller. *Electronic Musician* 7(10): 102–8.

Rothstein, J. 1995. *MIDI: A Comprehensive Introduction.* 2d ed. Madison, Wis.: A-R Editions.

Rowe, R. 1991a. "A Self-Critical Compositional Algorithm." In *Proceedings of the International Computer Music Conference.* San Francisco: International Computer Music Association, 250–53.

Rowe, R. 1991b. "Feature Classification and Related Response in a Real-Time Interactive Music System." In *Proceedings of the International Computer Music Conference.* San Francisco: International Computer Music Association, 202–4.

Rowe, R. 1993. *Interactive Performance Systems.* Cambridge: MIT Press.

Rowe, R., and T. Li. 1994. "Pattern Processing in Music." In *Proceedings of the International Computer Music Conference.* San Francisco: International Computer Music Association, 60–62.

Ryan, J. 1992. "Effort and Expression." In *Proceedings of the International Computer Music Conference.* San Francisco: International Computer Music Association, 414–16.

Ryan, J. 1992. "The STEIM Studio Report." In *Proceedings of the International Computer Music Conference*. San Francisco: International Computer Music Association, 325–28.

Scaletti, C. 1987. "Kyma: An Object-Oriented Language for Music Composition." In *Proceedings of the International Computer Music Conference*. San Francisco: International Computer Music Association, 49–56.

Schaefer, John. 1987. *New Sounds: A Listener's Guide to New Music*. New York: Harper and Row.

Settel, Z. and C. Lippe. 1994. "Real-Time Musical Applications Using FFT-based Re-synthesis." In *Proceedings of the International Computer Music Conference*. San Francisco: International Computer Music Association, 338–343.

Tanaka, A. 1993. "Musical Technical Issues in Using Interactive Instrument Technology with Application to the BioMuse." In *Proceedings of the International Computer Music Conference*. San Francisco: International Computer Music Association, 124–26.

Tanaka, A. 1994. "OverBow." In *Program Notes for the International Computer Music Conference*. San Francisco: International Computer Music Association.

Teufel, B. 1991. *Organization of Programming Languages*. Wein, NY: Springer-Verlag.

Vantomme, J. 1994. "Score Following by Computer: An Approach by Temporal Pattern." Master of Arts in Computer Applications to Music Thesis. Montreal: McGill University.

Vercoe, B. 1984. "The Synthetic Performer in the Context of Live Performance." In *Proceedings of the International Computer Music Conference*. San Francisco: International Computer Music Association, 199–200.

Vercoe, B., and M. Puckette. 1985. "Synthetic Rehearsal: Training the Synthetic Performer." In *Proceedings of the International Computer Music Conference*. San Francisco: International Computer Music Association, 275–78.

Waisvisz, M. 1985. "THE HANDS: A Set of Remote MIDI Controllers." In *Proceedings of the International Computer Music Conference*. San Francisco: International Computer Music Association, 86–89.

Wessel, D. 1991. "Improvisation with Highly Interactive Real-Time Performance System." In *Proceedings of the International Computer Music Conference*. San Francisco: International Computer Music Association, 344–47.

Winkler, T. 1991. "Interactive Signal Processing for Acoustic Instruments." In *Proceedings of the International Computer Music Conference*. San Francisco: International Computer Music Association, 545–48.

Winkler, T. 1992a. "FollowPlay: A Max Program for Interactive Composition." In *Proceedings of the International Computer Music Conference*. San Francisco: International Computer Music Association, 433–34.

Winkler, T. 1992b. *Three Interactive Etudes for Clarinet and Computer*. Doctoral Dissertation. Palo Alto: Stanford University.

Wishart, T. 1995. Keynote address for the 1994 international computer music conference. *Array* 5(1): 8–12.

Zahler, N. 1991. "Questions About Interactive Computer Performance as a Resource for Music Composition and Performance of Musicality." In *Proceedings of the International Computer Music Conference*. San Francisco: International Computer Music Association, 336–39.

Zicarelli, D. 1987. M and jam factory. *Computer Music Journal* 11(4): 13.

Index